AF394220

A Vast Horizon

Also by Anna Thomasson

A Curious Friendship

A Vast Horizon

Artists and Lovers, Freedom and War

ANNA THOMASSON

PICADOR

First published 2026 by Picador
an imprint of Pan Macmillan
The Smithson, 6 Briset Street, London ECIM 5NR
EU representative: Macmillan Publishers Ireland Ltd, 1st Floor,
The Liffey Trust Centre, 117–126 Sheriff Street Upper,
Dublin 1 DOI YC43
Associated companies throughout the world

ISBN 978-1-4472-4556-8

1 3 5 7 9 8 6 4 2

A CIP catalogue record for this book is available from the British Library.

Typeset by Palimpsest Book Production Limited, Falkirk, Stirlingshire
Printed and bound in the UK using 100% Renewable Electricity by CPI Group (UK) Ltd

Visit www.picador.com to read more about
all our books and to buy them.

For Trent,
and our boys

And by the power of a word
I begin my life again
I was born to know you
To name you

Liberty.

Paul Éluard, 'Liberty', 1942

Picnic, 1937

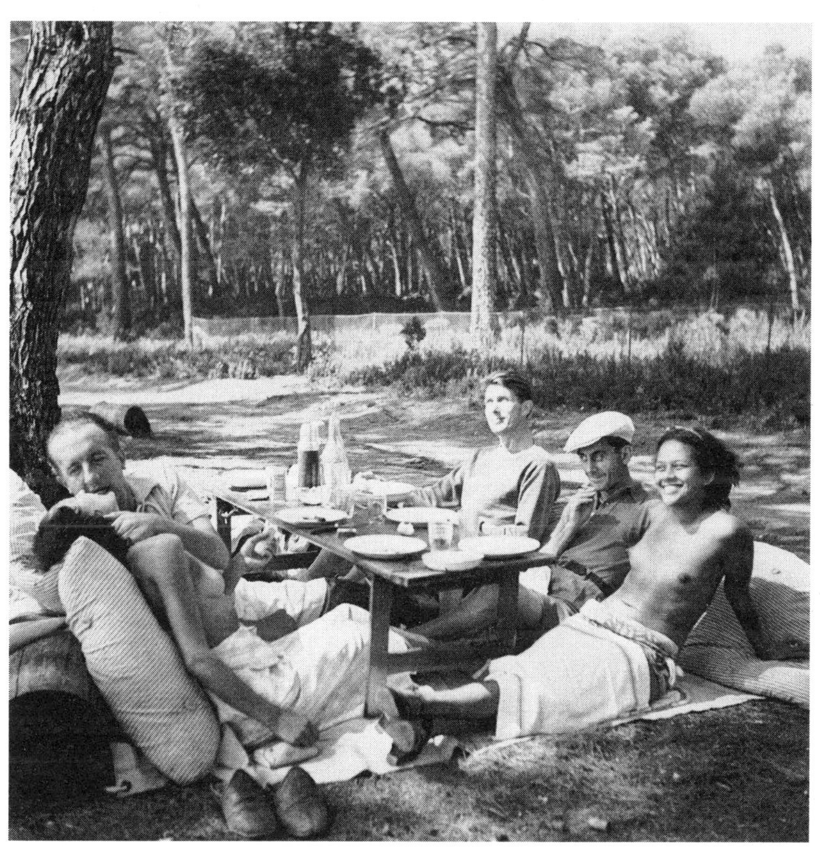

Picnic BY LEE MILLER.

'There is certainly another world, but it is in this one'

Paul Éluard

A woman tips her head back, laughing. Her dress is peeled to the waist and a pair of shoes lies discarded beside her. A man's hand wraps around her neck as he moves to kiss her. In one hand she is clutching what looks like a piece of bread, while her other hand lies inert at her side. This is a private performance. The unseen photographer, two clothed men and a topless woman who are sitting at the other side of the table make an audience of four. This second woman is grinning, her bare legs outstretched beneath a napkin as she leans back on her arms. The man to the right of her looks on amused and the man beside him smiles as he turns away and into the light. They're sitting on a blanket on the ground around a makeshift table, resting on striped cushions against tree trunks that act as backrests. The setting is a secluded clearing; sunlight is streaming down through the trees. The cork from a wine bottle lies discarded in the grass. The empty plates suggest their lunch is finished, and appetites have shifted.

A photograph is inherently, seductively unknowable. It obscures as much as it reveals. Our instinct is to pick apart the moment, to impose a narrative. And although we can look and invent and think we know what's happening it will never entirely yield its secrets. I've always been fascinated by this photograph, its sensuality, its enigmatic sophistication. It's as if we've stumbled upon a moment of intimacy in a sun-bathed and seemingly carefree world. Surely this is a spontaneous moment of desire and happiness, of men and women enjoying each other? This group, so at ease and unguarded, seems to invite us to stay and watch, to witness the spectacle. The atmosphere is charged, erotic, playful: an Arcadian idyll. But it's also a complicated image. There's a jarring asymmetry to half-naked women sitting amongst fully clothed men. Are they making themselves objects of desire, offering themselves up for the delectation of the men? Or is this brazen breast-baring a daring act of rebellion that goes far beyond the immediate company? It could be both. And, then again, it could be neither – merely an expression of complete ease, and freedom.

Two years after this photograph was taken the world would be at war and the lives of these friends thrown asunder. There lies its narrative. Not in the minutiae of its gestures but in what it represents, in the world beyond its frame. Set against the turmoil of 1937, the ephemeral moment captured in this photograph becomes an act of defiance, a riposte.

It's an image radiating with a shared joy and fierce hope, its subjects vibrantly alive. There's warmth and light and shade, food, friendship and the promise of conversation. It seems to spring from a world where pleasures supersede ordinary bourgeois cares. A world that's devoid of responsibility and childless, where communality is all. In an age of urgency and action, of political extremes, of nationalism and borders, of brutal racism, a time when contemporary art was dismissed as degenerate and decadent and women were to be tethered to their children and their hearths, here an international group of artists – amongst them a black woman, a Jewish man, a Quaker, women baring their breasts – sit around enjoying their right to do nothing. They're crossing borders. They're libertines par excellence. Perhaps there's an homage to Manet's *Dejeuner sur l'herbe*, so shockingly ambiguous and provocative in its day. They're making art of their lives.

However fleeting the moment, time is suspended in a photograph. They're always young and happy and the sun will always be shining. It celebrates, elevates and memorializes the moment. And yet it's an image that feels perpetually modern and defiantly immortal.

This photograph wasn't a public gesture. The two-and-a-quarter-inch-square Rolleiflex contact print would be squirreled away in an attic for decades. Rather, it was a private act of freedom. It's as if the group were thumbing their noses at fascism, offering a corrective for how to live. It's a manifesto for an alternative world to the one that was coming into being.

Lee Miller's iconic photograph of her lover Roland Penrose, and friends Ady Fidelin, Man Ray, and Paul and Nusch Éluard, was taken one day during a picnic on the Île Sainte-Marguerite – a lush, pine-wooded island off the coast of Cannes. It is the inspiration and starting point for this book and its themes of friendship, creativity, freedom, complicated gender dynamics, connection, bodies, sex, free love, desire, sensual exchange, action (and retreat), communality (and isolation). It's an exploration of photography, performance and play, and also the artist's commitment to sharing a new way of looking at the world, of living within art, and the limits of that life.

A Vast Horizon is the story of the picnic photograph, the people in it and other friends with whom they spent several weeks in the late summer of 1937 at a small hotel in the south of France, the Hôtel-Restaurant Vaste Horizon. It was the poet Paul Éluard and his wife Nusch, a model, who had discovered the Vaste Horizon several years before. That year, joining them were the photographer and artist Dora Maar and her lover, and fellow artist, Pablo Picasso. They had also invited the photographer and artist Man Ray and his lover Ady Fidelin, a dancer and model; the photographer Lee Miller, with her new lover, the artist and art collector Roland Penrose; and the artist Eileen Agar with her lover, the writer Joseph Bard. Éluard was one of the founding fathers of surrealism; Maar, Man Ray, Miller and Penrose were all surrealists too, some officially, others in all but name. Picasso and Agar, the group hoped to lure into the fold.

Hundreds of photographs were taken on that holiday; *Picnic* is one of many. Some were staged, others were spontaneous. Everything was recorded. The photographs offer a sense of the group's vitality, their elegance, their pleasure in friendship and connection, and their ever-evolving self-discovery. The quotidian, the ordinary, is rendered extraordinary in the hands of these photographers.

Some were old friends and others new acquaintances. Some were lovers or had once been. At the Vaste Horizon in Mougins their lives momentarily collided. They became a temporary community, brought together by a shared way of seeing the world, their elective affinities. When the group went its separate ways, some remained friends and others never saw each other again.

That year everything was in flux, febrile. Life felt provisional and urgent. There was a sense of living on borrowed time. And it was a momentous year for what it meant to be an artist. As photographers, artists, a poet, a model and a dancer, they had all, in different ways, deconstructed and reconstructed their own identities. They were in rebellion, against class, families, nationalities, fascism and the social dictates of gender. They lived outside and in defiance of convention. Fugitive spirits, their searches for independence and autonomy had sent some of them to the other side of the world, either in self-imposed or necessary exile from the place where they were born and grew up. There they embraced communism and/or surrealism, changed their names, eschewed the conventions of marriage, lived radical, reimagined lives and dreamed of a better future.

There were successes and failures; the things they sought, they did not always find. The vast horizon becomes something that they're striving for, a freer life, ever-shifting, a search without end.

And then the Second World War smashed into their lives. When Paul Éluard wrote 'Liberty' in 1942, France was under German Occupation and the poet, as a member of the Resistance, was in hiding from the Nazis. Within the repetition of the poem's emphatic refrain – 'I write your name' – Éluard writes the name of liberty on everything that surrounds him. It is this gesture of resistance in dark times, of reclaiming the world around him, and the redemptive power of creativity, which is central to this book. Creativity as an act of response, exchange and engagement. Creativity as something life-affirming, hope-inspiring and an agent of change, showing the promise of an alternative world, and evidence of our ability to make the world we want. The idea that freedom is not static but dynamic, something that must be practised.

The book follows those lives from that holiday, through the trials and deprivations of the Second World War and into the ruins, the rehabilitation and the new reality of the post-war world. When lives were at risk and culture was being policed or destroyed, how did this group of friends respond? What choices did they make in wartime? Do they advance into the world, take action and confront the darkness, or do they retreat from it? How did they see and make sense of the world? What did it mean for them to produce art and to be living through that moment? What freedoms did they seek and how did that seeking impact others around them? How did wealth, skin colour, gender, nationality, faith and power either buttress or undermine them? As for the women, though inevitably their lives were interwoven with those of their partners, what are their own stories, those which run alongside the ones that have been imposed on them by men and by history or mediated through art, as wives, mistresses and muses?

And what if there is little of their story that we know, as is the case with Ady Fidelin? The Martiniquan poet, writer and philosopher Édouard Glissant's theories were shaped by his experience as a colonized subject. He believed in a right to 'opacity', the right to not be understood, to be different, to hold complexity, to resist reductive categorization, easy interpretation, objectification. Opacity is humanity and enchantment, an antidote to 'transparency', which he considered flattening, deadening, a colonial method of suppression and control. 'It is impossible,' writes Glissant in *Poetics of Relation*, 'to reduce anyone, no matter who, to a truth he would not have generated on his own.' The gaps in Ady's archive demand this opacity. I'll write only what I've learned about her and describe only what we can see of her. I won't try to speculate, to impose a narrative upon her life, but instead acknowledge the unknowable shadows, the lacunae in her story.

These are vast themes, unfolding in epic times. Most of my subjects, about whom thousands of books have been written, were huge characters with stories, archives and bodies of work to match. It is not my intention here to be exhaustive, biographically or art-historically. I have a more modest claim. I'm spellbound by these people, drawn into their distant world by their photographs, their (to me) unfamiliar way of living, their (for some) commitment to surrealism, their paintings and their poetry. *A Vast Horizon* is an attempt to understand them, to dip into their lives, to look at the work they made, at the thousands of photographs they took of each other and the world around them. The book is an exploration – of ideas, images, artefacts, letters, poems, encounters and fragments. It is a collage.

THE TERRIBLE YEAR

Visions of new worlds on a grander scale were on display at the International Exposition of Art and Technology in Modern Life, which had opened in Paris earlier that year in May. Its optimistic ambitions were of inclusivity and internationalism, a celebration of innovation, of diversity and of cultural exchange between nations. Forty-four countries gathered to showcase the contemporary achievements of their arts and industries. Millions flocked to the national pavilions which had been designed and decorated by some of the most celebrated artists and architects of the day.

But what was meant to be a global village instead reflected a world in turmoil. International tensions and rivalries played out in microcosm along the banks of the Seine. Conflicting national ideals and ideologies jostled for attention. The Spanish Civil War had broken out in July 1936 and the Spanish pavilion was financed by the beleaguered Republican government, which was already losing the war. Belying the Exposition's technology theme, the pavilion was a single-minded exercise in propaganda which sought to show the world the terror that Franco wrought in Spain. Its centrepiece was Picasso's enormous *Guernica*, officially unveiled in July.

For all its retrospective fame, the Spanish pavilion was considered a failure at the time. It stood in the shadow, both literally and metaphorically, of the monumental German and Soviet pavilions, which faced off across the newly created Jardins du Trocadéro. Boris

Iofan's Soviet pavilion was clad in marble and topped by *Worker and Kolkhoz Woman*, Vera Mukhina's gargantuan sculpture of a man and woman striding forth, bearing a hammer and sickle in their raised hands. But eclipsing this with its sheer scale was the Nazi pavilion designed by Albert Speer, chief architect of the Third Reich. Hitler had contemplated withdrawing Germany from the Exposition but Speer convinced him otherwise and, on a trip to Paris some months before the opening, had secretly obtained Iofan's architectural plans. And so Germany's pavilion – a soaring monolith of granite topped with a giant eagle and swastika – towered over the Soviet pavilion and dwarfed the other buildings in the Exposition.

To the prophetically-minded this standoff was a terrible sign of things to come. Between the two pavilions, on the far side of the Seine, the Eiffel Tower, symbol of Paris and liberty, appeared trapped by the opposing force fields of the two totalitarian powers. Fascism was bubbling up in France, the left-wing alliance of the Popular Front was holding on to power only by a thread, and all the talk that summer was of war, but Paris was enjoying her freedoms while they lasted. It was as if everyone was dancing on the edge of an abyss. Nightclubs throbbed to the sound of jazz and on teeming cafe terraces people argued about how to make the world anew. For them Paris was still a city of fantasy and chance encounters. Though France had been pummelled by the Depression and there was mass unemployment, politics was dangerously divisive, anti-Semitism rife, and women wouldn't get the vote for another seven years, the idea of France, and particularly Paris, still meant liberty, democracy and revolution. It meant modernity and possibility, in art and in life. 'Paris was where the twentieth century was,' wrote Gertrude Stein in *Paris France: Personal Recollections.*

Artists had been flocking to the city for decades, escaping intolerance, persecution or the stultifying boredom of bourgeois life, lured by cheap rents and the chance to live differently. The freedoms they sought were social, sexual, creative, political, physical, psychological. Paris, with its libertine culture, was permissive and excessive. It was progressive, decadent and seductively impure. The city promised fellowship and the exchange of ideas. It proposed different models of community beyond the family and, for women, the potential for a life beyond marriage, motherhood and monogamy. It offered a space for experiments in living just as artists were experimenting with form and finding new ways to see and respond to the world.

If the real Paris was never quite the Utopia it appeared to be, it was still a city where people were striving to achieve it. Amongst the vanguard of its artistic life were the surrealists. Heavily inspired by Freud's theories – the unconscious, the interpretation of dreams, hysteria and of desire as a driving force – for them a radical freedom was to be found in liberating the unconscious as a wellspring of creativity. Surrealism meant embracing the irrational and the uncanny, rebelling against order and rejecting bourgeois values. It was both playful and deadly serious and it spilled out beyond art and literature, becoming an entire way of life. It was exactly this kind of art, and this kind of artist, which the Nazis planned to eradicate.

Nazi society was based on order, efficiency and blinkered subjugation to the state. It relied on violence, eliminating all opposition, the oppression of minorities and the lie that Germany was in the stranglehold of a Jewish-Bolshevik conspiracy. Freedoms were rapidly and brutally diminished. Individuality and identity were sacrificed in favour of collective subordination. Male superiority was all. And for the German woman, as Hitler declared in a speech in 1934, her world was her husband, her children, her home. Nazi dominance relied entirely on the ability to control. Germany was being held in the state's ever-tightening grip. The press, academia and the Church were all at its mercy.

From the early years of his rise to power Hitler understood the importance of harnessing the potential of culture and the aesthetics of politics in order to control minds. Art could be weaponized and used as propaganda. Ritual, ceremony, symbolism and theatre were paramount. Dissenting voices were silenced. Language was corrupted and meaning debased. What was truth and what was a lie was no longer clear. Certainties evaporated, opinion was discouraged, words were manipulated and became redundant except in their power to promote misinformation. Everything was simplified and reduced to the language of inclusion and exclusion. Books considered un-German were burned.

The Reichskulturkammer, the Reich Chamber of Culture, ensured that cinema, fine arts, radio, newspapers, literature and the theatre were all under the same aggressive control and all became cogs in the propaganda machine. Exploiting a growing antipathy for cultural liberalism in the ordinary German people who had voted them into power, the Nazis began to sanitize culture, promoting certain kinds of art and banning others. The German people and the world were to see that the Fatherland was culturally superior to other countries. In 1937 Hitler appointed his favourite painter, Adolf Ziegler, who specialized in kitsch Aryan nudes, to lead a commission charged with cleansing German museums of undesirable art.

What was acceptable and what was not became very clear that summer in Munich, with the opening of the Great German Art Exhibition on 18 July and the Degenerate Art Exhibition the following day. At the former, which opened to great fanfare in Hitler's newly designed House of German Art, Nazi ideals and Aryan aesthetics were on display in all their glacial glory. Floodlit marble halls were lined with paintings upholding racial purity, extolling the virtues of the bucolic ideal of German peasant life, promoting family and the home. There were folk paintings, sentimental scenes, statuesque nudes and fecund mothers. There was heroism, toil, muscular manliness and self-sacrifice. And there were plenty of landscapes, Hitler's favourite genre. Most were painted in a Classical style or in imitation of nineteenth-century realism. The message was explicit: youth, strength, optimism and victory. All was reason, realism, grandeur, order and facade.

Viewers weren't required to think or to form opinions. There were no invitations to explore the subconscious or use the imagination. There was only surface and sterility. Hitler declared at the opening that works of art needed to be understood without a user manual and that, thanks to him, the German people would no longer have to engage with art that did. There was no room for depth or doubt, for interpretation or nuance, for complexity and opacity, only a deadeningly unambiguous rationality. 'In the context of Nazi Germany, perfectibility is lethal,' writes Jacqueline Rose in *Women in Dark Times*, 'it is the death of freedom'.

Hitler planned for the opening of the exhibition and the House of Art to mark the beginning of a renaissance in German art. In his speech he railed against degenerate artists – modernists, decadents, communists and Jews – as enemies of Germany: 'From now on,' he ranted, 'of that you can be certain [. . .] all those [. . .] cliques of chatterers, dilettantes and art forgers will be picked up and liquidated. For all we care, those prehistorics can return to their ancestors and there apply their primitive international scratchings.'

The Degenerate Art exhibition, which opened the following day, was the brainchild of Reich Minister for Propaganda Joseph Goebbels. But it represented something of a personal vendetta for Hitler. As a young man in the early years of the twentieth century he'd been an aspiring artist, twice rejected by the Academy of Fine Arts in Vienna. His polite little paintings of landscapes and buildings failed to make any impact in an art world then dominated by the new abstraction and modernism. The avant-garde was dreaming optimistic dreams of a new world without social inequality and war, just as Hitler was beginning to formulate his own ideas. He would fix his hatred on Dadaists, soon to be at the peak of their celebrity, who represented a radical disruption of the old order, nonsense and anarchy. Over the years, Hitler's hatred of modernism became irrevocably interwoven with the fabric of his political manifesto.

In pointed contrast to the German Art exhibition, the Degenerate exhibition took place in dark, cramped rooms and the work was hurriedly and haphazardly installed in less than two weeks. Six hundred and fifty paintings, sculptures and prints by a hundred and twelve artists considered an offence to the Fatherland were exhibited, having been removed from museums or seized from private collections across the country. 'Degenerate' applied to most German modernist art, especially anything abstract or expressionist or by a Jewish or communist artist, and many works by international artists were also confiscated. There were pieces by expressionists, Impressionists, post-Impressionists, Dadaists (of course), Cubists, New Objectivists, fauves and the surrealists, amongst others. And compared to the relative obscurity of the artists in the German Art exhibition, the 'degenerates' were celebrities: Max Beckmann, Emil Nolde, George Grosz, Ernst Ludwig Kirchner and Otto Dix, as well as great international names like Edvard Munch, Henri Matisse, Piet Mondrian, Paul Klee, Oskar Kokoschka, Wassily Kandinsky and Pablo Picasso. The German artist Ernst Barlach was also included. The Nazis had confiscated almost four hundred of his works by the summer of 1937, and he renamed one of his sculptures *Das schlimme Jahr 1937* (The Terrible Year 1937) in response. Works were taken out of their frames and hung without care and without space. Walls were daubed with insulting slogans such as 'An insult to German womanhood' and 'Revelation of the Jewish racial soul' to emphasize the degeneracy and insanity of the artists.

This art was experimental, abstract, non-representational. And it was personal, irrational, sensual and subversive. Here were dreams and nightmares, sex and violence, chaos and death. Here was dissonance, and freedom: the freedom to shock and to get under the skin. Weimar Berlin, twentieth-century Paris, aspects of modern life revealed: queerness, nightclubbing, sex work, face painting, sexual deviation, poverty, misery, joy. To the Nazis this art was depravity. Minds were for controlling, not liberating. Individualism, irrationality, decadence and free love were all contrary to their master plan.

The exhibition travelled to twelve other cities over the next few years and the Degenerate Art Law was passed in 1938, placing a permanent ban on art of this kind and allowing art deemed degenerate to be confiscated from museums and collections, without compensation. Both exhibitions were popular – the German Art show had half a million visitors – but there were queues around the block for the Degenerate Exhibition. Of its two million visitors it's unclear who was for and who was against the modernist work on display. But, tellingly, though the Great German Art Exhibition was repeated annually, the Degenerate show was a one-off. Much of the art was locked away in a Berlin depot, or it was auctioned in Switzerland or burned. The Nazis rightly feared the power of creativity.

•

Where once for some people (not everyone), Europe had offered freedom, openness, internationalism, migration, the exchange of ideas and influence, now, increasingly, it meant borders, nationhood, distrust and disunity. In place of migrants there were exiles and refugees. More than ever, differences – of colour, ethnicity, faith, sexuality – mattered. Loyalties were being tested and limitations, moral codes, laws and labels were all to be considered. Artists of the avant-garde had been transgressing boundaries, disrupting the old order and dissolving the limitations of tradition, convention, gender and sexuality. They'd been exploring the frontiers of the self, the thresholds of the mind and irrationality.

But the Nazis were even infiltrating dreams. Not long after Hitler came to power in 1933, the German writer Charlotte Beradt began collecting accounts of the dreams of hundreds of Berliners. It became clear that the Nazi hold was so absolute that it even penetrated that most personal and intimate of places: the subconscious. Beradt described these dreams as nocturnal diaries whose authorship had been co-opted by the dictatorship. The collection would be published in the 1960s, with the help of Hannah Arendt, as *The Third Reich of Dreams*.

It was increasingly difficult to stop the outside world infiltrating the canvas or the page and be a private artist. The English poet and critic Stephen Spender, writing his autobiography after the Second

World War, recalled that he felt 'hounded by external events' in the 1930s. For artists and writers who found themselves out of favour and living in countries under totalitarian rule this was all too literal. They were persecuted, interned or forced into exile. Even for those in countries still clinging to democracy there was a feeling of anxiety and impending doom, of waiting for the inevitable war. For many artists, there was a conflict between private lives and public responsibility. Was it better to withdraw or engage? To retreat into what could be perceived as the ivory tower of introspection and aesthetics or to step up, take action, resist? And was it even possible to be immune to the outside world, to separate the personal and the political?

For the surrealists, who'd been mobilizing against fascism for some years, there was no debate. There was a necessity to question and an urgency to communicate ideas. There was a need to defend the right to create, to defend the right to live how they wanted and to dream without being controlled. Acts of creativity were a powerful weapon in the fight for freedom. Art gave agency, offered resistance, exerted influence, had consequences. Totalitarianism dehumanized and desensitized people, but art helped to make them feel again. It bore witness and offered alternative perspectives. It countered the separation and isolation, and could cross borders. Art and literature were more important than ever.

I

A Dance of Freedom

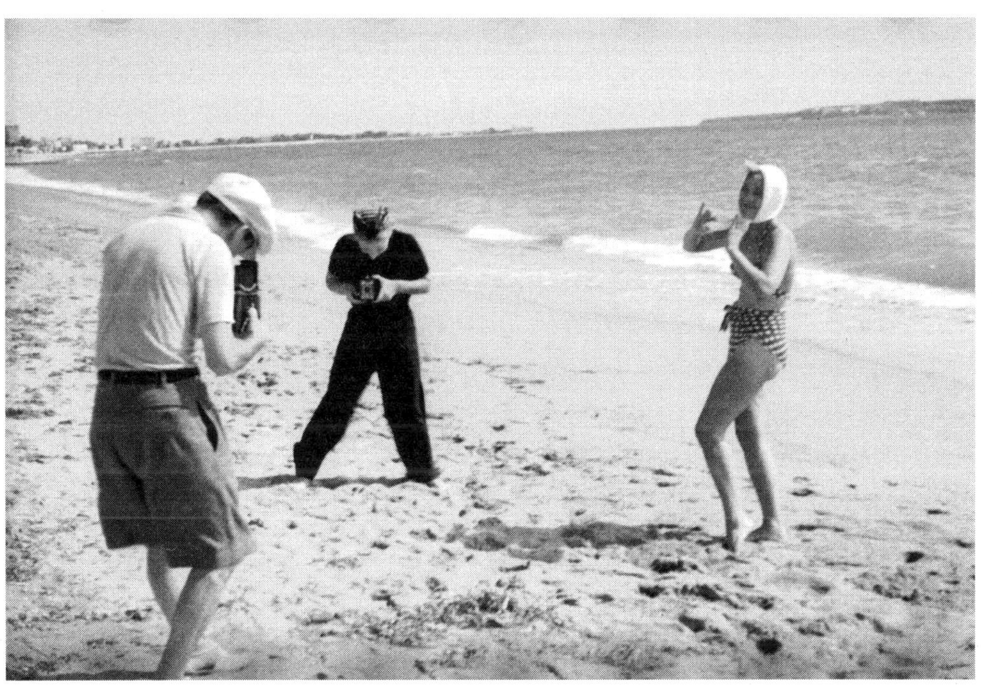

MAN RAY, EILEEN AGAR AND LEE MILLER, BY ROLAND PENROSE, 1937.

They all owed each other a tender nudity
Of sky and water, air and sand.
Everyone forgot their appearance
And that they had promised to see nothing but themselves.

'La Plage' from *Les Mains libres*,
Paul Éluard, 1937

———————

ROOFTOP

Eileen Agar is dancing on the roof outside her hotel room. Behind her a glimpse of tiled rooftops, chimneys and palm trees, hazy in the morning sun. She's turned away from the camera, absorbed in her dance, her head in profile and her arms aloft. The sheer slip of a dress she's wearing is belted at her waist with her breasts clearly visible. The fabric floats about her legs as she dances. Except for the prim 1930s bow in her cropped curly hair and her high, gathered collar, there's something Greek about her dress and her posture: a bacchant on a vase. She's dancing for her lover Joseph Bard and for the camera with which they're recording their trip. But this is about showing, not being seen. Perhaps she's dancing mostly for herself: her body, her canvas, her own.

They've spent the night in Cannes, en route to Mougins, a village tucked away in the hills a few miles inland, where Lee Miller and Roland Penrose will drive them later that morning. It's been a sleepless night, disturbed by bats from a nearby derelict church that invaded their room. Eileen would remember cowering under the sheets as Joseph leapt up naked to swipe at the swooping creatures. Perhaps she hadn't slept but she couldn't look more awake, more alive. In her autobiography she'd caption this photograph 'after a bat-infested night. A dance of freedom'.

'A HAPPY FAMILY'

The rhythm of their days was slow and simple. Each one much the same as the next. And yet from photographs and written memories of that time we get a sense of how intense, how inspiring it was for the people who lived through it; community as a modern counter to the long-held Romantic notion of the tragic artist, solitary in his garret. Everything, everyone, was photographed, recorded, memorialized: living as creation, as performance and collaboration. Daily life seen through the eyes and cameras of Dora Maar, Eileen Agar, Man Ray, Lee Miller and Roland Penrose transmuted – a kind of alchemy – into beauty, enchantment, spectacle. There are so many photographs in the archives that, seen together, they become a diary, like a flip book, reanimating their days and their nights. In those photographs there is light and shade, the powerful Provençal sun bestowing upon everything the drama of chiaroscuro. We get a powerful sense of physicality, of bodies, of limbs and breasts and bottoms and penises, alone or entwined, still or in action. We feel the warm sun and salt water on bare skin and sand between toes, intimacy and proximity and responsiveness and desire. The photographs crackle and shimmer with sensuality, kinship, happiness, creativity – reflected and refracted, all urgent, all interlinked.

After breakfast they would drive to the beach armed with picnic baskets, beach mats, parasols and cameras, piling into Roland's Ford V8 and Picasso's Hispano Suiza, driven by his chauffeur (and factotum) Marcel Boudin. Sometimes they went to the beach at Juans-les-Pins, west of Antibes, or to hidden coves along the coast. Other times they drove to La Garoupe, a secluded beach at the end of the Cap d'Antibes.

The women wear the elaborately folded and knotted two-piece swimsuit of the era then considered very modern and daring and soon to be known as a bikini. Sometimes they wear it with a matching sarong, as well as leather sandals, sunglasses, headscarves and traditional straw hats (perhaps bought nearby) tied with ribbons beneath chins. Sometimes they're topless or have rolled up their swimsuit tops to bare as much skin as possible to the sun as they sprawl on the sand. But never Dora, whose swimsuit remains resolutely intact in all the photographs. Often, she is wearing a chunky, gnarly necklace of bright white shells, crafted by Picasso from finds at Juan-les-Pins. He, the southerner, at ease on the beach, in tight white bathing shorts which contrast with his deeply tanned skin. The other men appear in varying states of undress: Roland Penrose and Man Ray in dark swimming shorts, the latter in espadrilles tied at the ankle and usually with a white cap on his head; Paul Éluard in trousers and a long-sleeved shirt. In several photographs taken by Eileen, Paul and Picasso sit on the sand beside an upturned boat. Next to Picasso, Paul looks rather formal and out of place, but for his bare feet. In one of these, Paul's eyes are closed but Picasso smiles at her and looks deeply into the lens, a penetrating gaze, as he toys with a cigarette in his fingers.

They're usually talking, often smoking, and sometimes swimming in the sea or dancing on the sand. The wind whips hair and sarongs and the sunlight glitters on the water. There are groupings, and regroupings, arms slung across shoulders, smiles, hands shading eyes from the glaring sun. Eileen's photographs best capture the spontaneous, the ephemeral and the unposed. But her observations, their informality, the skill of her perspectives and framing, reveal the art in the moments, the artist behind the camera. Nusch rearranges her swimsuit top, a cigarette clamped between her lips, her gaze caught directly by Eileen's camera. Flanking her, as if revealing her for an instant, Dora stands on one side, wisps of her hair caught in the breeze as she holds some piece of clothing aloft. On the other side, Paul in a jaunty hat, looking at Eileen, and in the foreground Picasso, his bare back to the camera. In another image Dora adjusts her camera as Picasso walks away from her along the beach. Something has been happening here. Perhaps a conversation. Does it hint at their complications, their arguments and power struggles? Or perhaps it was nothing of the sort. This photograph, like so many others, invites questions, imaginings.

In another photograph, Lee captured something of Dora and Picasso too. Lee must have been sitting beside him on the beach. Dora, her hair wet from the sea, leans down to speak with or listen to Picasso. Though it's Dora whose body fills most of the frame, it's Picasso who dominates it. Her pose though looming is somehow supplicatory. We see only a torso, a hint of head and nose, an arm bent to shield his eyes from the sun and a cigarette in his fingers, but the body, in the lowest part of the frame, with the hairy, puffed-out chest, the insouciant grip on the cigarette, is unmistakably Picasso.

Sometimes there's more; a frisson of some greater intimacy that exists or is yet to come between the subject and the photographer. Roland took many photographs of Ady swimming in the sea, she's smiling, laughing, splashing about or diving into the waves, the shapes made by her naked body refracted by sunlight on the water. In one image she's standing in the sea at the entrance to a cave and in another she is lying back on some rocks beside the water, the bottom half of her legs beneath it. Her arms are flung down beside her. She is topless, her breasts upturned and her face beaming at Roland and at his camera. In another photograph, of Lee, again by Roland, she is lying on her back on the beach, wearing only swimsuit bottoms and sunglasses. She has swung one leg up into the air; her arms are outstretched above her head. This is what ease looks like, and nascent desire.

Picasso, restless, ever itching to create, drew pictures with a stick on the sand. And with Eileen, a fellow treasure-seeker, he combed the beach for pebbles, shells, driftwood and cuttlefish bones that had been smoothed by the sea. All these objets trouvés he kept in his room in a black trunk he'd bought in Cannes. Eileen writes in her memoirs about her first encounter with Picasso. She'd been walking on the beach, gathering things for her collection as she went. Picasso, who was with Paul, was lying on his stomach on the sand. Paul introduced Eileen and she proceeded to offer up her finds to Picasso as a greeting, a tribute, an act of affinity.

And then back to Mougins, and to long lunches on the hotel terrace. The Vaste Horizon was a simple pension, with a few clean, spare and shuttered rooms. Different iterations of the group of friends had stayed there in the past few years. This year they had taken over the entire hotel. There was only one room with a balcony, bougainvillaea-framed and looking down beyond a hillside covered in vineyards, cypresses, olive trees and hot pink oleander to the red rooftops of Cannes and the bay of Juan-les-Pins, beyond it. This room was claimed by Picasso for use as a studio.

Meals were taken on the terrace that nestled between two right-angled sides of the hotel and a lane that led up to the village, seated at basic trestle tables, with wooden benches and wicker chairs. Much of this terrace was shielded from the sun by a vine-covered bamboo canopy that cast a tiger-striped shade over faces and tables. Several giant terracotta pots holding palms stood sentinel outside the hotel and sun loungers were scattered here and there.

In photographs their lunches and dinners look much the same. At the head of the table sat Picasso, naturally, their mercurial, tyrannical, charming host, 'le Peintre Soleil', holding court. His attentive, attendant courtiers, the 'bande à Picasso', were ranged around the table. He set the tone, not just for lunch, but for the pattern of their days. At the table he entertained the group with his effortless bravura, his restless fingers etching pebbles from the beach, crafting sculptures from torn and twisted napkins or scribbling portraits on tablecloths using wine, spent matches, lipstick or whatever material was within his grasp. One afternoon he broke apart a matchbox and reconstructed it in the shape of the landscape that rolled out before them to the rooftops of Cannes. Eileen marvelled at his dexterity and economy. His impish sense of fun was the prevailing mood. In *Picasso: His Life and Work*, Roland would write that Picasso had been 'seized with a diabolical playfulness' during those weeks.

Photographs show tables with white tablecloths, scattered wine bottles, half-drunk glasses, coffee pots, ice buckets and bread baskets. We feel the sensual pleasure, the intimacy as the friends eat together. They sit in animated conversation, often huddled or entwined. We see their gestures, their embraces and almost hear their laughter. They were, as Man Ray would recall in his autobiography, 'a happy family'. They smoked cigarettes, played cards or word games, discussed politics and collaborated in drawing 'exquisite corpses'. This was a technique developed by the surrealists to celebrate chance, in which a piece of paper was drawn or written upon and then folded, and then drawn or written upon once more, folded again, and so on, with each player ignorant of the preceding addition, until at the end of the game the paper was unravelled to reveal the result of this unconscious collaboration. Sometimes Paul improvised poems in honour of his friends or read aloud to them from what he'd been working on. Eileen was intrigued that, though Picasso had not long finished *Guernica*, which had dominated his life in recent months, she never heard him mention it at Mougins. She thought this was deliberate, that Picasso was sceptical about its reception. He told her that he would never return to Spain. He was no longer an immigrant; he was in exile.

John Richardson would later recall (in an article in the *Guardian*) how Picasso could be a great friend, when he chose to be, and quite the opposite when he chose to be too. He likens him to a vampire, who demanded – required – love. And somehow he absorbed the energy of everyone and everything around him, which he used to fuel his work. Picasso's strong sense of self-discipline dictated hard work and Eileen would remember him crying out after lunch that it was time to work, as the others dozed on the terrace or sloped off for siestas or to make love in the cool of their rooms. His afternoons were spent painting, occasionally landscapes, but mostly light-hearted, riotously coloured, carnivalesque portraits of his friends at the hotel, *à l'Arlésienne* (in the costume of traditional women of Arles), perhaps an homage to van Gogh, who loved the city and whom Picasso greatly admired. Were these paintings catharsis after *Guernica*, or did they represent more? That summer Picasso had discovered that he (along with van Gogh) was amongst the artists branded as degenerate by the Nazis. Perhaps painting such bold, playful, kaleidoscopic portraits and appropriating the colours and the costumes of the Dutch artist was an act of fraternity, an act of defiance.

If they posed for these portraits at all, it was brief. Lee later recalled how she didn't sit for Picasso; he just presented her with the finished work. He preferred to paint from the images that memory forms, essentializing and reworking their likeness into distorted and yet immediately recognizable versions of themselves.

Though perhaps with less commitment, the others worked too, at collages and drawings and paintings. That summer, Dora, with Picasso's encouragement, was favouring painting over photography, and producing polychromatic canvases. Man Ray worked on drawings, Roland on collages made from postcards. Eileen took photographs of her lover, Joseph. Other times they cycled or wandered through the narrow streets of the medieval village or sat in the shade of plane trees in the village square. Picasso sometimes wanted to be alone. Other times, accompanied by Paul, he would be driven off by Marcel to visit Matisse in Nice, or to explore the old pottery factories in nearby Vallauris.

At night, Picasso went for walks with Dora beside the sea at Antibes or Juan-les-Pins. Eileen, meanwhile, would recall a late-night drive; Lee dancing trouser-less in front of the car's headlights. And she would write of how small the world then felt, how free, how pleasurable. And though they knew that the apocalypse was coming they could still live in happy denial and swim and sunbathe and sit around a table in the shade of a terrace, eating lotus.

PICASSO AND LEE

There are six portraits in all. Perhaps he couldn't quite capture something he saw in her, so that he was drawn to paint her compulsively, again and again. Or perhaps it is that each portrait represents some different aspect of her. The French expression Arlésienne evokes the epitome of female beauty, but also the dangerously seductive power of that beauty, and it is in this spirit that Picasso painted Lee. He was clearly beguiled by her, her sensuality, her warmth, her vivaciousness, her impetuosity and her luminescent beauty. There's a photograph of Lee and Picasso at the Vaste Horizon where he's laughing at something she's saying — deeply, heartily laughing. It's a joy and rapport that carries into the paintings.

In all of the portraits she's wearing the headdress with its flowing ribbon and the fichu of traditional Arlesian costume (a square or rectangular shawl, usually of white lace or embroidered cotton), but each is different in mood. These paintings are the most saturated with colour of those Picasso painted that summer at the Hôtel Vaste Horizon: fleshy Pepto-Bismol pink, jade green, turquoise, red, azure blue and acidic yellow. Her face is there in each portrait, her almond eyes, her Cupid's bow, her huge, gap-toothed grin, the green tinge of her curly blonde hair. In one, her torso becomes a black triangle, like a witch's hat. Another is a grid of black lines and black-ringed breasts overlaid on the brightest of colours. There's a portrait in which Lee's skin is blue, and her breasts appear to float from her chest. And in one her vulva is also an eye. There's a sense of the urgency with which Picasso painted, of how provisionally he worked, in the still-visible drips of paint on the canvases. One falls from an eye like a long tear.

Roland delighted in the fact that Lee inspired Picasso. He later bought the pink painting with the weeping eye and gave it to Lee, uniting painter and sitter and the man who loved them both.

LEE AND PICASSO

Picasso looks at Lee, at her camera. His magnetic, unwavering gaze, the focus of the photograph, the punctum. He's sitting on the terrace of the hotel and has turned his head to glance at her. Immediately behind him there's an inexplicably upturned parasol, a surreal note. Further back we see plants in terracotta pots by the steps to an open door. He is wearing a jacket, its cuffs rolled back, and the sleeves pushed up to reveal his tanned forearms. Beneath the jacket is a polka-dot shirt; white spots on a dark background. There is someone sitting beside him, but we see only a part of their back in the foreground. They too are wearing white spots on a dark background and become a strange extension to, or echo of, Picasso's body. This is presumably Dora, as she wears a blouse like this in other photographs. It's a moment of easy intimacy, of complicity between Picasso and Lee. He is a little vulnerable, trusting, off his guard. Did they have sex from time to time? Lee's son Antony believes they did, but he thinks that it was the least interesting thing about their relationship, that it didn't matter. As if it was merely an organic aspect of their bond, rather than its raison d'être. Perhaps there is something of that in the gaze. But there is also respect, and friendship. Picasso considered Lee an equal. They would remain close for the next thirty-six years and this was one of the first of many photographs – more than a thousand – that she would take of him.

LEE AND ROLAND

Roland is crouching on the tiled floor in his bathroom at the Hôtel Vaste Horizon. Behind him the window shutter is open, and sunlight pours in. On the floor a suitcase, a pencil, papers, some screwed up and discarded behind him. A tangle of linens hangs on the wall, perhaps drying. Roland is wearing trousers, a short-sleeved shirt and strappy leather sandals, the traditional Provençal kind. He has a cigarette in his fingers, his head is down, focusing on the work at hand, a collage constructed from postcards with local scenes which he'd bought nearby.

Roland was layering copies of the same postcard, splicing them together, fanning them out to form bold, dynamic patterns. He was bursting with the urge to create. He had been in Mougins, less happily, the previous year with his wife Valentine. But this year, 1937, was different. Earlier in the summer he had met Lee for the first time at a fancy-dress ball in Paris. She had escaped her husband and a stifling life in Cairo for a summer in France. For Roland, whose hair was bright green and one hand dyed blue for the occasion, it was a coup de foudre, and they had been inseparable ever since. He would later give some of these collages to Lee and she hung them on the wall opposite her bed when she returned home to Egypt, as loved and loving souvenirs.

MAN RAY AND PICASSO

For Picasso everything was a surface on which to make his mark. At the beach one day he drew a woman with a stick in the sand. She's unmistakeably Picasso – all full, curved limbs and sinuous lines. She's reclining, or is she swimming? One hand reaches for the hair that sprouts like a fountain from her head. She's two-dimensional lines but for her breasts, which are tenderly, carefully crafted little cones of sand that look like walnut whips. And then one work becomes two (or three if we count the negative), as Man Ray photographs it and the ephemeral drawing in the sand takes on a new life as something fixed, a collaboration, a memory.

PICASSO AND NUSCH

A few sketched lines in pencil, coloured with wine and lipstick. It has been torn from a paper tablecloth, suggested by the honeycomb of tiny indentations on its surface. Nusch, immediately recognizable, a vignette in impromptu miniature, adjusting her little round sunglasses, a rosebud mouth and corkscrew curls held back by a slim band around her head.

GUERNICA

Picasso had arrived from Paris licking his wounds. Back in January he had been visited at his studio by a delegation from the Spanish Republican government, who had pleaded with him to produce a painting for their pavilion at the Exposition that summer. Though he'd lived in France since 1904, he was still a native son of Spain. They wanted him to create something enormous, a powerful piece of propaganda, something which would illustrate the extent of the fascist threat and tell the world that Spain was in peril.

Picasso reluctantly accepted the proposal. He hated working to commission and had, for the most part, sought to avoid making explicit political statements with his work. Though he was currently creating a series of prints satirizing Franco, had given money to the Republican cause and recently accepted the position of Director of the Prado in Madrid, it irked him to be used as a political puppet.

As the months passed, he was still struggling to fix on a subject. He'd begun sketching on a habitual theme, that of the artist in his studio, with himself painting Marie-Thérèse Walter, one of his lovers (who he kept a secret from most of his friends) and the mother of his infant daughter Maya, born in 1935. He had recently leased a studio on the top two floors of the seventeenth-century Hôtel de Savoie at 7 rue des Grands-Augustins, which Dora Maar had found for him. Balzac had set his 1831 story 'The Unknown Masterpiece' there (which had long fascinated Picasso). And it had more recently been used by Georges Bataille and André Breton for meetings of their left-wing, anti-fascist group Contre-Attaque, founded at the end of 1933. The vast, labyrinthine attics of Picasso's studio were reached by a spiral staircase. Balzac wrote that the daylight never made its way into the darkest depths. There Picasso could immure himself from the outside world. He valued and defended his freedom above all else, and perhaps the sketches of his studio were a celebration of that freedom, the liberty to paint and to live how he wanted.

But the brutal and merciless bombing of Guernica on 26 April, carried out by the Nazi Luftwaffe at the behest of the Spanish Nationalist forces, had changed his mind. It was market day in the Basque town and hundreds of people were gathered in the central square. For three hours bombs rained down and the town was swiftly reduced to rubble. In the wake of the bombing, anything that moved, even sheep, was then machine-gunned by low-flying planes. This was followed by incendiary bombs that set fire to the ruins. Guernica had no strategic value and its destruction was unnecessary. For the Nazis it was a flexing of military muscle; a test run for the coming conflict and a birthday present for Hitler. For Franco it was symbolic, a gesture of demoralization and dominance over the fiercely independent Basque people, for whom Guernica was a sacred place.

The next morning the headline of *L'Humanité*, Picasso's preferred newspaper, announced: 'MILLE BOMBES INCENDAIRES lancées par les avions de Hitler et Mussolini', alongside photographs of the death and devastation. Five days after the bombing Picasso started work on preparatory sketches inspired by eyewitness accounts he had read in newspaper reports. On 10 May he started painting. The canvas he had chosen was nearly eight metres wide.

Though his work was rarely political in the obvious sense, he too was feeling the force of events beyond the walls of his studio. The poet Juan Larrea, who was the director of information at the Spanish embassy, had dashed to see Picasso at the Café de Flore to suggest the bombing as the theme for his commission. And, undoubtedly, he was much influenced by Paul Éluard, his great friend of the moment, and by his lover Dora, both of whom were passionately invested in radical left-wing politics. But Picasso's earlier disinclination to make a grand gesture against the fascists had already sparked rumours that he supported them. The international response to the plight of the Spanish people had been so vociferous and yet Spain's most famous living artist was curiously muted. And so, now committed to a public gesture, he had issued a statement as he worked on the painting. It said that the Spanish people were fighting for freedom and that he had dedicated his life as an artist to that fight. He questioned how anyone could doubt his commitment and said that his new painting, which he was calling *Guernica*, was an expression of his repulsion for the military oppression taking a stranglehold in Spain and plunging the country into a sea of pain and death.

For the next few weeks Picasso worked on the painting at a furious pace. He invited a group of friends, artists and politicians, including Alberto Giacometti, Max Ernst, André Breton, Roland Penrose and Henry Moore, into the studio to watch him paint and to see the work in progress. This was uncharacteristic, but a political statement, a performance, a gesture in the name of the anti-fascist cause felt necessary. 'No, painting is not done to decorate apartments,' Picasso would later declare in an interview to hammer his message home, 'It's an offensive and defensive weapon against the enemy.'

Dora had been commissioned by Christian Zervos of the journal *Cahiers d'Art* to document Picasso's progress, and she captured its evolution from a white canvas to a progressively darker one in a series of photographs taken as he worked. Two years earlier Picasso had said that he'd be interested to have the metamorphosis of one of his paintings photographed as he worked on it, while adding that a picture rarely changes from the artist's initial vision of it, despite subsequent changes they might make. Each weekday Picasso retreated into his studio, often with Dora beside him. For both, these were feverishly intense and intimate days of creativity. Picasso spent his weekends with Marie-Thérèse and Maya. Dora remained alone.

Guernica was completed on 4 June; it had taken thirty-five days. Over that period Picasso had reduced and essentialized his ideas to some few characters, gestures and images in a chaos of devastation in the moments after the bombing. Amongst them we see a horse in its death throes; a solitary bull; a dead soldier and a dead child in the arms of its agonized mother; screaming women; a tangle of burning, broken limbs engulfed in licking flames; arms flung up to the heavens in abject despair; a light that might be the sun and an arm outstretched with a torch as if to light it with the heat of the sun. Everything is happening at once. There's no harmony; the viewer's gaze doesn't move seamlessly through each detail to the heart of the painting, but rather darts from image to image, searching for meaning, trying to make sense of the pandemonium.

There is devastation, brutality, solitude and absurdity. Picasso didn't paint the event; there is no history here. Instead he painted the essence of terror and pain, the corporeal, the human. It's universal. This was his response to the horror. Rendered in stark monochrome, the painting becomes a tableau or a monochromatic grisaille frieze (painted to imitate sculpture or stonework): mythic, ancient, eternal. 'Where is the protest then?' asks John Berger in *The Success and Failure of Picasso*. '[. . .] What has happened to them in being painted is the imaginative equivalent of what happened to them in sensation in the flesh. We are made to feel their pain with our eyes. And pain is the protest of the body.'

Even though the canvas was finished, Picasso continued to work compulsively, obsessively, on its themes. For months he had been working on paintings, prints and drawings of a 'weeping woman', a character in the spirit of the anguished women he painted into *Guernica*, and which were inspired by Dora. They continued to appear like aftershocks for years to come.

And yet, despite Picasso's fame and the enormous scale of the canvas, many at the time considered the painting a failure, specifically that it had failed in its propagandist purpose to draw attention to the tragedy of Spain. Except for the title there was no explicit reference to the bombing of Guernica. Many on the left believed that the times called for artists to suspend their individuality in favour of communication and political expedience, to produce art with a clear message, using representation and simplicity, the socialist realism expected of artists in the service of the communist message.

Writing in 1936, the French poet and communist Louis Aragon declared that 'for artists as for every person who feels like a spokesperson for a new humanity, the Spanish flames and blood put realism on the agenda'. And so *Guernica* was dismissed as cryptic bourgeois nonsense by some and as communist cant by others. The German government declared that it could have been done by a child. Only a few art critics responded enthusiastically. Michel Leiris, the ethnographer, wrote: 'Picasso sends us our letter of doom: all that we love is going to die, and that is why it is necessary that we gather up all we love, like the emotion of great farewells, in something of unforgettable beauty.'

Characteristically Picasso ignored all this, at least publicly. He refused to go to the opening of the pavilion. And at the end of the Exposition, he rolled up his canvas and took it back to his studio (though officially it belonged to the Spanish Embassy). After such a public gesture as *Guernica*, he retreated hurriedly into his private world.

As always with Picasso, Thanatos and Eros – death and love – danced hand in hand; a dance that both enthralled and appalled him. After weeks of painting war, his mood shifted to desire and companionship. He longed for the south, for the warmth and light of the Mediterranean, which for him held a mythic allure, and for friendship and ease. By August he had escaped to the Côte d'Azur in his Hispano Suiza, driven by Marcel. Picasso preferred to be driven, and to travel by night. Often he would decide to leave on a whim and his chauffeur had to be ready to go at a moment's notice. With him on the journey were Dora, Paul and Nusch Éluard, a heap of canvases, painting materials, an easel and his dog, Kazbek.

AMITY

Paul believed that loving was the only reason for living. He believed in the primacy of human connection, and in openness to encounters and relationships, both sexual and platonic, which had the power to renew and transform. He was a radical champion of love, of erotic love. But also, deep love for his fellow man, friendship, amity –

amitié. And so, for him, those weeks at the Hôtel Vaste Horizon weren't just a holiday, they were a time of profound and enriching interconnection, of serious pleasures. 'Éluard always has an air of availability, of sovereignty,' wrote his friend the poet and essayist Claude Roy, 'but [. . .] he believes in friendship, he needs friendship as he needs air [. . .] He seems to live only on love and cold water and poetry, and a little whisky when there is any.'

Paul was born in 1895, in working-class Saint-Denis, a rapidly expanding, industrialized suburb to the north of Paris, where factories relentlessly puffed out smoke and where the kings of France were buried. Strongly socialist, it became known as *la ville rouge* (the red town). Eugène Émile Paul Grindel (he later took his maternal grandmother's maiden name as a pen name) had a comfortable childhood. His father was an accountant and then an estate agent, buying and selling land. His mother was a dressmaker with her own workshop. In 1908 the family moved from the suburbs into the city. But in 1912 he became seriously ill and was diagnosed with tuberculosis. His parents sent him to a sanatorium near Davos in the Swiss Alps where he met and fell deeply – headlong – in love with Helene Dmitrievna Diakonova (known as Gala), the daughter of a Russian lawyer. At the same time as falling in love he was reading poetry, symbolists and avant-garde poets like Rimbaud, Apollinaire, Baudelaire and Whitman, and he began to write poems of his own. When he announced that he wanted to be a poet his parents were horrified. Gala was delighted, and encouraging.

In the spring of 1914, to their dismay, Paul was sent home to Paris and Gala returned to Moscow. By the summer Europe was at war and Paul was deemed fit enough to work in the auxiliary forces. He was mobilized into the hospital nursing corps, although his continuing ill health meant that he spent much of his time having treatment in a hospital near his home. In 1916 he was working as a medical orderly at a military hospital a few kilometres from the front line. Paul lived daily with death, having been given the horrifying job of writing letters to the families of dead and dying soldiers and to help dig their graves. Later that year he married Gala, who had persuaded her family to let her move to Paris. When he returned to the war it was to the front line, for which he had volunteered and where he again became ill and was sent to a military hospital. Like so many people, the experience of war never left him.

After the war, with reluctance, but out of necessity, Paul worked with his father in the property business. And he began publishing his poetry, poems filled with peace, happiness, love and hope. He met fellow poets André Breton, Philippe Soupault and Louis Aragon. They became great friends and allies, united by their pacifism, by the repulsion for war and its meaninglessness, for the corruption at the heart of Western civilization and for the society that had engineered and sustained that war for four merciless years. And as with many young people in the wake of the First World War, they shunned respectability and aspiration and morality and the constraints of conventional society and went in search of freedom. Together they were drawn to the Dada movement, which had begun in Zurich and New York, had spread to Berlin and Cologne, and then began taking root elsewhere. By 1920 it was exploding on the Parisian avant-garde scene. Dada sprang from disgust at the senselessness and hypocrisy of the war. It was bitter, mocking, nihilistic, subversive and frivolous in its contempt for religion, authority, the family and patriotism – the veneer of civilization. Its purpose: to entirely upturn the old order, to foment chaos, to blow up the past. It was anti-art, anti-society, anti-*everything*.

To Paul it offered creative and social liberation, and he threw himself into their seemingly madcap antics, their 'manifestations'. There were demonstrations, performances and provocations. There was dance, music, theatre, cabaret, poetry, recitations, artworks. These 'gestures', as they came to be known, were often satirical, wilfully nonsensical and absurd (like poems made up of meaningless sounds), and performed in wildly inventive costumes. Dada was a disorientating, confrontational mirror to the nihilism of the modern world. In this iconoclastic spirit Paul was unshackling himself from poetic tradition, from logic and from syntax. He was going to create a new language, to destabilize the old one, and he did, while allowing space for echoes of that tradition to resonate through his work.

Paul and Gala had a daughter, Cécile, born in May 1918, but the marriage was tempestuous. They promised each other absolute sexual freedom, and while spending long periods of time apart as Gala travelled, they wrote to each other. Paul was entirely obsessed with his wife. Their separation, and her having sex with other men, only heightened his desire for her to an achingly erotic pitch, just as he wanted it to. And his feelings are clearly evident in his letters to her; letters which he asked her to get rid of when the relationship eventually fell apart, but which she would later publish. Their relationship evolved into an intimate threesome with Paul's friend and fellow Dadaist Max Ernst, which lasted for several years.

In March 1924, Paul suddenly disappeared. Depressed, desperate to escape his current life, his current job with his father and his current self, he slipped away, sailing from Marseille to Tahiti, Indonesia and Ceylon. After seven months, he returned on a Dutch cargo ship that sailed from Singapore to Marseille, a little ashamed of himself, and with his eyes firmly opened to the realities of European colonialism, of which he became a vocal critic. His friends and family had thought him dead.

Paul stopped working for his father, and for the rest of his life he would never have another full-time job, always struggling to make ends meet. He and Gala quickly squandered his inheritance when his father died. For a while after Paul's return, the couple stayed together and Max Ernst found a studio elsewhere in Paris. Eventually though, Gala left Paul for Salvador Dalí. She effectively abandoned their daughter Cécile too; she was left in the care of Paul's mother. The Éluards divorced in 1930, freeing her to marry Dalí.

There were those in the surrealist circle, including André Breton and the filmmaker Luis Buñuel, who, no doubt threatened by the force of Gala's personality, her intelligence, her sexuality, and by the power of her ambition and her influence over Dalí and over their comrades, thought that Gala was a witch. She was likened to a life-draining vampire, a dominatrix who devoured and controlled men. But it appears that she remained the love of Paul's life, and he continued to write deeply loving, deeply moving and erotic letters to her almost daily for many years. This didn't change even after meeting Nusch Benz, whom he would marry in August 1934, who would inspire his finest poems and who would become a loved and loving stepmother to Cécile.

If Gala represented doubt and violent, volatile, complicated passion for Paul, then Nusch was lightness, security, ease and easy desire. For Paul, Gala was elusive, evasive; Nusch was present, amenable. Both had their erotic appeal. In writing about Gala, he often used the pronoun 'you'. With Nusch, it becomes 'we'.

Dada eventually burned itself out. It had lost its ability to shock and to provoke, having floundered on its lack of focus, its inherent negativity and plague of internal conflicts. Surrealism, founded by André Breton, sprang from its ashes. Charismatic and doctrinaire, Breton had attended medical school and though his studies had soon been disrupted by the war, he worked as an orderly and later studied in an army neuropsychiatric centre, caring for victims of shell shock. Breton never qualified as a doctor; literature and the lure of the avant-garde eclipsed medicine. But his experiments with patients – working with their dreams and with free association – helped to lay the foundations of surrealism.

If Dada was cynical, surrealism was optimistic. Instead of chaos and anarchy and futility, surrealism was about vitality and rebellion and a new logic, a new reality that drew from the depths of the unconscious and from dreams and the imagination. Their philosophy was heavily influenced by Freud and by the Marquis de Sade. Radically, passionately, de Sade rejected what he perceived as the artificiality of conventional morality in defence of absolute freedom, the liberation of desire and the pursuit of pleasure. To the surrealists he was a hero, a freedom fighter, a role model.

The movement became official in October 1924 with the publication of the *Surrealist Manifesto*. Paris was its crucible. Soon there were all manner of elaborate techniques and practices like automatic writing and drawing (which, in theory, bypassed the conscious mind) and investigations into sexuality that were developed to help in the process of mining those furthest reaches of the psyche, to liberate the imagination and overthrow the rational. Pure thought was unsullied by convention and reason and logic and morality. The surrealists' task was to release that force and let it out into the world. They believed in openness, in shunning censorship, in looking for the marvellous in the everyday, in the power of chance, in the need to *épater la bourgeoisie* – shock the bourgeoisie – and in startling juxtapositions from which new forms could spring. For the surrealists this ambitious, idealistic ideology became an entire way of life, of living. It wasn't a movement; it was a state of mind. And they wanted to incite a revolution.

Paul belonged to the group from the beginning, but from the beginning he refrained from participating in some of their practices. Breton called him the reticent disciple. Poetry, Paul believed, was not formed in dreams, but crafted consciously. He focused his surrealist energies on the subject of women and on politics; he was passionately against capitalism, colonialism and racism. He joined the French Communist Party, the PCF, in 1926, but was expelled in 1933, partly in response to an article he had edited denouncing Socialist Realism in Soviet films. Surrealism then aligned itself with the Marxist revolution; its contribution was to enable the liberation of the mind.

For a long time surrealism was a men's club, but 'woman' was the wellspring. Breton defined 'woman' in *La Révolution surréaliste* with a quote from Baudelaire: 'La femme est l'être qui projette la plus grande ombre ou la plus grande lumière dans nos rêves' ('Woman is the being who brings the greatest shadow or the greatest light into our dreams'). The group believed that women (considered less rational and inclined to hysteria) had easier access to the workings of the mind and were therefore conduits for creativity. Women's unconscious (but not their conscious selves) and their (invariably naked) bodies were the loci of inspiration. Female madness was celebrated as 'the marvellous', the purest form of the surreal. Women were muses, and only later in the 1930s, begrudgingly, were a few allowed in as artists in their own right. And although more joined later, it was always a two-tier system.

'The problem of woman', André Breton wrote in his *Second Manifesto of Surrealism* in 1929, 'is the most marvellous and disturbing problem in all the world.' In 1929, in a composite illustration in *La Révolution surréaliste*, Magritte's painting of a naked woman is at the centre, surrounded by photographs of the surrealists. They all have their eyes shut. Woman, it implies, is not seen, but imagined. The surrealist woman was an idea, not a reality.

Heterosexual desire (homosexuality was proscribed and denounced by Breton, lesbianism was tolerated), and the energy it unleashed, was harnessed and exploited at the service of surrealism. *Amour fou* – mad love – was magical, spiritual, transcendental, born of a chance encounter. To the surrealists this was love at its most powerful, its most productive. There was poetry in everyday life, in intensely lived moments, re-enchanting the world. And poetry was then at the heart of surrealism. 'There is no total revolution,' wrote Paul, 'there is only perpetual Revolution, real life, like love, dazzling at every moment.'

The surrealists, especially Breton, had been courting Picasso, seeing him as one of their own in his iconoclasm and relentless pursuit of freedom. He had grown close to the movement but refused to align with it in any formal sense. Breton was desperate to be friends with Picasso, but it was Paul, the tall, elegant, joyful, poet with the deep voice, the gentle eyes and the gentle manner, who appealed to Picasso. Paul was both intensely private and public, a man of both sensitivity and revolution. And Picasso loved poets. Two of his greatest friendships had been with Max Jacob and Guillaume Apollinaire. He had respect for very few people, but one of those was Paul.

Their acquaintance began in 1935 and grew into a deep and

reciprocal friendship, and Dora later told Roland that along with Jean Cocteau, Paul was the greatest influence on Picasso after 1920. They encouraged one another, discussing and exchanging ideas about art and poetry. Paul shared with Picasso his theories about the artist's responsibility in society. And they discussed politics, with which Paul had long been engaged but Picasso only since the war in Spain, which, for now, had turned him into a political painter.

Paul had the seasoned eye of an art expert. He loved painting and had over the years built up impressive collections of books and contemporary art, including a large collection of surrealist, Oceanian and African art bought from his many artist friends. And these he could sell at a profit when he needed to, often back to his friends (like Roland Penrose). Then he would start over. He had also been collecting Picasso's works since the early 1920s.

Paul understood art and, perhaps more importantly in terms of his friendships, he instinctively understood artists and their process. Over the years he would write essays and exhibition catalogues, dedicate numerous poems to artists and collaborate on illustrated anthologies of his poems. He delighted in responding intuitively to the work of others – both text and image – and initiating a dialogue, a relationship, with their creator from which sprang new collaborations. Paul and Picasso worked together on the first issue of the magazine *Minotaure* and, later, on the *Cahiers d'Art*. Paul's 1936 collection of poems, *Les yeux fertiles* (*Fertile Eyes*), was written as a celebration of his friendship with Picasso. He was devoted and often said that he was grateful to have lived in the twentieth century because it meant that he could meet Picasso. He believed deeply that everything changed in art with Picasso, that he pulled the walls down. Over the years around sixteen publications would result from their collaborations.

In return Picasso illustrated some of Paul's publications. But Paul often claimed that the role of the poet was to inspire rather than to be inspired, and during the first year of their friendship, Picasso began writing poetry, which coincided with a crisis in his painting.

It became an obsession and, for a time, words eclipsed images. His long-time champion Gertrude Stein was disapproving, perhaps fearing an encroachment on her territory, but Paul was encouraging.

Of course Picasso returned to his painting, and surrealism's increasing influence can be seen in his portraiture, in the focus on the perceived psychology of the subject, and the jarring distortion of bodies, but he continued to write poems (and later plays) alongside his art. Eileen Agar would later recount an amusing conversation she had with Picasso at Mougins about this period in his life. He told her that one night he realized that he couldn't continue to paint, and instead began to write poetry. He soon realized, he told her, that poems couldn't support his lifestyle, with his mistress and his penchant for good restaurants. And so he had returned to painting.

But perhaps what united Paul and Picasso most deeply was Eros. Both were driven by erotic desire; it was central to the inspiration and creation of their work. The early years of Picasso's friendship with Paul coincided with his relationship with Marie-Thérèse and the most visibly erotic period in his painting. Paul believed that he was bound together with his friends and his lover and that his poetry flowed from this unity. Perhaps surprisingly, much of his love poetry, especially from the mid-1930s, focuses on the sanctity of the couple. The couple as a fragile but erotically powerful ideal, but also as something more outward-looking, less self-limiting and personal. For Paul, love became a force of potential to be harnessed in the service of social change, though his idea of fidelity was far from conventional. Breton called him '*le partouzard*' ('the orgy lover'). Paul liked to offer Nusch to his friends as a gift, a gesture of friendship, an *hommage*, he called it. This (which has at times been linked to Candaulism, a specific kind of voyeurism) greatly aroused him. Sometimes writers have sought to find greater meaning in the act, to interpret it as evidence that Paul was a repressed homosexual, that Nusch became a proxy for his desire. Others suggest that his years of illness had left him impotent.

Inevitably Nusch was offered to Picasso too. He loved to paint her but whether or not they slept together is unclear. In *Life with Picasso*, the artist (and Picasso's later partner) Françoise Gilot suggests that Picasso accepted, but only to avoid insulting Paul. In *The Minotaur Years*, the fourth volume of his biography of Picasso, John Richardson tells a different version of events, quoting the artist, who claims that Paul encouraged him to have sex with Nusch and when Picasso refused it angered Paul, who saw it as a rejection of his friendship.

Paul had visited Picasso in his studio almost daily during the creation of *Guernica*. In dialogue with the painting, he wrote 'La Victoire de Guernica' ('Victory at Guernica'), his responsiveness and reciprocity a testament to his admiration for the painting and the painter. It was a consciously anti-fascist gesture. And the title of the poem was ironic, but hopeful. It was exhibited alongside the painting in the Spanish pavilion. And later he would write a book called *À Pablo Picasso* as an impassioned tribute to his friend: 'You hold the flame between your fingers,' he wrote. '[. . .] All is reborn before your just eyes.'

PAUL

They would evolve throughout his life, but his poems were almost always a celebration of love, of desire, a mapping of intimacy. Or they were about the longing for social change, inspired by his life, by the world he lived in or by historical events. Often the two – heterosexual desire and activism – were interwoven in a deeply personal embrace. It is sensuous, dreamlike, and feels deceptively simple. And it is real, fluid, spontaneous, almost provisional. Images and ideas fuse and morph. His poetry was always too lyrical for surrealism, just as his warmth and gentleness and generosity of spirit didn't entirely fit the surrealist mould. His poetry is a radical, transgressive fist in an elegantly wrought glove.

There's a prosody that demands to be read aloud, to be listened to, sounds and sentences to savour, to delight in, and to linger on the destabilizing, unexpected and yet crystalline images he crafted.

He writes with urgency and attention, mostly free of punctuation and with everyday words. He writes of the moment, of now, and of feeling – in its deepest sense – and of things tangible and elemental, of light and shade. And he writes of beloved bodies and of his desire and encounters with them, almost as if we're having the experience with him, gazing with him. But then his instinct was always to share, even – perhaps especially – the women he loved. Living, and living well, were paramount to him, and superseded notions of morality. For Paul, goodness expressed itself in good living, and evil in submission and defeat.

There's little that is lofty, arcane or elitist about his poetry. Just as there was nothing of the ivory tower about Paul. More than anything he wished to communicate – to commune, to write for all, for his words to be read and his sentiments understood, perhaps recognized: to show and make seen, to connect. In the years to come, this instinct would become more urgent. More necessary.

VASTE HORIZON

Eileen and Joseph were the newcomers that summer of 1937, which is perhaps why of all the guests at the Hôtel Vaste Horizon she had the most to say about Mougins, and dedicates a chapter in her memoirs to it. As a relative outsider Eileen was in a good position to observe the group that gathered that September. She's a shrewd, irreverent and engaging storyteller, at once of the group and yet a little removed, a little cynical, perhaps amused by her recollections of that time. 'Am I a surrealist?' she calls one chapter, asking herself the question as the group had sought to claim her.

Early the previous year Roland Penrose and Herbert Read, a critic and poet and fellow British surrealist, were choosing work for their International Surrealist Exhibition that was to be held in London at the New Burlington Galleries in June. In its early days surrealism was predominantly a literary movement, and dominated by men. Over the years it was evolving to allow for artists who were gradually moving to its forefront, and slowly, tentatively allowing for women artists too. Eileen was having an affair with the British surrealist painter Paul Nash, having met him in 1935 in Dorset, where she was renting a house for the summer with Joseph. It was probably Nash who suggested that Penrose and Read should visit her studio. They selected three paintings and five objects. She had thought her work unique, highly personal, and now, suddenly, she was seen as a surrealist.

She was undoubtedly an ally to the movement. Vivacious and intelligent, she lived openly, freely, poetically, and was receptive to the 'marvellous', and to chance. Her studio flat in Earl's Court, filled with her vibrant, cerebral paintings and collages, her extraordinarily eclectic collection of found objects – shells, fabric, stones, skulls – and her fantastical sculptures and assemblages, resembled an ever-evolving *Wunderkammer*, a cabinet of curiosities. She likened it to a shipwreck offered up by the sea.

Eileen questioned her affiliation. Breton's beloved automatism (whereby techniques were used to bypass the conscious mind so that the unconscious became the principal source of creativity) left her uninspired. But if association with the surrealists meant exhibitions and publicity, then she was happy to go along with it. Her work was exhibited alongside Brancusi, de Chirico, Duchamp, Dalí, Ernst, Klee, Picabia, Giacometti, Miró and of course Picasso. Meret Oppenheim's *Object*, her wittily erotic play on notions of femininity and female sexuality, a fur-covered teacup, saucer and spoon, was the talk of the show – T. S. Eliot was obsessed.

The exhibition drew huge crowds, brought the traffic on Piccadilly to a standstill and provoked passionate arguments. Augustus John walked out and slammed the door when Paul Éluard began a panegyric on de Sade during his poetry lecture. Dalí, lecturing in a diving suit and helmet on an incredibly hot day, almost suffocated, while the audience laughed and applauded, thinking it was all part of the spectacle. Inevitably there was a lot of publicity and controversy. The British press (and soon the British public) was baffled, scandalized and fascinated. Eric Newton, a critic writing for *The Manchester Guardian*, was more open-minded than many, reassuring his readers that they needn't be shocked by surrealism, that they need only look at the work of Lewis Carroll, Hieronymus Bosch and William Blake to see its predecessors.

A photograph of several exhibitors and associates was taken one afternoon in the gallery. Eileen (who was invited by Paul Éluard to join them) sits in the centre, in the front row beside Nusch and several other women. Behind them stands a row of men: Paul Éluard, Salvador Dalí, Roland Penrose and other surrealists. It's terribly serious, curiously formal – the men in their buttoned suits and ties, the women elegant in skirt suits and jaunty hats – but that was very much the point. Eileen writes about the care with which surrealist women dressed, and it could equally apply to the men. Out in public they delighted in wearing eccentric but highly elegant dresses (or well-cut suits) designed by the avant-garde couturier Elsa Schiaparelli, which contrasted with their astonishing behaviour and their shocking art. This antithesis was unsettling, unexpected: surrealism in action.

For the most part (with some notable exceptions), British surrealism never had the fervour of the French contingent. It was never quite as serious. Perhaps it was more romantic, less dogmatic, and more aligned with Blake and Carroll (as the *Guardian* critic noted) than with Freud and free association. Writing in her memoirs, Eileen blamed this on the English temperament, a certain complacency, a reluctance to disrupt the status quo and the urge to turn every event into something social rather than serious.

In July 1937 Eileen and Joseph were invited by Roland to a gathering at Lambe Creek, his brother's Georgian house hidden between woods and water near Truro in Cornwall. Paul and Nusch were there, fellow surrealists Leonora Carrington and Max Ernst, Man Ray and Ady, and the Belgian surrealist E. L. T. Mesens. Roland of course was host, with Lee, in the very early days of their relationship. The mood, as established by Roland and described by Eileen, was ludic, orgiastic. She writes of being invited to watch Lee have a bath but that there was not enough room in the tub for Eileen and everyone else to join her.

She began a brief, casual affair with Paul Éluard, and claims Joseph wasn't jealous as he was having sex with Nusch. Paul Nash, however, was driven wild with jealousy. He could share her with Joseph because Nash believed that there was some lyrical part of Eileen's spirit with which only he could connect, but it was a part that Éluard had now usurped. Eileen was beguiled by the poet's joie de vivre and devotion to the erotic life. The deeply serious, sensitive poet could also take delight in the smallest, simplest of pleasures. In her memoirs she writes that Joseph took Paul for lunch at the Savage Club when he was in London. At the end of the meal he was given orange jelly which wobbled and quivered on the plate like a breast. This sent Paul into paroxysms of erotic delight as he nudged it again and again with his spoon.

It was because Eileen and Joseph had proved such willing participants in the surrealist spirit of the house party in Cornwall that Paul Éluard decided to invite them to come to Mougins in September. For Eileen the invitation to join Picasso at the Vaste Horizon meant she'd finally arrived in the art world. She was thrilled to be meeting him. And after the delights of Cornwall, she was reluctant to return to London, to the ordinary world.

At the Vaste Horizon, Picasso became the master of revelries. He suggested that they should all swap names. He became Don José Picasso. Joseph Bard became Pablo Bard, Man Ray became Roland Ray, Eileen Agar became Dora Agar. And if they forgot their names they were fined. The name swapping was playful, permissive, allowing for both the familiar and the strange, imbued with the disruptive spirit of misrule. Soon, as well as names, and as at Lambe Creek, they were swapping lovers. This was living surrealism, an openness to experience, to the experience of other bodies and a belief in sexual pleasure as a catalyst for change. As it was in their art, so it was in their lives: exchange, experiment, connection and collaboration.

In these fluid, casual, sexual encounters, these temporary, provisional pairings, there's a sense of the chance meeting, of conscious disruption and complication, of fresh juxtapositions that created unexpected, intriguing new dimensions and discoveries to inspire the imagination. Beyond the exclusivity of the couple, fidelity didn't have to mean monogamy, which they considered bourgeois. There was a sense of communal love, a loving community, a collective spirit. And perhaps there was safety in being amongst like-minded people, the security of mutually felt, mutually respected openness and freedom.

The men had their well-documented kinks. The women's desires are less known. Roland was interested in restraint and liked to handcuff his partners to the bed. He bought Lee a gold pair from Cartier and in her memoirs Peggy Guggenheim (with whom Roland had a brief affair in 1938) recalls him using a pair of ivory bracelets to tie her up when they had sex. He didn't mind the reference to the cuffs, but pointed out that they were the ordinary police type, not ivory. Man Ray had at least a theoretical and creative interest in BDSM and Picasso, as Marie-Thérèse would later discuss in an interview, was experimental and enjoyed novelty.

For Éluard, polyamory was central not just to his erotic vision but to his way of life. John Richardson writes that Picasso recalled sitting with Nusch in a cafe while Paul went off to a hotel with a sex worker. And Claude Lanzmann, the French filmmaker (who is best known for his Holocaust documentary *Shoah*), writes in his memoirs *The Patagonian Hare* of visiting the Éluards' apartment just after the war. Paul invited him into the kitchen. Nusch was in the bedroom. 'I heard moans from the adjoining room, the door to which was ajar,' he recalls. 'In the bevelled mirror, I glimpsed the red pompom of a marine's beret. Éluard seemed to have quickly thrown on pyjamas before opening the door to me.'

We know Lee and Eileen had affairs, and shared the same instinct for openness as the men. In *A Look at My Life* Eileen insists that she didn't have sex with everyone who asked her, but that she disagreed with absolute fidelity, writing that she saw her relationships with Paul Nash and Paul Éluard as opportunities for love. As for Ady and Nusch, were they free (or did they even want to be?) or under instruction from their partners? We don't know what they enjoyed. For Dora, most probably, there was only Picasso, and whatever he wanted.

Perhaps inspired by Paul, Roland offered Lee to Picasso as a mark of his devotion. Again, it's not clear whether Picasso accepted the *hommage* and we don't know what Lee thought of it either. But it's difficult to imagine her doing anything she didn't want to do. Eileen writes in her diary of a flirtatious frisson between herself and Roland, and how when Lee caught wind of this, she sprayed Eileen with a water siphon. Eileen responded by telling Roland to control his girlfriend. It was all playful, perhaps.

Realities and cares and fears of a coming war were for now suspended, but time was running out, and they knew it. Even Éluard, the most politically engaged of the group, had cancelled his plans to attend the International Writers' Conference in Spain to join Roland at Lambe Creek, favouring friendship over politics. But then, for Éluard, the personal was political. Eileen writes of her happiness at Mougins, swimming and taking photographs and living amongst friends for whom art and poetry were not aspects of life but life itself. And yet the distant rumbling of war was getting ever louder, ever closer.

But it was not just war that they swept aside in those weeks. There were husbands and wives and children and fears about assets and money. Man Ray was in the process of divorcing a wife back in America. Picasso's discarded wife Olga continued to plague him, he felt, and was threatening to break up his estate. His son Paulo felt abandoned by his father, and he had Marie-Thérèse and Maya tucked away in a house in the countryside outside Paris at Le Tremblay-sur-Mauldre. Lee's patient, loving husband of three years was in Cairo, awaiting her return.

At the time, the friends believed that their affairs with each other only helped to strengthen their friendships and their romantic relationships. But freedom is always relative. For the surrealists, the Marquis de Sade was a heroic libertarian, but his sexual fantasies of torture, rape and murder illustrate how the liberty of one person can mean the oppression and degradation of another. Invariably that other was a woman.

In a moving letter Roland's first wife, Valentine Penrose, writes to her husband, discussing the breakdown of their marriage and the previous summer of 1936, which they'd spent with Picasso and others in Mougins. She says that she has lost faith in life, and wants to regain it, to seek beauty rather than novelty, experimentation and sensation, as he does. She tells him how difficult she has found living with him in his pursuit of these things, especially during that previous summer, and how painful it had been to try to live like that too, which she has been attempting for his sake. Eileen writes of the hypocrisy amongst the surrealists, that the men's sexual freedom was encouraged, but not so the women's. She gives as an example Lee, who, while in a relationship with Man Ray in Paris earlier in the 1930s, had decided to free herself, to much disapproval in the surrealist ranks.

In photographs taken at Mougins, Dora is rarely smiling, although there are a few exceptions. In one image, taken by Lee, Dora and Picasso are standing in the sea. The water's up to their waists. Picasso, bare chested, an easy smile, squinting against the sun. Dora, beside him, smiling too, in a two-piece swimsuit and nuggety necklace Picasso has whittled for her, her hair wet from the sea. But she often seems somehow detached and wary, and even in this photograph there's a sadness or perhaps a reticence in her eyes. Eileen observed there seemed to be something condemnatory that remained unarticulated beneath Dora's elegant, restrained demeanour. Evidently, she lived in constant fear of being abandoned by her lover. When they returned to Paris after the summer she wrote to Picasso, trying to justify her outbursts, telling him that her jealousy was making her mad and causing her pain. She promises to redeem herself and begs for his patience and forgiveness.

Looking back at this time – all so seemingly carefree – it's tempting (and easy with hindsight) to speculate as to what might have lain beneath, what is not seen in photographs, what is not written about in memoirs. Was there power play at work? Were there frictions, tensions, rivalries, jealousies, rages? It's easy to lose sight of how radical the group were, that these were experiments in modern living, and loving. And perhaps, like all experiments, it's the attempt we must admire, not their ultimate success or failure.

PICASSO AND PAUL

She's sitting on a bright red van Gogh-like chair in a dark room, the wall behind her is black. It's presumably Picasso's hotel room; the window shutter is the same as in photographs. The shutter is open and letting in warm and golden, perhaps sunset-sunlight. It becomes a glowing block in the black, composed of stripes of gold and amber and outlined in red. The light falls on the woman and on the wall behind her, which is salmon pink. As in Picasso's portraits of Lee, she's an Arlésienne in traditional costume – a black and white striped skirt fans out from her waist, an orange shawl with a black fringe is tied around her shoulders and on her head is a traditional straw hat in darkest blue and yellow. Her hair is perhaps a bun, tied with a green ribbon. Her skin is mostly pea green – face, neck, arms and hands spread out like chubby claws with yellow fingernails. One breast, heavy with milk, is also green with a blue and white nipple, and at which a small striped yellow kitten is suckling. Her other breast and her upper torso beneath the shawl are salmon pink like the wall behind her. She has pretty eyes with long lashes, and ruddy red cheeks to match her red teeth, showing through a smile. Her distorted face, with its strong nose, high forehead and gentle eyes, belongs to Paul. Apparently, the friends were shocked when Picasso presented this latest portrait at lunch. Roland thought it was a joke. An in-joke, perhaps with some oblique allusion now lost. Maybe this was Picasso laughing at surrealism. Or perhaps Paul-as-cross-dresser was Picasso's way of making some kind of comment on his friend's sexual practices.

LEE AND NUSCH

Perhaps they were about to leave after a morning at the beach; this was taken at Golfe-Juan and Nusch is wearing a swimsuit and a sarong. Lee must have been sitting on the ground to take the photograph because we're looking up at Nusch. The grille of the car becomes a looming edifice and behind it we see only sky. Nusch is perched on the fender, one hand's resting on it and the other's in her lap. Her head is tipped back and she's laughing; a hearty kind of laugh that shows her teeth and gives her a double chin.

Women photographing women. This photograph is not about Nusch's body, this is about her personality. Something's amused her. In Lee's lens she's a subject not an object. For women photographing women there's perhaps a greater possibility of finding something more than an image that bounces back with a reflection of the photographer's own desire. This image speaks of tenderness, camaraderie, ease, complicity, connection. How differently the men photographed the women that summer, as a form of sexual possession. Here Nusch is real, not surreal.

For some women, within the limited freedoms they had access to in the 1920s and 1930s, the avant-garde world would have had a glittering allure – the prospect of freedom, of passionate debates clustered around cafe tables, an invitation to rebel, to belong, perhaps to create. A promise of something other than conventional domesticity, of alternative arrangements. A woman in the surrealist orbit, if she was not an artist in the conventional sense (and sometimes even if she was), fell into one category or another, almost mythological, like the women in Arthurian romances, or tarot card characters that represent different destinies. She was adored, an exalted muse. She was a helpmeet, a model, an erotic site. She had to be able to inspire the man who had chosen her, either as the virgin or the whore, the angel or the witch or the sybil or the hysteric or the femme fatale or the child or the child-woman. To be welcomed in, she had to be beautiful. Deference, subordination, abdication were expected. She was a vassal, a vessel. Because, although some were artists, mostly they were bodies – to have sex with, to share with friends, to pose, to tie up, to photograph, to panegyrize. Man-handled. Women in the slipstream of famous men. 'Headless. And also footless. Often armless too; and always unarmed, except with poetry and passion. There they are,' writes the art historian Mary Ann Caws in her essay 'Seeing the Surrealist Woman: We Are a Problem': 'the surrealist women so shot and painted,' Caws says, 'so stressed and dismembered, punctured and severed: is it any wonder she has (we have) gone to pieces?'

Women and their bodies: unavoidable, ever political, ever problematic. A woman and her body coexist in the world. She's public property, disputed territory. Dora's likeness was being appropriated and used and reused as the epitome of grief. Lee had been raped as a child. In the past, when she'd needed to, Nusch had done sex work. Ady was a black woman negotiating life in a fundamentally racist, as well as sexist, society. But these were also bodies that painted, performed, danced, photographed, felt pleasure. It was left to these women to make space for themselves within that world, to struggle to find their own ways to make freedom and to live creative and meaningful lives. To make themselves the subject and not the object.

DORA MAAR

An early self-portrait from 1930. Dora as she saw herself, and how she wanted to be seen. She's looking into a mirror and it's her reflection that we see. The mirror is standing on a bookcase, its frame white-fluted, a fan in front of it that partly conceals her face, books stacked on the shelf below. Her black hair is fashionably cropped, a short fringe across her forehead, and her light-coloured blouse is unbuttoned at the neck. She's standing by a window and light falls on her face, a look of determination, a direct gaze returning a direct gaze. She looks self-assured. Perhaps one hand on her hip as the other clicks the shutter. Some said she had pale blue eyes; others remembered them as hazel, or dark. Here they are bright. And a pale, serious, oval face with thick eyebrows, a strong jaw and a slightly downturned mouth.

Dora's look was central to the self that she presented to the world. Over the years it evolved, became more severe, more dramatic, more elegant. Armour, perhaps. Longer hair, swept up, and often beneath a Schiaparelli hat; black Balenciaga suits, long, painted nails at the end of her long, beautiful hands. At the time of this self-portrait she was very social. Though later she was remembered as reserved, volatile, intransigent and proud, she had many friends, friends who loved and admired her talent and creative passion, her conviction, her wit, her independence and perhaps, above all, her acute intelligence. By the time Françoise Gilot knew her, she would marvel at Dora's demeanour, her stillness, and that she spoke little, gesticulated even less. She was proud, dignified, but more than that, there was a strictness, a rigidness, a disquieting solemnity.

But that was later. Had she always been like this? Or is this how she became?

'Some lives', writes Olivia Laing in a review of a biography of Ted Hughes in *The Observer*, 'fall into dangerous shapes, patterns that dominate and overcome any individual involved, turning them into archetypes, divesting them of their complexity, the swarm of possibilities that all of us contain.' Before Dora was turned into an archetype, an epithet, before she became one in a mythologized line of women in the 'divorced, beheaded, died, divorced, beheaded, survived' mould, her life was a swarm of possibilities and complexities. Dora the radical, the artist, the celebrated photographer, the political activist, the friend, the lover and, almost uniquely, the woman embraced and respected by the surrealists for her work and not for her body.

She was born in Paris in 1907. Henriette Théodora Markovitch was the daughter of a French mother who owned a fashion boutique and a Croatian father who was an architect, and who gave Dora her first camera as a child. When she was three, the family moved to Buenos Aires in Argentina, where she learned to speak Spanish. She could also speak English, learned from an English friend at school. Her childhood was spent travelling between South America and France, and her first photographs were of the long sea journey between the two. In the 1920s she moved to Paris to study painting and applied arts at the Union Centrale des Arts Décoratifs and the École de Photographie. She also enrolled at the Académie Julian. These were some of the city's most progressive art schools. But by the early 1930s increasingly she found herself drawn to photography, and painting was sacrificed in its favour.

For women, photography meant freedom, and potentially a career. Since the turn of the century camera companies had been actively marketing to women, as a way to celebrate their increasing emergence from the home, to see the world outside and to capture it. Photography was empowerment – the photographer's vision, their choice of subject matter, their framing. For women it meant independence. Lee Miller thought that women were particularly suited to photography, particularly portraiture, believing them to be more adaptable to the moment, more intuitive than men. Perhaps too because they are used to being looked at; they know how it feels to have a lens pointed at them.

In 1931 Dora opened a professional studio in the fourteenth arrondissement with fellow photographer and set designer Pierre Kéfer. She was bursting with ambition and ideas. She was a working woman, and she gave herself a new name: Dora Maar.

Soon she was as successful as her friends the Hungarian photographer Brassaï (with whom she shared a darkroom) and Henri Cartier-Bresson, balancing her personal photography with her commercial work. She was popular on the Parisian art scene, spending much of her time with her friend Jacqueline Lamba from her days at the Beaux-Arts and socializing with the surrealists at the Café Cyrano on place Blanche in Pigalle, their favoured haunt. She was fascinated by Breton and no doubt flattered by his appreciation of her work. When Jacqueline Lamba began a relationship with Breton it drew Dora closer still into the heart of the group. Paul Éluard became her closest male friend. Nusch she loved, and loved to photograph.

Dora became entrenched in surrealist ideas, ideas which began to show in her work. And she was heavily influenced by the photography of the avant-garde and by their technical innovations. By then she was taking portraits, taking photographs on the streets – both as personal work and as reportage for clients – and making images for advertising, couture houses and fashion magazines like *Madame Figaro*. The same spirit runs through all of her work; she was experimenting, manipulating images in the darkroom, exploring surrealist ideas, and she was drawn to the dangerous and the transgressive. She loved to shock, to provoke.

Dora's photography is filled with drama, a mysterious ambiguity and frequently a dark, unsettling, almost macabre humour. Landscapes are filmic, oneiric. There are reflections and vertiginous, often eerily gothic perspectives, looking down onto empty tree-lined streets or up the stone steps of Mont-Saint-Michel, half in light, half in shade. Peopled street scenes look natural, seemingly spontaneous. But there's always something extra-ordinary about them, the photographer's chance encounter, the everyday made marvellous.

There are visual tricks, there's clever tight framing and there's playing with words. In Dora's photographs the ordinary is rendered enigmatic and uncanny, inherently surreal. There are queasily upturned spaces and indistinguishable amorphous shapes. One of her most famous and shocking images is of an armadillo foetus, a little being, vulnerable and grotesque in its nakedness. A tiny boat dances across shimmering waves of golden hair in an advert for hair oil; a sensual, subtle, clever image. A model is dressed in a beautifully draped and gathered evening dress, her back turned, her arms pulling back curtains to reveal a star-filled darkness; there's a glittering star in place of her head. Dora's work in fashion and advertising is intelligent, elegant, fun and fantastical. Fashion, she implies, is not about perfection but imagination. A spider's web has been superimposed onto a photograph of Nusch's face, which is in ethereal, contemplative mode, the painted nails at the end of her delicate fingers pressing into her cheeks. A spider sits on the bridge of her nose at the centre of the web. This photograph she gave the title *The Years Lie in Wait for You*, which would have a kind of prophetic irony because, sadly for Nusch, the years did not.

The Kéfer–Dora Maar studio closed in 1934 and, with financial help from her father, Dora opened her own studio at 29 rue d'Astorg in the eighth arrondissement. This gave her the freedom to become even more experimental. She began working with photomontage and the strange, ludic quality of her work only increased. All is fantasy, cutting and pasting to satisfy the whims of her imagination: a hand emerges tentatively, elegantly from a seashell; a sky is filled with eyes; people do unnervingly ambiguous things in complicatedly erotic but also ridiculous scenarios. There's a knowing, perhaps slightly subversive use of surrealist tropes, of the disembodied woman. The head and shoulders of a very modern woman with a perfectly painted face and perfectly set white-blonde hair has been detached from her body and set onto a pedestal. A pair of shapely legs hovers above the Seine, a hand in the foreground, its fingers reaching to pinch one dainty, floating foot.

Dora was highly committed to political engagement and became involved in the October Group, a Marxist theatre troupe, along with her friends Éluard, Louis Aragon and the poet and screenwriter Jacques Prévert. Political conviction suffused her photography and in the early 1930s she travelled across Europe on self-commissioned photojournalist trips, highlighting the plight of the poor in Barcelona and Paris and London with her easily portable Rolleiflex. She attended and photographed rallies and demonstrations, and signed manifestoes, all in support of the anti-fascist movement and of the surrealist cause. She signed her name to *Appel à la lutte* ('Call to the Struggle'), a tract written by Breton in affiliation with the far left in response to fascist riots. It was signed by many of her surrealist friends and by the screenwriter Louis Chavance, with whom she had a relationship. She also joined the anti-fascist movement Contre-Attaque, and had a brief affair with its founder Georges Bataille, the surrealist, author and intellectual. Bataille was also founder of Masses, the ultra-leftist association, and a sadomasochism enthusiast. Though the affair was brief, it was probably quite enlightening.

And then everything changes, the metamorphosis begins. But in this myth, almost Ovidian, she doesn't become an animal or a plant, but an idea. Winter, in early 1936, Dora sits at a table at Les Deux Magots on place Saint-Germain-des-Prés. Elegantly dressed, perhaps in a hat, lipstick, nail polish. She is alone. She takes off her gloves – black, and embroidered with rosebuds. One hand rests on a wooden table, the other is clutching a penknife. This she drives between her outstretched fingers, stabbing into the wood between them, faster and faster. Sometimes she catches herself, and drops of blood begin to appear. Eventually she puts her gloves back on and here and there the rosebuds begin to darken.

DORA

A man in a suit is walking along a pavement, beside a brick wall; it looks like any London street. In front of him is another man. He's looking down an inspection hole in the pavement, obviously having lifted the cover with the tool he's cast aside on the pavement. His head and an arm are already in there, and it appears as if the rest of his body is about to follow. As if he's about to disappear. He's wearing what looks like a suit and seemingly smart leather shoes. He looks entirely incongruous. It's as if he's a businessman, much like the man walking behind him, but that he's escaping the workaday world for an alternative, something more exciting beneath the streets. And it's like a metaphor for so much of Dora's photography, for how she herself – like the man in the street – sought and found those holes or fissures in the ordinary world and glimpsed the surreal beyond them. Her photographs invite the viewer to imagine. Look closer, they seem to say: can you guess what's happening here?

ISLAND

They're at the picnic table on the Île Sainte-Marguerite. Eileen and Joseph aren't with them. And neither are Dora and Picasso, they've had an argument. This is after lunch and the plates have been cleared. There's a flask (presumably coffee) and a wine bottle and scattered glasses. Ady has her arm around Lee's head and another hand inside her swimsuit bottoms; they're lying on the ground. Ady's grinning up at the camera, a look of complicity. Paul is squatting beside them, watching, his hand somewhere in Ady's groin. And then Lee's top has been pulled down to expose a breast and her hand now cups Ady's breast. They moved location, perhaps to be more private, to a hidden gap in the rocks at the shore. They're lying on pebbles. Ady and Nus-ch are naked, Paul is wearing a shirt and trousers, he's taken off his hat, which sits on the rocks. He's lying upside down beside Ady, his head between her thighs. Nusch stands beside them watching. In another photograph, taken from a different angle, they're intertwined; Paul and Ady seem to be kissing, Nusch is crouching beside Paul whose trousers have been pushed down, his penis in her hand. She's leaning forward as if moving to give him oral sex.

These are Man Ray's photographs, now in the archive at the Centre Pompidou in Paris. He believed deeply in the transgressive and poetic potential of erotic imagery and in the right to, and the celebration of, sexual liberty. Nudity represented freedom in surrealist parlance, and sex was an act of ecstatic, Dionysian inspiration. Speaking in an interview with Arturo Schwarz, Man Ray discussed the influence de Sade had on him and how much he admired his dedication to his beliefs, and for spending so many years in prison in defence of them. From there, with only quill, candlelight and his imagination, 'he wrote the most passionate defence of individualism and freedom', says Man Ray. 'And by so doing, he revealed a universal aspect of our nature, an aspect that only hypocrisy and puritanism refused to acknowledge. Sade helped us understand ourselves.'

These photographs are the photographer as voyeur and sex as performance, as art. Was this Man Ray orchestrating or staging his fantasies, or are these images spontaneous souvenirs? He was probably exploiting the moment and the mood, because this was nothing new for him. And the mood that day on the island was erotic, intimate, almost primal. Earlier he'd taken photographs of Lee and Ady gleefully brandishing speared octopuses on a fishing boat. Lee's wearing shorts and a swimsuit, Ady's wearing only swimming bottoms, their hair wet from swimming in the sea. Later the fisherman cooked their catch on an open fire at the beach. Roland took a photograph of Man Ray at the picnic. He's at the very bottom of the frame, still reclining at the picnic table. Lee, Nusch and Ady are crouching behind him in a row, perched on the tree trunk backrest. Nusch is in the middle behind Man Ray, she's got her arms around the other two women. They're all still topless, laughing, huddled towards him, their breasts hanging down in a row behind his head. Man Ray has his hand on Ady's thigh and an impish hint of a smirk on his face. He's in his element.

For many years he'd been making graphic images of sex and nudity, often putting himself into the action. There's a photograph taken in his room at the Hôtel Vaste Horizon with Nusch, they're both naked, she's sprawling by the window, he's crouching beside her, his face on her breast. Nusch frequently posed for erotic photographs for Man Ray, working with him to realize the images he envisaged. In hindsight the photographs he took at Mougins that summer resonate with greater meaning. In a world that encouraged isolation and conformity, that was becoming increasingly dehumanized, increasingly controlled, they hold a deviant, libertarian power.

And they're a testament to the mood of collaboration, of community. He was amongst like-minded friends. Man Ray was a provocateur and a narcissist, but at the same time he excelled in the art of friendship, and befriending people who he admired, or who might be useful to him. He was loyal and kind to his friends and managed to maintain a benign neutrality amidst the squabbles and shifting loyalties of the notoriously combative Dadaist and surrealist factions. In his autobiography, *Self-Portrait*, he presents himself as a determined tough-talker; there's something of a Hemingway character in his voice – brusque, cynical, witty, misogynistic, a veiled vulnerability and a reticence beneath the machismo, the bravado.

Man Ray – Emmanuel Radnitzky – was born in 1890 in south Philadelphia; his parents were working-class Russian Jewish immigrants who'd escaped persecution and pogroms for a freer life in America. His father was a tailor who worked in a factory; his mother was a seamstress. They moved to Brooklyn just before the turn of the century and, in 1912, as a gesture of assimilation and no doubt to avoid discrimination, the family changed their surname to Ray.

Soon too, at twenty-one, Emmanuel became Man, and Man Ray became a single name, a modernist metamorphosis. It was a new identity. He had ambitions, he was going to live life to his own design. He continued this process throughout his life. He was fascinated by himself, and the selves he dismantled and constructed. This self-reinvention, as well as his adaptability and his determined autonomy, would prove central to his success and the length of his career. Later he'd try to renounce – to escape from – the narrative of his early life in America. He was contemptuous of his upbringing, resentful that his family were immigrants, that there was little money, that he was an outsider. He didn't like to talk about it and there's very little of it in his memoirs. But it was these things that informed his entire life, and that drove him. He wanted to be enigmatic, and an insider. In obfuscating his origins, he would be the master of his past as well as his future.

As a youth in New York, Man Ray spent his time in galleries poring over Old Masters, as well as drawings by Rodin, paintings by Cézanne and etchings by Matisse in Alfred Stieglitz's 291 gallery. He was longing to become a painter too. Eventually he threw over the possibility of a career in architecture in favour of a life dedicated to art, which his parents reluctantly agreed to support. In 1913 he visited the legendary Armory Show, the International Exhibition of Modern Art in New York. The exhibition marked a turning point, introducing modern art to its American audience. It entirely changed Man Ray's worldview, opening his eyes to a contemporary European world of Cubism, fauvism and post-Impressionism, to the avant-garde. Most of all, it was the radical work of French artist and Dada pioneer Marcel Duchamp, and his attempts to depict movement in the motionless, that thrilled him.

In 1915, when Duchamp moved to New York for a time to bring Dada to the New World, they quickly became (lifelong) friends and allies. Duchamp opened Man Ray's eyes to possibilities beyond painting, to sculpture, film, assemblage, photography and to the found objects which Duchamp used in his 'readymades'. These were mass produced, often utilitarian objects to which he gave titles, thus elevating them out of the ordinary, the functional, and into the realms of art, the most famous of which was *Fountain*, a porcelain urinal he submitted to (and was never shown publicly by) the Society of Independent Artists exhibition in 1917. It was a gesture that shattered the traditional idea of the artist as craftsman – the artist's eye rather than his hand at work. He believed art's function was not to be pleasing: it was to make people think.

Throughout his life Man Ray thought of himself primarily as a painter, but for now painting was sacrificed in favour of other forms, the object and photography. This had been true for Duchamp too, who had shrugged off the strictures and limitations of painting to engage with ideas, not just in artistic production. Through Duchamp, Man Ray discovered Dada and its radical spirit of disruption, of destruction: the shock of the new. The painter became the polymath. He was passionate in his pursuit of novelty – new forms, experiments, iconoclasms, technical innovations, mechanisms – ceaselessly driven to invention. And he was fascinated by kinetic art and by the potency of the found object. The photographer Alfred Stieglitz, with whom Man Ray had been friends since his earlier days frequenting the 291 gallery, had also introduced him to photography and, having mastered the technical side of it, he was soon working professionally. He found the medium of light more liberating than paint.

In New York he had become an art celebrity, but he felt like a fish out of water. Instead, he longed for Europe. For an American seeking escape (and it was escape he sought) there was only Europe (though before long the tables would turn and America would become the sanctuary, a means of survival for many Europeans) and in July 1921 he moved to Paris, which he considered the apex of the art world. He knew no French, but he had a little money, and the support of his parents. He left behind his old life and a wife, the Belgian poet Adon Lacroix (Donna Lecoeur) who he'd married in 1913 and from whom he'd separated in 1919 after she'd had an affair.

In Paris, Duchamp gave him immediate entrée into the epicentre of the avant-garde. And his friend (who lived in New York and Paris and back-and-forthed between the two) was at the Gare Saint-Lazare to greet him, and he was soon whisked off to the Café Certâ, where the Dadaists liked to meet, and where there were many gathered to meet Man Ray that day. And they were all in attendance at an exhibition, at Philippe Soupault's Galerie Six several months later, which included paintings and collages Man Ray had brought with him from New York.

In its championing of individualism and in the way that it encouraged the shrouding of one's own past, Dada was the perfect fit for Man Ray. Soupault's invitation for the exhibition was written with a witty evasion worthy of the artist himself. 'No one knows any longer where M. Ray was born', it declared. 'After having been a coal merchant, several times a millionaire, and chairman of the Chewing Gum Trust,' it continued, 'he has now decided to accept the invitation of the Dadaists to exhibit his latest work in Paris.' The private room was filled with balloons which entirely obscured the view of the paintings. To shrieks of 'hurrah', Soupault and his friends burst the balloons with cigarettes. And thus Man Ray was announced to the art world of Paris.

He was in a privileged position, and yet none of the paintings sold, which made him more determined than ever to shift his focus away from painting. Photography satisfied his need to experiment, his need to be modern, and it could be lucrative too. He set to work photographing, socializing and collaborating with its most celebrated figures including Cocteau, Dalí, Breton and Ernst. For Man Ray it was a new world.

As for many of his friends, surrealism eclipsed Dada. Surrealism unleashed new ideas, new impulses. Its spirit of revolt aligned so entirely with his own. In late 1921 and early 1922 he started making camera-less photograms in his studio by placing objects on photosensitive paper and exposing them to light, a technique that had been developed in the nineteenth century. For Man Ray it suited his impulse to make the familiar strange, abstract, elevated, and – like Duchamp – choosing everyday, functional objects for his images. Though he was employing an old technique he was refining it and, in doing so, he claimed it and called the results 'rayographs', after himself. And he also began making technically and thematically experimental films and using increasingly radical cropping, lighting and perspectives in his photography. With many of these same techniques, as well as the light room processes he'd mastered over the years, he managed to create a career for himself, capturing the mood of the moment, and sustaining his fine art with work as a fashion and portrait photographer for *Vogue* and *Harper's Bazaar*. By the 1930s he was highly sought after and commanding impressive fees for both his portraiture and his fashion work. He was both slumming it at cafe gatherings with his surrealist friends and swanning about at parties with the avant-garde branch of high society, for whom a Man Ray portrait was de rigueur.

Man Ray had moved to Montparnasse, 'the Quarter', he called it, and soon he was in a relationship with the queen of the quarter, Alice Prin, known as Kiki de Montparnasse. Kiki (slang for vagina), with her voluptuous body, her heavily painted oval face and sensual, sloping eyes, had modelled for everyone in Paris from her early teens. Man Ray took possession of her, claimed her as his muse. She would model for him and indulge his sexual obsessions for the next fourteen years. Every night before they went out, he would paint her face with make-up, or dress her according to his whim. He took countless erotic photographs of her, with her. She helped to unleash and give form to his interest in the erotic, which was to become the fulcrum of his creative life, probably his whole life.

It was Kiki who posed for two of his most famous photographs. In *Le Violin d'Ingres*, the contours of her naked back and bottom echo the shape of a violin. Once printed, he painted the f-holes of a violin onto her back in the image, and then rephotographed the print to make the final artwork. She's draped in fabric beneath her bottom and over her thighs and she's wearing an oriental-style turban. She's a modernist odalisque, an object, an instrument waiting to be played. In *Noire et Blanche* her neat head with its glossy black hair and pale, painted face rests, as if detached from her body, beside a black African mask. Man Ray had been swept up in the negrophilia of the period and he was heavily influenced by *L'Art Nègre*. For

Man Ray, as for other surrealists, blackness meant otherness, wildness, untamed sexuality and both modernism and primitivism. For him, it meant freedom and transgression. The surrealist movement supported anti-colonialism while simultaneously exoticizing black people and black culture and they saw nothing contradictory in that.

In 1929, Lee Miller, the model turned photographer, sought out Man Ray in the hope of becoming his assistant. Soon they were lovers and collaborators. Lee, and her lovely body, became his new obsession, the encapsulation of surrealist amour fou. She posed for him, and played at being his possession. Together they created images of a seemingly shared interest in BDSM and the Marquis de Sade, fetishizing, idealizing the female body, displaying it, cutting it up, objectifying it. Their photographs together oscillate ambiguously between power and subordination, freedom and restraint, often using props – ropes, shackles, collars, handcuffs. The master of light, forever attempting to possess, to harness, to claim Lee's radiance. When she left him and returned to New York, he was inconsolable and claimed to be suicidal. For a while he carried a pistol in his pocket and photographed himself with it, and a rope and other violent objects, romanticizing, fetishizing his pain. His wife's affair had been the first (and probably the greatest) blow to his manly pride. He writes about it in his memoirs with a characteristic bluster and with unbridled bitterness. Lee's departure must have been a blow upon an old bruise.

Soon after Lee had left he re-made a 1923 work, *Object to Be Destroyed*. In the avant-garde journal *This Quarter* he published a drawing of the work and wrote new instructions to accompany it: 'Cut out the eye from a photograph of one who has been loved but is seen no more.' This was to be attached to the pendulum of a metronome and then the tempo set as desired. 'Keep going to the limit of endurance,' he adds, and 'with a hammer well-aimed, try to destroy the whole at a single blow.' The insistent, interminable beat of the metronome was a perpetual reminder of absence. The image of the eye was now Lee Miller's, the 1932 addition. Their relationship is barely mentioned in his memoirs.

At Mougins in the summer of 1937, they were reconciled as friends. By then Lee was married and had just met Roland. Man Ray was living a domesticated life with Ady, who was said to have a calming effect on him, and perhaps that is partly why we know so little of Ady: contentment is less of a story than drama in the narrative of Man Ray's life. He had vowed never to enter into a relationship again but with Ady there was none of the tempestuousness of his relationships with Kiki and Lee. By the late summer Lee and Man Ray were with everyone in Mougins and it seems they were comfortable with each other, enough to spend time together, and to collaborate in the making of erotic photographs at picnic tables.

Paul Éluard had been one of Man Ray's first friends and allies in Paris, they'd met at the Café Certâ on one of his earliest days in the city. He thought Paul looked like a young Baudelaire. He loved spending time with him, creating work with him, and admired the contrast between the revolutionary sentiments of his poems and the elegance of their form, rather like the man himself. And, of course, they were united by and perhaps matched each other in their dedication to the erotic. They understood each other.

For some time, inspired by surrealist automatic drawing, Man Ray had been filling notebooks with pen and ink drawings, mostly with lingering feelings of himself as the spurned lover, conjured in his imagination late at night before sleeping or inspired by his dreams as he woke up in the morning. The drawings are mostly of women, mostly nude, mostly in beseeching, vulnerable poses. One nude, her arms thrown back above her head, lies beside a huge fish as if they are two sardines in a tin; another is about to be cut by giant scissors, and another, comprised only of horizontal lines, resembles an artist's mannequin, to be manipulated at will. Hair falls, hands clasp, body parts are isolated. One woman is a head and shoulders attached to a single leg, emerging from or bound to a rock. Sometimes we glimpse Ady, her face, her hair and possibly her hands. Man Ray described these fifty or so drawings as evidence of his hands dreaming and they would become the basis of his next collaboration with Paul, *Les Mains libres*.

In response to the drawings Paul wrote short but dynamic poems. And this collaborative relationship was made clear on the frontispiece to the book – 'drawings by Man Ray, illustrated by poems by Paul Éluard'. It speaks of imminence, apprehension, and it became a paean to freedom, of free hands, free play and the limitlessness of the imagination. In the introduction to the book Paul wrote about Man Ray revealing himself in these drawings, offering his eyes and hands; drawing to make his mark in the world, to be loved. The book ends with an imaginary portrait of the Marquis de Sade. *Les Mains libres* would be published by Jeanne Bucher several weeks after the friends had returned from Mougins on 10 November 1937, in Paris. There was an accompanying exhibition of drawings at the Galerie Bucher in Montparnasse.

Like Paul, Man Ray believed passionately in the need for fellowship amongst artists and it was in this spirit that they were all together at Mougins, and taking photographs, being photographed on the Île Sainte-Marguerite. This was their communality, their shared vision, their Utopian ideal. In 'La Plage' ('The Beach') from *Les Mains libres*, Paul wrote, as if echoing, and perhaps inspired by, the photographs from that day:

> They all owed each other a tender nudity
> Of sky and water, air and sand.
> Everyone forgot their appearance
> And that they had promised to see nothing but themselves.

MAN RAY

On the day of his first exhibition in Paris (as Man Ray tells it in his autobiography) the French composer Erik Satie came into the gallery and swept Man Ray out for a drink at a cafe nearby. Returning to the gallery together, several drinks later, they passed a shop selling household goods and Man Ray spotted a traditional flat-iron in the window. Suddenly he had an idea for an assemblage. He bought the iron, along with a box of thumb tacks and some glue. Back at the gallery he glued the tacks in a row along the base of the iron. He called it *Cadeau* (*The Gift*) and planned to give it to Soupault as a present for holding the exhibition. But it had disappeared from the gallery by the end of the opening night, never to be recovered. Perhaps this was by design; it was the only time this happened. He had already photographed the object and later made reproductions. Man Ray thought that *The Gift* was erotic. The subliminal, violent potential of its underbelly to rapaciously tear at a dress foreshadows his affiliation with surrealism, with the irrational, and his preoccupation with tropes of sadistic desire. But mostly it was a classic Dadaist gesture – the witty, savage subversion, the stymieing of the functional object. And he knew its functionality well; for his tailor father it must have been in constant use. And so perhaps it's not just a negation of function, but a brutal rejection of his parents – his past – too.

MAN RAY

He's lying in bed, appearing to be asleep, his head resting on a bent arm. A hand pressed against the mattress in febrile dreams. He's at the bottom right of the frame, dwarfed by a studio lamp that points at his head and which stands on the bedside table to his left. Above him, sweeping to the top of the frame, is an expanse of bedroom wall. It's painted a colour but rendered grey by the black and white film. Mounted on the wall above his head is a plaster cast of the Venus de' Medici's torso – the original dismembered goddess – pure, smooth white, against the greyness of the wall. It's the spot above the bed where a Christian might put a crucifix. But this was Man Ray's religion – woman as ideal, but this one is accessible, possessable, his household deity. And this is surrealism in action. Self-reflexive. The dream of woman brought into the light, made manifest, staged for a photograph.

DANCER

According to Eileen, when Ady Fidelin first met Picasso in Mougins, she flung her arms about his neck and quipped that she had heard that his painting was rather good. That summer she would be photographed at the beach, laughing, perching against his back, a hand resting on his head as he sits on a jetty with Dora Maar, who is clutching his foot. In other photographs Ady is riding a tandem bicycle with Dora Maar, she's in animated conversation with Lee Miller, or sitting on Roland Penrose's shoulders at the entrance to the hotel. In this photograph she is wearing short shorts, and he looks amused, his head clamped between her bare thighs. Man Ray himself later recalled how he and Ady had been so welcomed by the friends at Mougins.

And yet, in the memoirs and biographies of Man Ray and of these friends whom Ady had enchanted and who had welcomed her so warmly, she is mentioned briefly, if at all, and recalled – perhaps because she was younger than the others – as a spirited child, a vivacious naif, an exotic creature or, as in Man Ray's case, a sexy housewife. In his biography of Man Ray, Penrose, who was apparently very charmed by Ady (they were possibly lovers that summer), wrote of 'the delightful girl from Guadeloupe, who could swim, laugh and dance like a brown angel'. In Neil Baldwin's biography of Man Ray she's 'a self-effacing young woman with modest needs'.

Eileen has the most to say about her, recalling in her memoirs Ady's charm, her youth, her laughter. She tells an anecdote about over-exposing photographs of Ady and making her skin look darker than it was, which, she writes, upset Ady. To compensate, Eileen and Joseph took Ady for lunch in Cannes where, according to Eileen, she ate Creole rice which she rolled into little balls with her fingers. Eileen writes that at lunch one day at the Vaste Horizon, Man Ray teased Ady that horses were eaten in Guadeloupe. A (presumably playful) argument ensued, ending in Picasso shouting that they eat bicycles in Guadeloupe. Playful, perhaps, and yet, as with Eileen's observations, it gives an insight into how Ady was perceived. In *Man Ray: Writings on Art*, Jennifer Mundy quotes a letter from the artist to Roland Penrose, a little window into his relationship with his girlfriend: 'Ady is in fine shape, doesn't miss a Saturday at the Bal Blomet, and keeps me from being pessimistic. She does everything – from shining my shoes and bringing my breakfast to painting in backgrounds on my large canvases! All to the tune of a beguine or a rhumba.'

The memory of Ady exists almost entirely in pictures – photographs, engravings, drawings and paintings – some very famous and mostly by Man Ray. In these she is almost always laughing. That year Man Ray painted her portrait, its Creole title *Maime quand i qua domi i qua ri* (*Even When She Sleeps, She Laughs*). Bright sun illuminates her face as she laughs in her sleep (her closed eyes rendering her both inscrutable and vulnerable, an object of desire – the surrealist archetype) and her head casts a deep shadow behind her. The painting was sold by Christie's for €201,000 in 2024.

There are around four hundred photographs of Ady by Man Ray. And in those photographs she is a beautiful (invariably smiling) face, a beautiful dancer's body (often naked). She is swimming in the sea or dancing or smoking in bed or washing herself in a bath. In an intimately domestic fantasy, she is outstretched on a bed with a bowl of ripe fruit resting on her groin – an offering. She dances, leaps, licks an ice cream as she sprawls on the sand, posing seemingly without effort, bending, coiling, shapeshifting to satisfy every whim of her lover's image-hungry eyes. Sometimes they're together – sunbathing on a balcony, walking in a park, amongst friends.

But for these glimpses, Ady is without a story. She is seen, but unseen, 'hidden in plain sight', as art historian, Wendy A. Grossman, describes it in her essay 'Unmasking Adrienne Fidelin: Picasso, Man Ray, and the (In)Visibility of Racial Difference'. Her life has been lost in history, reduced to an image, her story truncated to the few years she lived with Man Ray until his camera was turned from her.

We have very little of her voice, her lived experience, except for a few letters written to him during and after the war.

Ady, the willing housekeeper, the biddable model, the laughing girl blithely perched on Picasso's shoulder at the beach, was also Adrienne, the dancer, the immigrant, the orphan. Most of those friends that gathered at the Hôtel Vaste Horizon that summer had, over the years, sought to escape the lives into which they had been born. Their escape had been a luxury, a privilege, Ady's had been a necessity.

Casimir Joseph Adrienne Fidelin was born in 1915 on the island of Grande-Terre in Guadeloupe, which was then a French colony. Her father was from one of the oldest Creole families on the island and worked in a bank. When a cyclone devastated the islands in 1928 it killed her mother and swept Ady from the comfortable middle-class life she had known. Her father died only a couple of years later and Ady travelled to France in one of the waves of emigration from Guadeloupe in the wake of the cyclone. In Paris she joined her siblings who had gone before her. She was then fifteen.

Eileen Agar would observe at Mougins – perhaps amused by the perceived incongruity – that alongside Ady's propensity for happiness she had a more pensive side too. Ady, she writes in her memoirs, had a habit of stopping by cemeteries, not because she was gloomy but because they made her feel peaceful. In 1925 Josephine Baker had made a similar journey to Ady's, leaving behind her home, sailing for France and changing her own destiny. Leaving the racism and restriction of segregated America, Baker was delighted to see the Statue of Liberty disappearing behind her as she sailed from New York. Suddenly she felt free. 'What was the good of having the statue without the liberty, the freedom to go where one chose, if one was held back by one's color?' she wrote in her memoirs. For Josephine, Paris was a city alive with promise and possibility, somewhere she might determine her own life, live on her own terms.

But though inhabiting a black female body in 1920s and 1930s France was less restrictive than in the US, it was still political: elevated and exoticized in some quarters, ostracized and denigrated in others. Though the city was not without racism it welcomed the dancer and her vital, comedic, sensual performances with open arms. She became a star overnight. 'Paris is a dance,' she would later declare in *Les Mémoires de Joséphine Baker*. In a city gripped by negrophilia, she zipped and vibrated across the stage. The nightclubs of Montparnasse pulsed to the sound of black American jazz and swayed to the mournful rhythms of the Antillean beguine, and crowds flocked to exhibitions of African art, whipped into a *tumulte noir*.

To white Parisians, black culture and black people were novel, erotic, they were art to be appropriated, bodies to be objectified, commodified, projected upon. As Josephine Baker realized, and very quickly turned to her advantage, and as she later declared 'the white imagination sure is something when it comes to blacks'. Baker learned to play the system to her own advantage; tapping into the French colonial fantasies of her white audience made her one of the highest-paid performers in Europe. Shimmying bare-breasted across the stage in feathers or her iconic banana skirt to the tribal beat of African rhythms, hunting down a white man in safari gear, Baker performed the sexual savage. But there was something more. This was not, as the author, theorist and activist bell hooks describes it in her essay 'Selling Hot Pussy', 'a silenced body'. This was Baker noisily, joyfully, playfully disrupting colonial stereotypes with comedy, daring and misrule. This was black female agency boldly and brazenly on display, Baker owning and celebrating her sexuality, her erotic potential, her black heritage and her black body. This was the Paris into which Ady arrived.

Le Bal Blomet in Montparnasse was a smoky, boozy, bohemian melting pot of colour and class, where countesses and carpenters, black and white people, danced with each other to the sultry sounds of jazz, blues and Caribbean music. Long frequented by the Antillean diaspora community, it had since been 'discovered' by the Parisian avant-garde. The poet Robert Desnos, who lived near the club and visited with his fellow surrealists, christened the club 'Le Bal

Nègre', which is how it became known to many. There Josephine Baker, Ernest Hemingway, Henry Miller, F. Scott Fitzgerald, Brassaï, Jean Cocteau, Maurice Chevalier, Mistinguett, Man Ray and others gathered. There Ady Fidelin made her way some time in the early 1930s, drawn by the promise of work in Josephine Baker's wake. And there she performed the beguine and the traditional dances of Guadeloupe: the rhythms, the movements and the gestures of her old world, her old life.

There is freedom in dance, the freedom to move in space. Photographs and fleeting comments in letters and memoirs create a strong sense of Ady's physicality. She is always using her body: to dance, to leap on the beach, to swim in the sea, to respond to a camera, to show love.

It was probably one night on the dance floor at Le Bal Blomet that Ady met Man Ray. He had photographed several well-known Guadeloupean performers before, so perhaps they were introduced by mutual friends. Their first two encounters were recorded in his diary. One day in late December 1934 he wrote 'Ady' and another day in the following year he wrote down her phone number 'Odeon 79-95' and took some photographs of her. Soon they were lovers and Ady had thrown in her lot with him, moving into his apartment in Montparnasse. She was twenty and Man Ray, still technically married, forty-four. The age of majority in France was then twenty-one, so she was still a child in the eyes of the law. Living with Man Ray, modelling for him, meant that she was defying the conservative values of her family and the Guadeloupean community in Paris. Such immodesty, such affrontery – it was a bold gesture.

They lived between Man Ray's apartment, his house in Saint-Germain-en-Laye and, later, an apartment he rented overlooking the sea in Antibes during the summer. Ady was now amongst artists who lived experimentally, now she was living experimentally too, and she moved in circles to which a young woman like her would rarely have access.

Man Ray scribbled MANADY ADYMAN in pencil on the cover

of his diary and made a short film of them both in the apartment at Antibes. He is in the foreground, wearing only a short sarong around his waist. A cigarette dangles casually from his lips and he's clutching a paint brush. From time to time, he applies paint to the easel beside him and then glances out of the window. In the background Ady sits at a desk writing; she appears to be naked, her back to the camera. She drops something on the floor and stoops to pick it up, and then carries on with her task. The camera turns to the window to show an uninterrupted view of the sea and then pans across the rooftops of Antibes.

Over the years of their relationship, Ady modelled for Man Ray's paintings and for hundreds of photographs, often naked or topless, holding props and poses. There are studio portraits and informal, intimate, often erotic moments. She posed alongside 'primitive' African art from his personal collection and in one series of photographs, in a nod to the costume of her Guadeloupean heritage, with a scarf around her groin, a headscarf and necklaces. In another series, Man Ray posed Ady with Nusch Éluard, both naked, their bodies – one black, one white – intertwined as if in a homoerotic embrace. There's nothing of the idealized woman in these photographs, as there is in images of Lee with their artificial tricks. Ady's photographs are naturalistic, with Man Ray perhaps trying to capture the intrinsic primitivism he perceived in her.

This was not the first time Ady had modelled; so she knew what to do, what was expected of her, the transaction. She had also posed for other photographers, including Wols (Alfred Otto Wolfgang Schulze) and Roger Parry, and worked as an extra in films, including *The Secrets of the Red Sea*, a colonial adventure set in North Africa adapted from a book by Henry de Monfreid. Sala Elise Patterson and Wendy A. Grossman believe that Man Ray was helping Ady to build a portfolio with which to develop a modelling career.

Looking at Man Ray's photographs, Ady has the ease of a performer, an embodied knowledge of what she is capable of doing. She uses her body; moving, exerting, collaborating responsively, giving herself to the camera as a dancer offers up their performance to an audience. But a performer is always changing presentations, never one thing or another, always opaque. Ultimately these photographs of Ady are pictures of desire. Man Ray's desire. They are images drawn from his erotic lexicon, a language in which his models needed to become fluent. Man Ray was older, white, wealthy, a domineering personality. In one photograph Ady is standing in front of a window. Beside her, on the windowsill, is a 'primitive' African sculpture. She is wearing a dressing gown and her feet are bare, her toenails painted. Her hair is bound up in a hat, she has lipstick on and pearls in her ears. She is smiling, one hand resting in her pocket, and another wrapped around a plaster bust of Man Ray, her head tilted towards it, a playful priestess at the altar of her lover. Together they attended the masked ball where Lee and Roland had met that summer of 1937. As if role-playing one of his fantasies (or perhaps it was closer to the truth than that), Man Ray had arrived dressed as a Barbary pirate, with bare torso, a turban and harem pants. Beside him was Ady, his bare-breasted slave.

In early September 1937, as the friends were gathered at the Hôtel Vaste Horizon, a series of photographs taken by Man Ray was published as a two-page spread in the American magazine *Harper's Bazaar*. In 'The Bushongo of Africa sends his hats to Paris', four women are modelling Congolese hats alongside an English translation of an essay by Paul Éluard. The hats had been exhibited in a recent surrealist exhibition in Paris. One of the models – the main photograph and the only black woman in the article – is Ady. The photograph of her is cropped to show only her head, her smiling face, her bare shoulders and an arm which she holds up behind her head as she gazes into the middle distance. In the original, uncropped image she is naked to the waist. The other women are all dressed. Ady wears the hat at a jaunty angle, as well as a tiger's tooth necklace and an ivory bracelet on her upper arm. This is Ady as African native, her Creole heritage sacrificed to the service of Man Ray's negrophilia.

This was nothing new. Black women's bodies had long been considered a symbol of white men's desire and colonial dominance. In photographs Ady's ethnicity is not obvious (and is often still misattributed). Her indeterminate skin colour meant that she could perform the role of a kind of generalized exotic other in these images. Sala Elise Patterson, writing about Ady in *The New York Times* in 2007, sees this less as a sacrifice and more of an expedience, which enabled her to break new ground. *Harper's Bazaar*'s publisher William Randolph Hearst had previously banned black models from its pages and all the other key fashion publications had followed suit. Ady Fidelin was the first black model to shatter this dictate, to appear in a major fashion magazine. She was a pioneer.

MAN RAY, NUSCH, ADY, PAUL (AND UNIDENTIFIED MAN)

A party, a tableau. Nusch is wearing traditional Antillean dress – a shawl, a draped and tucked checked madras dress, a white petticoat beneath it, an elaborately knotted madras head scarf and big hooped earrings. She's posing and dancing happily alongside Ady, who'd presumably dressed Nusch in her own clothes. Ady's in boldly patterned beach pyjamas, a matching cropped top and a huge bow whittled from a scarf in the same fabric. She's wearing big white earrings that look like glowing flowers against her dark hair, and a huge necklace of delicate white flowers that looks almost like a Hawaiian lei. She's beaming at the camera, a hand on her hip. At the women's feet is Man Ray, in shorts and shirt and sandals. He's balanced on one knee and playing a ukulele, a cigarette in his lips. Beside him sits Paul cross-legged on the ground, in a polo shirt, trousers and white espadrilles tied around his ankles. He has a glass cradled in his hand, and he's smiling up at the women. Behind them all is an unidentified man, also with a glass, glancing over to Nusch.

This is Man Ray's photograph. It's dated as possibly 1937, perhaps it was then, or a year either side. It was almost certainly taken on the balcony of the Antibes apartment he shared with Ady. Of course, on the face of it, this is a typical Man Ray image, his blithe appropriation of 'exotic' cultures (in other photographs from the same series Nusch is dressed in a kimono, clutching a paper umbrella and with eyeliner at the outer corners of her eyes, a breast peeping out from the open gown).

But perhaps it's interesting to see this photograph in a different context. Ady had worn the traditional Creole clothes in which she had dressed Nusch for studio portraits by Man Ray. They carried within them a link to the home, the childhood, the culture that she had left behind. And beyond their personal resonance, these clothes are associated with a proudly defiant, post-emancipatory history of women's dress in the French Caribbean. Wearing madras in its riotously patterned, multicolour glory had been a rejection of the white of enslavement dress codes, a gesture reclaimed by Guadeloupian and Martiniquan women in the early twentieth century. Perhaps for Ady, dressing Nusch in the traditional clothing of home was a celebration, an assertion of her heritage and of the language of freedom imbued within its folds.

PICASSO AND ADY

Her face and body look like the inner workings of something, an elaborate network of interconnected lines and stripes – vertical, horizontal and diagonal – and of triangles, circles, rectangles and other, more organic forms. There's blue and black and yellow and red. She's sitting in what looks like a black metal-framed chair. She's beside the window shutter in Picasso's room, the pink light (perhaps another sunset?) is so bright that the wooden bars are all but bleached out and the room behind her is bright yellow with hints of green at the left edge of the canvas and elsewhere. Her shoulders and neck are a triangle, an arrow that points into her head. One arm swoops away from it like the arrow's shaft. Her hands are starfish-like. Her lower torso is a rectangle with a navel. Her hair is a dense block of black with little loopy curls at the edge and on the top of her head are three black spiky cartwheels picked out with blue. Curls perhaps? Her face in parts is black and her body skin, beneath the bright stripes and shapes, is a grey mauve. She is smiling, a smile that floats across the middle of her face.

For many years this wasn't Ady, merely an anonymous seated woman in pink and yellow. Trawling the archives while researching Ady's life, the art historian Wendy A. Grossman came across a reproduction of this painting (the whereabouts of which is currently unknown) and immediately recognized its likeness to a photograph Man Ray had taken of Ady holding a washboard, taken by a rendered wall outside the Hôtel Vaste Horizon. Picasso rarely painted black people, and so this reattribution has been important for Picasso's oeuvre but more important still for helping to rehabilitate Ady's place within art history. Looking at the painting and at Man Ray's photograph of Ady with the washboard, it's easy to see how the former echoes the latter. Others disagree with this reattribution. Antony Penrose, Lee Miller's son, believes the portrait is of Nusch. But the evidence – especially the link to Man Ray's washboard photograph – is compelling, convincing.

The painting's many years of misattribution are testament, like many black models before her, to how the story of Ady's life and her presence in the work (and lives) of Man Ray, Picasso and the others has been lost and disregarded over time. Picasso gave the painting its title, *Seated Woman on a Yellow and Pink Background II (Portrait of a Woman)*, which meant Ady was detached from it almost from the beginning. Grossman adds that in the 1950s, long after Ady had lost contact with her friends from this time, Picasso requested another print of the washboard photograph from Man

Ray, her influence, if not her presence, still felt. And Picasso kept the painting of Ady all his life.

LEE, ADY AND MAN RAY

Ady and Man Ray are sitting back-to-back on the ground, perhaps on a pavement in Mougins. There's a pole between them, almost as if they are attached to it and to each other, a single unit. Ady, in the foreground, is wearing a headscarf with stripes and anchors knotted around her head, and a cropped halter top and high-waisted shorts patterned with little clusters of flowers. In her ears are tiny stud earrings. She has chipped polish on her nails and around one finger is wrapped something that looks organic, spiky, perhaps found at the beach and whittled into a makeshift ring by Man Ray or Picasso. She leans against Man Ray and turns her head back towards him with a smile. Man Ray leans in too, turning towards her, smiling, affectionate. He's wearing shorts, a light vest, a metal watch and white espadrilles tied on with twisted cord. In his hands he is clutching a walking stick.

Lee often photographed couples, or friends, or groups united by a common cause like the surrealists and, later, teams at work together in the war. She was drawn to capture their dynamic, their collective energy, the intimacy and, here, the evident love between them.

'WOMB MAGIC'

In the 1980s when Eileen was collaborating with the writer Andrew Lambirth on her memoirs, she gave him a book, *Assorted Articles* by D. H. Lawrence, published in 1930. Inscribed on the title page in intricate, foreign-looking handwriting it says: 'Bought it from Harold Monro at the Poetry Bookshop in 1930. Joseph Bard.' The book is a collection of essays and occasional pieces with titles like 'Is England Still a Man's Country?' and 'Give her a Pattern'. In the latter, Lawrence writes of woman: 'It isn't that she hasn't got a mind – she has. She's got everything that man has. The only difference is that she asks for a pattern,' he writes. 'Give me a pattern to follow! That will always be woman's cry. Unless of course she has already chosen her pattern quite young, then she will declare herself absolutely, and no man's idea of woman has any influence over her.' This is one of only a few passages that Joseph marked in the book, the last sentence is marked twice.

Eileen (who, presumably, Joseph had in mind with his emphatic marking) had chosen her pattern quite young and remained entirely her own woman, her own person, all her life. She chose never to be defined, never to be confined, and to defy expectations and convention. It helped of course that she was born into a charmed world of wealth and comfort. And so she might have continued, a cosseted child, later a debutante. She could have married grandly, lived well, politely. But Eileen had other plans. She spent her time drawing and thinking. She felt that she was different from the people around her, and that she must do something different with her life.

Eileen was born in Buenos Aires in 1899. Her father was a Scottish industrialist and her mother was an American biscuit heiress, a strict matriarch with a keen sense of social propriety. She greatly disapproved of her daughter's drawing and thinking. Eileen's childhood was exotic and eccentric. With her two sisters, she was brought up in a house called Quinta La Lila (The Villa of the Lilacs) in a rich, elegant, polo-playing expatriate community. They had ponies, wore furs, even in the mild Argentine winters, to denote their wealth, and travelling from Argentina to Britain, their mother insisted on taking with them a cow for fresh milk and an orchestra to keep them entertained. At six she was swept off to boarding school in England in an effort to curb a burgeoning rebelliousness, but at some point an art teacher noticed and nurtured her talent and helped to set Eileen on her single-minded course of freedom, encouraging her to always live with art. After school she went to study under the painter Leon Underwood at the Brook Green School of Art in west London. From there she took up a place at the Slade in 1921. Her parents were appalled by these decisions (her mother suggested she should buy art rather than make it) but had been persuaded of Eileen's talent by one of their grand friends.

Even art school was too restrictive for Eileen. In 1924 she left home and ran away to Cornwall, shaving her head to unshackle herself from the debutante life for which she had been destined, to slip out of that skin, and as a celebration of the freedom she needed to claim for herself. In the following year she went travelling in Europe with Robin Bartlett, a fellow student from the Slade, with whom she lost her virginity on the Isle of Wight. She married him in 1925, probably because she was bored and wilful and because she wanted to annoy her parents, who were irked that he was working class. They lived for a while in a little cottage in Normandy and in London. For Eileen at least, it was a temporary situation. She later described the marriage as 'an escape-hatch'. In 1927 she left Bartlett (and would soon divorce him) for Joseph Bard, a thirty-four-year-old Jewish Hungarian writer and editor whom she had met the previous year, and they moved into a flat together in Fitzroy Square.

Joseph (born József Diamant) was very much a man of the Viennese coffee house, of Mitteleuropa, that loosely defined, central European concept that evokes ideas of multiculturalism, of Habsburg territories, of old-fashioned civilities and modern ideas, of Freud, of writers like Joseph Roth, Stefan Zweig, Franz Kafka and of people who are polyglot, cultured, sophisticated, superior, intellectual, opinionated. Joseph had written a novel, *Shipwreck in Europe*, published in 1928, about an American who travels to Europe for psychoanalysis. He'd been in a relationship with a Hungarian woman with whom he had two children, and was then married to the American political journalist Dorothy Thompson, who would interview Hitler in 1931 and, in 1934, would be the first American journalist to be expelled from Germany. They divorced in 1927.

Eileen thought Joseph was handsome, cosmopolitan and clever. He had European ideas and elegant European manners, and he also had thoughts about her work, criticism which she found encouraging. He became a muse for her and his likeness would often appear in her work. She felt liberated by their relationship and would later write that he opened her eyes to different ways of thinking. Eileen was all too aware of her limited worldview and felt that Joseph expanded it.

'People were very shocked to hear Joseph and I were living together,' she would recall in an interview in *Colour of Dreams*, a 1989 documentary about her life and work, still with an air of delight in the unconventionality of it all those years later. There was an openness to her relationship with Joseph, an elasticity. Later they would live in two flats, side by side, Eileen always insistent that she should maintain a room, or rather a studio, of her own. Later, in 1934, she would begin her passionate affair with Paul Nash, and it would continue, on and off, into the war years. Later, writing of her mother's own lifelong monogamy, Eileen would lament in her memoirs that she never knew the pleasure of having a lover, as she herself had done.

There is an urgency, an impetuosity about Eileen in the late 1920s. She was still trying to find herself. But she was beginning to feel her own freedom, personally and creatively. She found a new sense of direction, and that coincided with meeting Joseph. She destroyed her work from the Slade, deciding it was academic and overly influenced by others. Now she felt free. She painted a self-portrait to mark this watershed moment: bold blocks of colour and a bold gaze on her brightly lit face, painted in impasto. She thought it was the first successful work she had made.

Her father died at this time leaving her with an inheritance, which meant that she (and Joseph) could live comfortably, freely, despite his disapproval of her choices when he was alive. They lived between London and Portofino, and in 1929 they moved to Paris, where Eileen trained with the Czech Cubist artist František Foltýn and where she would meet André Breton and Paul Éluard.

Those two influences, Cubism and surrealism, began to weave their way into her work. But she was a slave to neither. For Eileen they remained influences rather than doctrines. Though there are plenty of geometric forms and planes of colour in her work, she thought total abstraction too rational, too clinical. And though there is much in her work that is surreal – dreamlike, irrational, ludic and juxtapositional – she could never entirely align herself with the movement, even after her inclusion in the 1936 exhibition in London. She described her practice as the work of both an inner and an outer eye moving in tandem, which meant that her work was a synthesis, a dance of the seen and the imagined, the rational and the irrational.

Eileen had her own ideas about creativity, her own entirely independent philosophies and personal mythologies. She saw a difference between male and female artists. Women are freer, she believed, less dedicated to the technical, pragmatic side of painting. Women combine both thought and feeling in their work, allowing for lyricism and liberty in their work and in the way they see life. For Eileen creativity came from a deeply female, deeply sensual place. She believed in the power of the imagination, particularly the fertility and fecundity of the female imagination, a kind of atavistic intuition. She called this 'womb magic' and believed it was a force capable of countering the rising tide of militarism in Europe. This philosophy preceded her engagement with the surrealists and extended beyond women's creativity to include womankind in general. She believed that with the increasing threat of war, women's role in the world became ever more necessary. Her powers, her instinct and the complexity of her mind offered a counterbalance that would stop the world destroying itself. She lamented that this potential had for so long been (and continued to be) held in check by the mores of society, and by marriage.

Womb magic was about creation rather than procreation. Eileen said that she didn't want to be a mother, believing it would impinge on her freedom and her work. Other than a time in the early 1930s when perhaps she had engaged with the thought, when ideas of family and reproduction infused her work, she was emphatic about it, believing that having children would get in the way of her career. She said that she wanted to be a painter more than she wanted to be a mother.

In 1933 she began a painting called *The Autobiography of an Embryo*, one of her best-known works, a large and densely layered canvas about the biological development of an embryo, split into four sections which represent the four seasons. The painting is rich in symbols, of life and death, ancient civilizations, cogs turning, shells, birds and their outspread wings, fish and marine plants. It's all-encompassing, projecting a feeling of evolution and deep time embedded within the embryo, as if it carries the kaleidoscope of history and geology and life and the cosmos within its germinal forms. And it has a metamorphic energy, almost like fission, of new life bursting into the world.

Though she didn't want to become a mother, Eileen was fascinated by the development of a foetus growing inside a womb and this painting celebrated that and humanity itself. But the painting isn't prescriptive; instead there's a liberating ambiguity to it, as with much of her work. It's an ambiguity that seems to invite interpretation from the viewer while simultaneously resisting it. Her work is open and defiantly universal, just as she wanted it to be. But it's easy to perceive in her work the relationship she anticipates with her audience. She wants to communicate, to shock into new thinking, to seduce, to persuade others to her way of seeing the world, to offer a conduit into the collective unconscious. Her work is personal, but purposeful.

Eileen never limited herself to painting, her curiosity and experimentation always pushing her into new forms, new expressions: collage, frottage, found objects, photography, sculpture and assemblage. There's a lightness to her work, not in the fatuous sense, but in terms of a lyricism, a deftness. She thought that one shouldn't take life too seriously and believed in the importance of play as a liberating, creative force. In that spirit she made herself what she called a *Ceremonial Hat for Eating Bouillabaisse* in 1936. She had bought a cork basket in Saint Tropez which she upended and made into a hat, which she then adorned with a lobster, a tiger fish, a prawn, a fishbone, seashells, marine flowers, starfish, bark, coral, a bead and a piece of jigsaw puzzle. It's a joyfully absurd celebration of femininity, and perhaps an ode to her mother, who she remembered wearing highly embellished and extravagant hats to the seaside. There's a Pathé newsreel clip of Eileen wearing her hat to walk down a London street. She saunters along elegantly, feigning formality in the encrusted carapace on her head, as passers-by turn to stare at her and her strange creation. There's a distinct look of pleasure on her face.

Eileen drew her greatest inspiration from nature, for her the natural world was Eros, the greatest source of erotic, and therefore creative, inspiration. She wove images of nature into almost everything she created, often held in check by geometric shapes and networked forms. The organic objects she collected were imbued with a talismanic, animistic, ensorcelled power, a potential, something ancient and fundamentally female. There are sycamore seeds, leaves and horns, and a bestiary of beetles, birds, spiders. And the flotsam and jetsam of the sea and the shore – seaweed, shells, rocks, which she used to create works that resemble encrusted treasures from a sunken pirate ship, its treasures long claimed by the sea. And then there were bones, horns, fossils, a classical amphora bought in the south of France – things ancient, once concealed and unearthed, perhaps a link to the subconscious, and what lies beneath. For her, they carried within them their own ancient narratives and mythologies. And there was something liberating and disruptive about using them that entirely bypassed a classical idea of making art.

She juxtaposed these objects with others, creating new forms, in collages and assemblages, akin to the surrealist chance encounter. While she reappropriated these forms, like a witch she sought to harness their inherent energies for her own ends, in the pursuit of her own transformations. She believed collage allowed for an elasticity, an openness of meaning and interpretation for the artist and their audience. For Eileen nothing was more surreal, more marvellous than nature, which she thought represented freedom, and produced shapes and forms in the wild ferocity of storms and the sea or at the beach or in woods, that could never be conjured by the imagination. It was why she rejected pure abstraction. Nature's inspiration was all.

In many ways she was a neo-Romantic like her lover Paul Nash, who like Eileen had a profound love of nature. In the early years of their affair, Nash shared with her his fascination for the spirit of place, of the deep and distinct energies of landscape, which suffuse his surreal, visionary landscapes. On holiday with Joseph in Brittany she bought a camera and photographed the vast, anthropomorphic rocks at Ploumanac'h in which she playfully perceived the shape of a face, a bottom, a thumb and other body parts. Later she shared prints or postcards of these photographs with Nash and he would use one image in the background of a painting. Eileen saw shapes in everything, personal references that add to the layered complexity of her work. Her impulse was not so much about responding to specific places, but rather about harnessing the spirit of the sea and the world beneath it, and of the shore and rocks, her geographies of the mind.

She carried this energy into the biomorphic world of her canvases, with their organic and marine forms, their thrumming, pulsing, dancing rhythms, their radiating mandalas, whorls and swirling, swooping skeins of colour that endlessly turn into themselves like an ouroboros – a snake or a dragon eating its own tail. Almost rococo in its ornate aesthetic, but liberated, as if reclaimed by nature. Eileen used blue repeatedly, the colour of dreams and of infinite distance and infinite desire and the sea and the sky. And green – leaves, trees, new life. In her collages and assemblages everything is tactile and sensual – the crunch of dried leaves, the rustle of silk, the iridescence of feathers.

At Mougins, Eileen had bonded with Picasso over their shared delight in objets trouvés. She would cherish a cork he gave her, which he had told her to put between her teeth to stop them chattering when the bombs started falling. In 1940 she would incorporate it into a work called *The Object Lesson*. Having spent time with him that summer, she also painted Picasso. In 1939, inspired by a photograph she had taken of him sitting on the beach, she painted *Muse of Construction*, a monumental, almost Classical figure, rendered in Cubist planes of colour. Typically playful, perhaps a little irreverent, she has claimed the master muse-maker as a muse of her own.

In *Ladybird*, a 1936 work, Eileen used a photograph that Joseph had taken of her standing naked in a shaft of sunlight while holding up a transparent material through which we see her illuminated body. Onto the print she painted swirling black and white lines and dots and stars and radiating forms, with gouache and ink, as if she is metamorphosing into a ladybird, as if she is also becoming a part of nature. Because her greatest muse was herself, what she conjured from the arcanum of her imagination, her body, her sexuality, her desire, her own image – as canvas, as performance – clothed or naked. As when she had danced in a sheer dress on the rooftop of her hotel in Cannes: for Eileen this meant freedom.

Eileen and Joseph

Joseph is sitting in a cane chair on the balcony which had been, until recently, Picasso's balcony. He's naked, his head turned to the sunlight, his face in profile. His arms are flexed behind his head, making his biceps bulge. A plant on the balcony has cast its shadow across his groin, a playful and ineffectual fig leaf, as his penis is clearly visible. There are others in this series of photographs by Eileen. Joseph's standing, his arms bent aloft in bodybuilder mode, the shadow of leaves again playing across his groin. There's another of Joseph's groin in which his genitals are at the centre of the photograph and clearly the focus. He's lying on a bed, there's no upper body and only the top of his legs. In her memoirs and elsewhere, Eileen expresses how beautiful she found Joseph, his body, the shape of his head and his profile. Here she is foregrounding that desire. There's a feeling of loving and intimate complicity, and also allowance and acceptance of vulnerability between them. Amongst all the images of male desire, of the male gaze that summer at Mougins, these are refreshingly, strikingly, passionately female. A celebration, a counterpoint.

LEE AND EILEEN

A section of moulded Coade stone column fills the photograph. Light falls on the column and casts the shadow of a woman onto it. She is standing in profile, a sharp nose and mouth slightly parted. She is wearing a hat with a point, like a pixie, and a little bush of hair pokes out from beneath. Below her waist, at her belly, the shadow bulges. The fanciful, swollen curved ridges of the column's moulding further reshape the shadow, like distorting mirrors at a fairground. At the other side of the column there's another shadow, presumably the photographer.

Earlier in the summer of 1937, perhaps after they'd been in Cornwall, Lee and Eileen went to Brighton where Lee took this playfully surreal photograph of Eileen carrying her camera, the shadowy bulge at her waist. Later, at Mougins, Picasso demanded a print and declared that this was Eileen, 'pregnant with a camera'. A lucky accident perhaps – though Lee had an uncanny knack of noticing and capturing these pertinent, biographical details – but one that perfectly encapsulates Eileen's concept of 'womb magic', and its inherently female creative force. At Mougins Lee used this photograph in a collage in which she incorporated a postcard with an illustration of the coastline of the Côte d'Azur. She mirrored Eileen's form with a white paper silhouette. And, from the side of this silhouette, the back of Eileen's head and neck, she has formed another head in profile, unmistakeably Dora with her long dark hair and a band around her head. She looks like an Egyptian hieroglyph. Lee also included a photograph of her own sarong. She's there in spirit too. It's a tribute to their friendships, to the collective, creative spirit of at least some of the women that holiday, a sense of unity and affinity.

EILEEN, JOSEPH, LEE AND ROLAND
(AND OTHERS)

DEAROLANDLEE
WE ARE STILL SITTING
PRETTY ON THE MOUN
TAIN TOP AT MOUGINS.
ONE SLEEPS SO SOUNDLY
IN PICASSO'S BED. THE
WEATHERS WUNDERBAR.
BARD SENDS LOVE + KISSES AGAR

Eileen and Joseph, the latecomers, were staying on after everyone else had left, and they'd upgraded to Picasso's room. Perhaps she'd had her photographs printed in Cannes. By way of a postcard, Eileen wrote these words in the blank space beneath a photograph that she had taken of Lee and Roland sitting beside each other at the beach. It must have been sent to one or the other of them; Roland was returning to England and Lee to Egypt. At the end of the holiday, there had been many photographs of their departures. Paul and Nusch returned to Paris by train and there's a photograph of Nusch waving from a train window. There's another of Picasso with Lee and Dora beside his car. Dora looks pensive, Lee happy. The Hispano

Suiza would have been filled with Picasso's canvases and painting equipment, as well as the engraved stones and shells and the skull of an ox that he'd found at the beach. Roland writes that the day before they left, the art dealer Paul Rosenberg, who had been staying nearby, had visited Picasso, who had shown him all the paintings he'd been working on. He was given his pick and reserved a large number of them. Every holiday was a working holiday for Picasso.

ADORA

> Picasso is sitting on a rock at the beach that summer of 1937. He's in his short, tightly fitting white swimming trunks, tanned skin, knees bent, legs spread apart, testicles weighing heavily, barely contained by the white fabric that holds them. In his hands he has the skull of an ox which he has found on the beach. He's holding it up in front of his face. Picasso, the man-beast, the Minotaur.

Dora, who was then twenty-eight, knew exactly what she was doing as she stabbed the penknife between her gloved fingers at Les Deux Magots. This was a manufactured chance encounter, no doubt carefully planned, the surrealist performance as seduction. The fifty-three-year-old Picasso, beguiled, asked his companion Paul for an introduction. And he asked for the bloodstained gloves, which he then kept in a display cabinet like a martyr's relic. Dora and Picasso perhaps knew each other by sight. They'd probably met on the film set of Jean Renoir's *Le Crime de Monsieur Lange*, for which Dora was set photographer, or at a surrealist gathering.

Picasso responded to gestures like this; he liked to make them himself. In the self-mythology of his life, women were ideas, 'female figments' as Siri Hustvedt describes them in *A Woman Looking at Men Looking at Women*. They became leitmotifs, symbols, metaphors for the phases in his work and the periods and moods in his life.

And he had a gesture to match each woman. Fernande Olivier, artist, model and Picasso's first muse, was offered a kitten. Later, in 1943, he would present Françoise Gilot, who for him represented fecundity and youth and a return to happiness, with a bowl of ripe cherries – his *temps des cerises*.

Dora understood this. And in trying to seduce him, and later to please him, she became complicit. She too became a mythmaker, a symbol-spinner, Picasso her muse. Sometimes Picasso depicted himself as a faun or a satyr, but it was the Minotaur which enthralled him. The photograph with the ox skull was fantasy in action. This is exactly how he saw himself, how he wanted to be seen – masculine, powerful, priapic, savage. Into this mythopoeia, he wove his symbols and his preoccupation with the bullfight (which he'd loved in Spain) and its association with passion, machismo, cruelty, danger and death. There was a ritual, a choreography – a danse macabre. First the chase, the battle of the corrida, and then surrender, which inevitably became entangled with sex and submission.

In 1936 he drew himself as a rapacious Minotaur; huge, dark, hairy and lustful, overpowering a naked Dora, her legs spread in waiting. And in turn Dora became a mythological creature in his work. She's a sphinx, a female Minotaur, a buoyantly breasted bird-woman, often with talons to imitate her long, painted nails. Picasso had first been drawn to her strong, mysterious face because he saw how adaptable its image could be. And he was fascinated by her moods, which changed like the weather. For him she was a palimpsest. For years (and even after their relationship began to falter) there was drawing after drawing, painting after painting of desire and love. Sometimes lustful and erotic, at other times gentle. Starry-eyed Dora, wood nymph Dora crowned with flowers, contemplative Dora, windswept-at-the-beach Dora. In one, a simple line drawing, Dora's naked and lying with her hands behind her head. She's wearing a necklace (presumably one of the love tokens he made her) and her legs are spread wide apart, her vulva at the centre of the picture. 'ADORA' he wrote beneath this, punningly – to Dora, adored, adoring.

Eileen discusses Picasso in her memoirs, having observed him at close quarters at Mougins. His paintings of women, she writes, are evidence of his love for them, for his capacity for gentleness. She describes him as a small and pleasant man, who didn't radiate sexuality as much as a domineering masculinity, and who to some people was enthrallingly monstrous. And yet in spite of this his life appeared to be relatively ascetic, eating modestly, drinking only water and keeping his intimate social circle small.

And yet monstrous indeed. John Richardson, in his biography of Picasso, recounts a particularly vicious tale Picasso told with glee about how he'd ejected his wife Olga from his life, some years earlier. She had been a ballerina with the Ballets Russes, and they had married in 1918. Olga had beautiful hair, which she believed Picasso admired. She began to talk of cutting it and Picasso became bored of her discussing this repeatedly. He reached for some scissors and cut it all off. And then, in a second part to the story, one evening he took Olga and their son to the opera. That night he undressed her tenderly and made love to her. The following morning, they were awoken by the announcement of a visitor. You go, he wants to see you, Picasso told Olga, though she was not dressed. She returned carrying a summons to appear in court. Picasso was bringing a divorce suit against her. Apparently, he then sauntered off singing lyrics from the opera of the night before. There is such cruelty in this anecdote, and more shockingly, in his evident delight in the cruelty. When Picasso had introduced Olga to his mother many years before, in 1917, she was warned that Picasso was entirely focused on himself. María believed he could never make any woman happy.

Dora wrote to Picasso in 1936, wondering what she had dared to begin by coming into his life. For the women in Picasso's orbit, it must have been so hard to reconcile the profound and disarming tenderness, as well as the talent to create such beauty with the misogyny that twisted within him and his capacity for extraordinary, unpredictable cunning and aggression. Impossible to negotiate with someone like that, like being forever at sea.

Picasso's idea of freedom sprang from an ego that had been lovingly nurtured from birth and must have been fuelled as his fame, celebrity and notoriety grew over the years. Genius exonerates, exempts, permits, vindicates. Freedom for Picasso meant the acquiring and throwing off of women to suit his whim; freedom that benefits one to the detriment of the other. He wanted women, claimed them, used them, tired of them and then disposed of them, but of course the process was never so clinical, so transactional. There was desire and love, intensely intimate periods of creativity, and then violence, emotional abuse, cruel mocking, rejection. And, in the end, a merciless amputation. In life, as on the canvas, he grappled with the irresolvable woman problem which haunted his interior. With women (and sometimes friends) he was like a little boy goading insects in the grass, burning them with a magnifying glass for his own entertainment.

In Dora, Picasso knew he'd found an intellectual equal, someone incredibly talented, independent, an experienced lover who moved with ease in the same circles as him. And yet his instinct was to dominate. Dora was drawn to egotistical men: Bataille, Breton, who fascinated her, and now Picasso. It was with an almost masochistic urge that she threw herself headlong at Picasso. A self-immolation. Perhaps she thought she could withstand the heat, match it. Instead it seemed to consume her.

Dora was Picasso's *maîtresse-en-titre*, his public girlfriend. But throughout these years of their relationship Marie-Thérèse and Maya were in the background, living a bourgeois existence in the countryside, a sequestered secret. Devoted, domesticated, maternal Marie-Thérèse, who was responsible for cutting her lover's fingernails, who then treasured the clippings and whose image represented peace, innocence and unbridled sensuality for Picasso. One day while he was painting *Guernica* in his studio, Marie-Thérèse arrived unannounced and told Dora that she must leave, that her claim to Picasso as the mother of their child outweighed Dora's. According to some writers Dora had been told that she was unable to have children.

True or not, it seems that her (possible) infertility was weaponized by Picasso and often thrown at her as an insult. And so this showdown with Marie-Thérèse must have been doubly painful. But Picasso apparently took great delight in the event, and no doubt delighted in later recounting this story to Françoise Gilot, who recorded it in her memoirs. Marie-Thérèse told Picasso to choose between her and Dora. Picasso (as he tells the story), paused to contemplate and no doubt to savour the moment. One was biddable and gentle; the other was formidably intelligent. Rather than deciding he told them that they would have to fight it out, and so they did.

So many of these stories about Picasso are well known, polished and hewn like pebbles on the beach. They feed his myth. Yet they're worth telling, and it's worth remembering that at the heart of these stories were not archetypes, not fauns and satyrs and sphinxes and monsters, but women, children and a man.

Not long after he had taken the studio on the rue des Grands-Augustins, Dora moved to an apartment at 6 rue de Savoie, a small street that crossed the road where Picasso lived. She wanted to be as near to him as she could, though they would never live together. Françoise Gilot writes that Dora was expected to always phone him before she could visit, and she could visit only rarely, for some special reason. Working alongside Picasso was Dora's ideal scenario; an active, creative partnership. Particularly in the first months of their relationship this was how it was. They worked together on photographs, manipulating the prints, as well as printmaking, collaborating intensively on projects. And she was with Picasso almost every day as he painted *Guernica*, documenting its development, making suggestions and influencing its design (the monochromatic scheme and the chiaroscuro were possibly inspired by her photography and the brutally bare light bulb was taken from one of her earlier paintings); her greater political engagement quite probably influenced its existence. She was willing to devote her life to him and to her passion for him. She wanted to be his official, his only photographer, to record his work and to help him in the darkroom. Picasso's old friend and collaborator Brassaï would later recall, in *Picasso & Co.*, how Dora was very protective of this role and wary of other photographers who might impinge. Knowing of her emotional volatility, and to avoid her wrath, he decided not to step on her toes.

But evidently this collaboration was not what Picasso wanted in the long term. Increasingly he was wanting to use her face, his idea of it, and the energy, the personality that he perceived in her, to realize his paintings. As his paintings were his life, a part of him, he began to see Dora as a motif, a symbol in the mythology of his life.

After Mougins, back in Paris in the autumn of 1937, Picasso began to revisit, repeatedly, the image of the 'weeping woman'. The political situation in Europe was intensifying and painting this Pietà-like motif became a compulsion. For the original he'd been inspired by Dora, and as he painted, her likeness was more and more swept into the paintings. He told Françoise Gilot, who recounted it in her memoirs, that for him Dora had always been a weeping woman. He claimed that this wasn't a sadistic gesture, that he took no delight in it, but that in painting her like that, he was merely responding to what he saw in the depths of her. 'Women are suffering machines,' the novelist André Malraux quotes his friend Picasso as saying.

Though it seems Dora was in Picasso's thrall, she was later able to disassociate herself from the paintings and the sobriquet to which history has tethered her. 'All his portraits of me are lies. They're all Picassos. Not one is Dora Maar,' she told her friend the writer and critic James Lord.

Though Dora took photographs of the group at the Hôtel Vaste Horizon in the summer of 1937, for the most part she had set her camera aside. This was prompted by Picasso, who believed that photography was secondary to painting, and encouraged her to return to the canvas. He said the same thing to Brassaï. Perhaps he meant it, perhaps it was another form of control. But Dora dutifully put down her camera and took up her paints.

And then there were her own paintings of the 'weeping woman'. These were not a gesture of collusion, of imitation, but rather of reclamation. Dora's biographer Mary Ann Caws sees this as evidence of Dora's strength, and of the independence of her art, her creative vision. These paintings are an act of collaboration. And they (both his, and mine) are a metaphor for universal grief and sorrow, Dora was saying. These are not portraits of me.

PICASSO

This is not weeping, which implies a steady stream of tears falling in cathartic release. She is grief, and not the abstract idea of it but the act of it, the gesture of it, performed like a Greek chorus. Behind her a claustrophobia of striped walls in bands of yellow and ochre. Her hair is smooth black lines interspersed with coloured stripes of blue and violet and green. She's wearing a black jacket, all sharp lines and edges and shoulders with heavy stitches at its seams. Her face, painted in shades of green, is in profile and broken into angular, disjointed shapes, a splintered chaos of forms and colours. On her head a hat with a feather held on by a clasp. Her wide open, tear-filled eyes reflect the silhouetted shape of an aeroplane. Her hands are raised to her face as if forever held at the moment of terror. At the centre of her face, her fingers and mouth and the agonized lines of her misery are painted in white and black and blue, the concentration of her emotion centred in these cold, colour-drained forms that resemble icicles or shattered glass.

DORA AND PICASSO

His face – in her hands, on her canvas – becomes dissected, distorted, abstracted; the front and sides of his head a flattened plane manipulated into the outline of an artist's palette. Within this shape his face is broken by red lines, reduced to segments and wedges of sinister, muddied colour to mark the distinctive features of his face – deep green, darkest aubergine, sage, cold blues and a murky chartreuse. His nose, with its wide, flaring nostrils, becomes a cylinder which dominates his face like a rocket shooting up towards the top of his head. His mouth, aslant, looks as if it's speaking. His prominent chin is a chartreuse oval outlined in red, which becomes the thumb hole of his palette-face. There's a black oblong emerging from the top of his head. Dominating all this are his eyes – two large almonds whose inner points meet each other, outlined in red. Their whites are yellow-orange. There are no irises – only pupils – huge pools of empty black which touch the outline of the eyes. He is staring, blankly and yet all-seeing. Not a living thing. He is sight, and paint. A redress.

DORA AND MARIE-THÉRÈSE

Two women dressed in shades of grey are sitting in a red room. Above them a bright lightbulb protrudes from a shade in the ceiling. One woman, with blonde hair, her face illuminated by the light, sits behind a table facing outwards. Beside her the other woman, with dark hair, is sitting on a chair; she's in the shade and her back is turned to the viewer. She's leaning towards the blonde, their shoulders touching. The gesture isn't adversarial, it's almost sisterly. They are apart but connected, united. The brunette was Dora's portrait, and the face of the blonde was that of Marie-Thérèse. Dora called this *The Conversation*. Picasso is not in the room, and there is no goading, no fighting. Instead there is stillness and a kind of dialogue. An alternative reality.

PORTRAIT OF SPACE

There's a frame, perhaps this was once a window, but the frame is there to focus the gaze, force it within its boundaries. And so we look within it, and beyond it to a barren desert landscape, a sharply defined horizon and above it sky and a cloud shaped like a bird in flight. There's a gauze – perhaps it was once a fly screen? – fixed into the frame. Towards the top there's another, much smaller frame within the gauze, suspended at an angle, like a window within a window. The gauze is unravelling at the edges and it has been torn apart in the centre, almost as if someone has leapt through it and into the outside world. Through this fraying, ragged rent we see the same landscape, but brighter, unfiltered.

Lee called this photograph *Portrait of Space*. It was taken near the Siwa Oasis at the edge of the Great Sand Sea in Egypt. As ever with her work it's enigmatic, enticingly ambiguous. It's easy to see in this image a surrealist-inspired portal between the conscious and the unconscious mind, or the promise of escape, of freedom. But perhaps it is just what she says it is – space – emptied, unpeopled. In late 1937 when this picture was probably taken (the year is definite, the precise date is not) Lee's world was her husband's world – high society Cairo – and her life had been reduced to a claustrophobic round of cocktail parties, tennis matches, drinks at Shepheard's Hotel, polo, pearls and gossip. She had not long returned from France, from the art world, from her friends and lovers, from Mougins, from Roland, from freedom. Having escaped Cairo earlier in the year, an escape granted and funded by her rich, indulgent and understanding husband, Aziz Eloui Bey, she was now back in the fold. Though she had little social freedom at this time, she still had creative freedom. Her husband's wealth meant that she didn't need to work as a photographer but just be one, to photograph nothingness and perhaps her loneliness if she chose to, instead of the socialites and celebrities and models that had filled her studio in New York. For now that life was a distant memory, having abandoned it all to marry Bey and decamp to Egypt. France had been a welcome interlude, and now she was ready to flee again.

The narrative of Lee's life is often packaged and polished into a fable. She's likened to a Greek goddess, beautiful, golden, a perfect body and many talents. And with her self-assurance and her freewheeling recklessness, she was dashing through life, beset by monsters, saved by heroes, adored and revered, capturing it all on her camera as she gradually descended from Parnassus to the Underworld. This narrative, like Dora and her 'weeping woman', doesn't allow space for a real person, for the messy complexity of living. Rather, Lee was always moving – hurtling – as if from one level of a computer game to the next, a buccaneer pinging between constraint and freedom, between the urge to settle and the urge to flee, having tired of someone or something or achieved all she wanted from it, and moving on, and on. Her story is one of escape, freedom, autonomy, ambition, renewal, reinvention and, most of all, an extraordinary way of seeing. 'There is certainly another world, but it is in this one,' wrote her friend Paul Éluard in *Donner à voir*, in 1939. Lee saw the world similarly, and she photographed it so others could glimpse it as well.

Inevitably, *inevitably*, it's the story of a body too, of Lee's body, its strengths and limitations. Of how it was used – photographed, adorned, objectified, reduced to parts, painted (sometimes literally) – and abused. And how she also used it and reclaimed it – to photograph, to photograph her own body, to get herself ahead in the world, for pleasure, to push boundaries, to face danger. Later to be in the first advert for sanitary towels. Later still to sully the memory of a dictator.

Lee was born Elizabeth Miller in 1907, in Poughkeepsie, New York. Her father was an engineer, with a fascination for innovation, both technological and ideological, and progressive ideas, and her Canadian mother had been a nurse before she married. They were comfortably middle class. She spent her early childhood playing with her two brothers, constructing things, inventing things, fishing, climbing trees, dreaming of far-flung places.

But then, when she was seven, Lee was raped by a family friend while staying in Brooklyn and contracted gonorrhoea. In *Women in Dark Times*, Jacqueline Rose writes: 'There are acts of cruelty towards women which wipe out [. . .] all freedom of mental life.' Rose suggests that abuse brings a brutal cessation to the mind's ability to dream, to wander, to create. It closes in on itself, holding only the memory of that violence like a stuck record, and it may be from this point in her life that Lee turned outward from her imagination, became fearless (now that the worst had happened), became restless, seeking sights, sensation, stimulation beyond herself and her fractured interior world.

Perhaps that's too tidy an idea, a slide back into the reductive neatness of myth. But she must have become hyper-aware of her body, of her embodied self at that time, and carried the experience with her in some form all her life. Certainly, the horrifically painful and invasive treatments – douching and bathing in acids and anti-septic – administered by her mother made her fearful of maternity. Her brother remembered her screams ringing through the house as she received her treatment. It must have perpetuated the initial damage and made her feel inherently unclean. And her parents, on the advice of a psychiatrist, encouraged her to dissociate love and sex (preparing her well for a life amongst surrealists). The event and subsequent treatment became the family secret. Lee's secret.

Her father Theodore, who adored Lee, was an amateur photographer. He repeatedly photographed her clothed or naked, from childhood into adulthood, apparently in part to encourage her to see the unsullied beauty of her own body. At least this is sometimes given as explanation for the many photographs he took of her. In one, taken just before her eighth birthday, she's standing naked in the snow, her eyes screwed up against the brightness, and she's clearly shivering. As images they seem violating, invasive, exploitative. Perhaps they helped her to feel comfortable in her body, or perhaps they only exacerbated her defensive detachment from it. And yet Lee adored her father all her life. He was the only man who ever made her feel safe.

Whatever the attempts to help Lee find peace, after her assault she became wayward. She was expelled from school after school, and as the years passed was increasingly bored by Poughkeepsie. Eventually, in 1925 when she was eighteen, she persuaded her parents to let her travel to Paris. She wanted to live as if she was in one of the novels that she read. And she felt at home as soon as she got there. She studied stage design with Ladislas Medgyes, a Hungarian artist and a radical designer, and when she was not studying, she was happily learning to live in Paris and having unsatisfactory affairs. When she returned home she enrolled in a drama course at Vassar, but Vassar was dull by comparison, and she spent more and more time in New York where she just wanted to live and to create and to be a modern woman.

One day in New York, just before her twentieth birthday, Lee was in Manhattan and stepped out into the street and into the path of a car. Pulling her back to the safety of the sidewalk was Mr Condé Nast, the all-powerful owner and publisher of *Vogue*, who was immediately beguiled by the gorgeous, swan-like, flaxen-haired flapper girl he'd just saved from impending doom. It was a charmed chance encounter. Soon Lee was on the cover of *Vogue* in a drawing by Georges Lepape and shortly after that she was swept up into the world of high fashion and was modelling for, and in great demand with, the most famous fashion photographers in the business, particularly Edward Steichen, perhaps the most celebrated of all. Having posed for her father since her childhood, she knew what to do, how to hold her body, how to withstand the scrutiny, perhaps how to detach herself from it. She later said that though she looks angelic in photographs from this time, inside she was a devil, not of her own making. All the while she was also learning how to take a picture. Soon she was famous and a star of the New York social scene. This is when Elizabeth became Lee – short, peppy, androgynous.

Lee's modelling career came crashing to the ground when her image was used in the first advert for Kotex sanitary towels. She had unwittingly signed the release form and so there she was, photographed by Steichen, dressed in a clinging white evening dress to prove the product's efficacy. She was essentially blacklisted in the fashion world. At first she was appalled by the association, but she later changed her mind and took pride in it. But by then she'd had enough of being in front of the camera. She wanted to be behind it.

It was Steichen who had first suggested Lee could be a photographer, and it was Steichen who suggested that she should go to Paris and seek out Man Ray. Theodore had bought Lee her first Box Brownie when she was ten and from then she'd shared her father's darkroom, becoming conversant in, and experimenting with, the process of making photographs. Lee set sail for Paris in 1929, just after her twenty-second birthday, armed with the fame of her modelling career, her knowledge of set design and lighting, and introductions to the Parisian fashion world from Steichen and Condé Nast. As the ship sailed down the Hudson one of her boyfriends flew low over the deck in his plane and showered it with roses as a grand farewell gesture – the kind of extraordinary event that isn't uncommon in the story of Lee's life. And yet it's almost a throwaway detail, a footnote.

In Paris, Lee found Man Ray and introduced herself as his new pupil. He had always refused them but for her he made an exception. He had been dumped by Kiki the year before (although he remembered it the other way round) and they began a relationship, one that lasted for the next three years. Lee found Man Ray incredibly magnetic. He was almost seventeen years older than her, which suited Lee; she often preferred older men. He was famous and in huge demand for his portraits, he drove a sports car, was well connected and stylish. Lee seems to have been happy to pose for Man Ray in any way he asked of her, for her body and its parts to be itemized, fetishized, tied up, laid bare.

She, meanwhile, was learning all the tricks of his trade – techniques, portraits, fashion photography. Lee would later acknowledge how much she had learned about photography from Man Ray. She was working alongside him in the studio, acting as his receptionist, and then working in the darkroom, developing film, printing and retouching photographs. One day, in the darkroom, she felt something crawl across her foot and rushed to turn on the light. In doing so she exposed some of Man Ray's negatives to extra light. When they looked at the negatives, they realized that the exposure had created a dark, dynamic, almost eerie outlined effect on the image, a deep nimbus. Man Ray named it solarization and claimed it as his own invention. They worked together so closely that perhaps it felt like a collaboration. Often they didn't know which photograph had been taken by whom.

In time, as Man Ray was more and more drawn back into painting, he offered the lesser commissions to Lee to shoot in his place. And as Lee grew more confident in her work, she began to assert her independence, to draw away from Man Ray, creatively and emotionally. She grew tired of his possessiveness, his jealousy and his instinct to control her. And she was tired of being Madame Man Ray, as they called her in Paris. She was gaining clients of her own, including *Vogue*, Schiaparelli and Paramount Pictures. She rented her own studio with a darkroom. And she starred in Jean Cocteau's film *The Blood of a Poet* as a plaster cast of a classical statue, her body painted entirely white but for the black eyes drawn onto her eyelids. Cocteau had been overwhelmed by her beauty.

But she was also photographing herself (and other women) nude, reclaiming her image and her body, bending and twisting it into erotic poses in the surrealist manner but entirely bypassing the male gaze. It was a reclamatory gesture, rather like Dora would make with her own weeping women. There were ironic photographs too – a woman's head trapped inside a glass jar, another woman as a knife-thrower's target.

Lee was always surreal and never officially or exclusively a surrealist. Her eye for the uncanny was there long before she talked her way into Man Ray's studio and into the surrealist world he inhabited. But though she seems to have had little time for the unconscious self, her work is inherently surreal. Like Dora Maar, Lee liked to wander the streets of the city with a portable camera. It took her away from the stifling atmosphere of Man Ray's studio – he preferred to shoot indoors. Outside she sought out and photographed strangeness, fractures in the ordinary, creating slippery, unsettling images that undermine the concreteness of the world and our understanding of it. A woman's hand reaches for the handle of a glass door (the entrance at Guerlain, the cosmetics house). We are seeing it from outside. A patch of the glass through which we see her hand has been scratched and the fingers all but disappear behind an opaque haze. It looks as if the hand could be shattering the glass, or the glass somehow shattering the hand. She called this *Exploding Hand*.

In December 1931, Lee joined her friend Charlie Chaplin and others at Saint Moritz, Switzerland's glitteringly fashionable ski resort. There she became reacquainted with a friend, Aziz Eloui Bey, whose beautiful wife, Nimet, Man Ray had photographed in Paris. Lee and Aziz began an affair, which would end his marriage and her relationship with Man Ray. Perhaps it was the catalyst she needed. By the autumn of the following year, she was determined to leave Man Ray and Paris and return to America, alone, to set up her own studio.

In October 1932 she arrived in New York, a celebrity in a beret and fur coat. Reporters were there to greet her. In response to a journalist's comments about her being one of the most photographed faces in New York she replied that she'd 'rather take a picture than be one'.

She found a studio in Manhattan and employed her brother Erik as assistant. Soon the opening of Lee Miller Studios Inc. at 8 East 48 Street was announced. She had stationery designed. And she advertised the studio, shamelessly, as the Man Ray school of photography's American branch (she was Madame Man Ray when she wanted to be), which appalled her erstwhile lover. Celebrities began flocking to her studio for portraits. She resurrected a lot of her old connections, working for commercial clients in fashion and for luxury beauty brands and for magazines. She also held her first (and last, in her lifetime) solo show, at the gallery of her friend and sometime lover, Julien

Levy. But in spite of all this she was struggling financially. In all the glitter and the gloss, she'd lost sight of her surreal instincts, become too slick, too polished. Perhaps, though she was only twenty-six, a certain ennui had set in. And in the America of the Depression tastes were changing, becoming more parochial, more insular. Realism was favoured over foreign whimsy.

In June 1934 Aziz turned up in New York and asked Lee to marry him. Aziz was then forty-three and Lee twenty-seven. She agreed and they were married in a civil ceremony in July. They were also married at the Egyptian consulate on the same day, in accordance with Muslim law, which entitled Aziz to more wives, and the freedom to divorce Lee at will. He could also forbid her to leave the house without his permission. Perhaps Lee knew that in Aziz, paternal and forbearing, she'd marry someone who would respect her liberty in spite of these cultural differences. After a honeymoon at Niagara Falls, they departed for Egypt, Lee leaving her brother Erik to close down her studio.

Though, as a foreigner and a non-Muslim, Lee wasn't confined to quarters once she arrived in Cairo, she was soon restless in what, after New York and Paris, felt like a stagnant backwater. At some point towards the end of that first year of marriage, she possibly suffered a miscarriage, which can only have compounded her mood. By the spring of 1937 she was making plans to escape the city's summer heat. She sailed for Marseille in May. Arriving in Paris she contacted Julien Levy who invited her to a fancy-dress ball that night. Having had no time to devise a costume she quickly unpacked and dressed herself in a dark blue evening gown. That night she would meet Roland. And then Cornwall and Mougins followed that summer, and her life shifted once more. In 1938 Lee wrote a letter to Aziz telling him of her longing for the seemingly impossible: to feel both secure and free. And she told him that she was determined to fight for it.

MAN RAY AND LEE

A triptych, a sequence. Lee stands in a room beside a window. To the left of her the darkened room, to the right, the window. From this light pours in and bathes her face, which is turned away from the camera towards the light, a distant, dreamy gaze. It bathes her upper body too; she's naked to the waist. She's pushed down her clothes, a giving of herself. She's wearing a dark skirt that melts into the darkness of the room and her arms are tucked to her sides, her hands behind her back. And so she's a head and a torso and breasts – a Venus de Milo or de' Medici, a mannequin. The shadow of the sheer, openwork curtain at the window falls on her body, its grid-like pattern emphasizing the lines of her body like contour lines on a map, a mapping of desire. Territory. But in the second image, a subtle shift – an arm raised to the window, her head tilted down a little, the skirt removed. Now she's embodied, not a body, her fierce face with its dark-ringed eyes that no longer gaze but stare. The straight arm aloft, and her naked groin girdled in the shadow of balcony railings, she's no longer submissive, she's an Amazon. And in the third, a shift again. She's entirely behind the sheer curtain, neither Venus nor Amazon, but a woman at a window, filtered, veiled, inscrutable – perhaps for Man Ray the most unattainable of all.

LEE

After witnessing a radical mastectomy one morning at the American Hospital in Paris, Lee returned to French *Vogue* from the operating theatre. She was carrying the detached breast under a cloth, the surgeon having agreed to let her take it. According to Lee's son Antony Penrose, the surgeon, Dr Dax, had become a good friend of Lee, having treated and finally cured her gonorrhoea with the newly invented antibiotics during her early days in Paris. It was thus that she had unique and privileged access to his operating theatre and could leave with a severed breast in her hands. Once in the studio, she put it on a plate and placed it upon a napkin on a table, laid a knife and fork either side of the plate, and a spoon above it, and began to photograph. It's a simple, honest sort of image. The plate, the cutlery, the checked napkin, shot diagonally from above and a little away from the table. In the background there's an out-of-focus chair. And at first glance what is served on the plate could be a slice of pie, its glistening meat escaping from beneath a pastry lid, and there's a little lump on it which, if this was a pie, might be a leaf whittled out of the pastry as decoration. Except we know from the photograph's title – *Untitled (Severed breast from radical surgery in a place setting 1)* – brutal in its clinical, macabre economy, that this was a woman, her flesh, her skin, her nipple. And so any thoughts of appetite shift quickly, queasily, in recognition, to repulsion, pity, horror.

This was entirely Lee: transgressive, subversive, unsettling. The photographs that she took that day are witty, grotesque, almost baroque. They're an elegantly economical riposte to surrealist dismembering and to the gluttony to which her body, and the bodies of the other women in the surrealist world (and beyond it), were subjected. This was a repudiation of their objectification. And this was a woman's reality too. Lee always sought the real woman in her photographs. Lee (whose own perfect breasts were photographed time and time again, and the shape of which was used to design a set of champagne glasses) shows us not 'the eternal feminine' but the grim reality of a body taken apart and ready to be devoured.

ACROBAT

The contemporary artist Kaye Donachie paints portraits of women, ideas of them, 'spectres' she calls them, inspired by old photographs. They are beautiful, ethereal, intangible, and they radiate emotion, a feeling of someone. She is fascinated by women who were muses to other artists, famous men, who have been marginalized, and about whom little is known but everything is seen. Nusch is one of them. In an interview with the writer Francesca Gavin for *Beauty Papers*, Donachie explains the appeal of women like Nusch. She tells Gavin that she usually discovers them through the prism of those men's work, their art or poetry, and that she admires their relationship with, their understanding of, fashion and beauty. 'Their life is like art . . .' she says of the women, 'they have a real sense that they understand themselves as performers. [. . .] They are active.'

Nusch was a performer almost all her life. Her story is that of her body. She was born in the Alsatian city of Mulhouse in 1906. Her father was a street acrobat, and in her childhood, Nusch performed with her parents in a travelling circus. Her name was Maria Benz; it is possibly her father who gave her the nickname Nusch. For him she learned to bend and leap and use her body to entertain an audience. In her act Nusch was chained up by a comedian and also by a spectator. She would break free, and dance in triumph to much applause. Eileen later quipped in her memoirs that this prepared Nusch well for a life spent with Paul Éluard. At fourteen Nusch moved to Berlin to become a stage actress, but with little success. And instead, for a while, she made a living posing for erotic postcards, before returning home to her parents.

In 1925 she was in Zurich and in a relationship with Max Bill, the Swiss architect and designer, who had studied at the Bauhaus. It's also possible that it was Max who nicknamed her Nusch. He wanted to marry her to save her from being extradited, but his father vetoed it, and when her residency permit expired after several months their relationship ended.

In 1928 she moved to Paris, calling herself Maja Benaro, and found work performing as a hypnotist in a gruesome horror show at the Grand Guignol theatre in Pigalle. Nusch rented a small hotel room near the Gare Saint-Lazare and was often hungry, living hand-to-mouth, donning a dress she'd stolen from the theatre and a little black hat to walk the streets to do sex work. Sometimes she performed acrobatics or played at being a fortune teller on the pavement instead.

One day in May 1930, when Nusch was twenty-three, she was performing (or perhaps looking for clients) outside the Galeries Lafayette when she was approached by Paul Éluard and his friend, fellow poet and surrealist René Char. They took her to a cafe where she hungrily devoured a basket of croissants. Paul asked her to come home with him, and she never left.

At Mougins Picasso inscribed an ink portrait of her with 'Pour Nusch, pour Nusch', which Patrick O'Brian, in his biography of Picasso, believes is a play on pour (for) and the English word, poor. Françoise Gilot recounts Paul and Nusch's meeting in her memoirs of her time with Picasso, saying that Picasso was moved by the story of it. For him she seemed to spring from his Blue Period: a vulnerability, a frailty, perhaps a certain melancholy, a lost child. Eileen thought her charming, untameable. From the start Nusch was an encounter, a woman seen, a motif, a fantasy, a projection.

For Paul, meeting Nusch on the street was more than just luck. The surrealists loved to approach women; the chance encounter was at the very heart of their aesthetic. Paul and René would often frequent the Grands Boulevards to watch the women walking, to enjoy the theatre of the streets, to revel in the erotic tensions and the possibilities of the city. A man wanders the streets, flâneuring with no route or destination in mind, when he happens upon a woman. Ideally, she has a wild, mysterious, melancholy air. Preferably, she is mad, and their fevered encounter, in the realms of the marvellous, provides the man with enough erotic inspiration to fuel a lifetime of creativity.

Breton had one such encounter, which he reworked into a novel, *Nadja*. The woman he met was mentally unstable and was later committed to an asylum. In one scene she encourages Breton to drive with his eyes closed and, when he refuses, she accuses him of being bourgeois. It was in this spirit that Paul met Nusch. He was overwhelmed by the force of this encounter, this 'discovery'. As for Nusch, perhaps she was just hungry. For the surrealists, Nusch, and her ease with nudity and her sexual openness, would become the incarnation of female freedom and sensuality. It's ironic that many of her choices in the early part of her life seem to have been made out of expedience rather than liberty.

Nusch's presence filled Éluard's poems from the moment he met her. For him, Nusch becomes an infinite and overflowing fount of erotic, and therefore poetic, inspiration. They married in August 1934, Paul still longing for Gala, the woman who had left him for Salvador Dalí. In one of his letters to his ex-wife, near the beginning of his relationship with Nusch, he fantasized about having sex with her while Nusch looks on. There are many letters like this, and these types of encounters were not just imaginary, but often acted out. It seems Nusch devoted herself entirely to Paul, to his surrealist way of life, to his creative ambitions and to the whims of his libido and erotic imagination. Paul shared Nusch's body with all those who read his poems and, more literally, with Picasso and also with René Char, Man Ray and other friends. That is to say he encouraged her to have sex with them, for his pleasure. Whether it was for hers too isn't known. We don't know what she liked, and it's wrong to presume that she was a victim; submission can be a choice, a pleasure. Her biographer, Chantal Vieuille, writes that Nusch cut holes in her bra to let the nipples protrude, that she and Paul would caress each other in public, that Nusch felt deep physical pleasure and that Paul, with his weakened body, celebrated it. Woman as incarnation of or conduit for male desire was nothing new in the surrealist movement but perhaps theirs was an erotic partnership, a collaboration. But it's unknown: one of Nusch's many unknowns.

Nusch's likeness appears in a number of paintings by Picasso, and also in works by René Magritte and Joan Miró. But it's perhaps in Dora's photographs of her and in Man Ray's, for *Facile* (a 1935 collaborative book with Paul), that we get a glimpse of Nusch as a collaborator, of how she worked with these artists, using her body and her inscrutable, sphinx-like face, helping them to realize their own visions. She's not inert, passive, but active, creative. Surrealism objectified women but it also gave them space to assert themselves, to express themselves – a two-edged sword.

Nusch was not an artist in the conventional sense. With its emphasis on the importance of personal reality, of an entire way of life, surrealism allowed her to make living her art. Her art was the way she dressed, the way she held herself and gave herself, the way she wanted to be seen, the way she used her body to collaborate with artists, an identity, an aesthetic vision, a creative way of being in the world that was radical and brave and modern. To look at Nusch directly is to see her lovely, fragile body and her lovely, delicate and enigmatic face in paintings and photographs and poems, an image almost entirely mediated through the male gaze. To understand her we need to catch glimpses of her beyond her written history or the countless photographs, to imagine her obliquely, as Donachie does. We need to grasp the ephemeral things – emotions, gestures, playfulness, elegance, vivacity and laughter and friendship, and love-making and modelling – that aren't recorded because they aren't deemed important by posterity. These things lie between the lines of her story.

PAUL, MAN RAY AND NUSCH

Silvery images of her naked serpentine body or of individual, venerated parts of it, often hauntingly solarized, weave together and embrace sensuously with words of love across its pages. They called it *Facile* (*Easy*), a photobook Paul and Man Ray made together, an intimate dialogue between artist and poet, between photographs of Nusch and love poems about Nusch – her pliable body, her apparent ease. *Facile* became one of the iconic photobooks of the era, and a testament to Paul and Man Ray's friendship and collaboration. It is also (usually unacknowledged) a testament to their individual dialogues with Nusch, as both model and poetic inspiration, and to the extent to which she gave herself. Quite literally – one special edition of the book had curls of Nusch's hair trapped between two plates of glass, like a relic or a specimen.

'You are resemblance', Paul wrote at the end of 'You Rise the Water Unfolds', a poem that dips into the hollow of her solarized back and then wraps around her bottom on the page. Nusch is herself, he implies, and she's also the reflection, the projection, of his desires. A duality. She's transformation. His.

PICASSO AND NUSCH

The painting is unmistakeably Nusch, with her pointy nose and mass of tight curls, picked out in dots and dabs and swirls of blue. The frizzy ends have perhaps caught the light and are little white flicks around the outline of her hair. Her body is a pyramid, sharp lines to echo sharp limbs. Half is in strong white light and half in correspondingly dark shade. And the shade, a thick black line, traces up her neck and around her face. Picasso painted her several times – elegant, beautiful Nusch, a Schiaparelli harlequin in a sharp double-breasted jacket and a jaunty hat and, later, melancholy Nusch, a wan and fragile nude.

In this portrait, painted in his hotel room at Mougins, she's grinning, her mouth open to reveal a grille of white teeth. This is joyful Nusch, whose ringing laugh was loved by her friends. Her nostrils are dainty quavers, and her eyes are lively fish, one above the other, swimming in the green and white sea of her face beneath the black arches of her thinly plucked eyebrows. Her blue-lipped mouth could be a boat. The tones are different from Picasso's portraits of Lee, far more restrained; she's lightness and elements. There's an expanse of white, there's sky blue, sea green and areas of red that perhaps suggest the warmth of her face. On her head, Picasso's idea of a traditional Niçoise straw hat is black outlined in blue, adorned with yellow stars and finished with a flourish of red that curves and loops around its brim.

London

Guernica arrives in Britain on 30 September 1938, the day that Chamberlain signs the Munich Agreement and promises 'peace for our time'. Signed along with France, Italy and Germany, the agreement allows for Germany's annexation of a large area of Czech territory, but not its entirety. And it is hoped by some – not many – that this is enough to curtail Hitler's territorial demands. In October 1938, *Guernica* is on display at the elegant New Burlington Galleries, scene of Roland's triumphant surrealist exhibition two years earlier. But times are different. And suddenly no one is in the mood for looking at war. Reviews are divided, as they had been when the painting was first exhibited in Paris – it is an image of extraordinary tragedy, it is pure propaganda, too obscure, too personal. *Guernica* attracts only three thousand visitors during its time at the New Burlington Galleries before being sent off on a tour to Oxford and to northern cities.

In 1938 Roland had established The London Gallery with E. L. T. Mesens to promote surrealist art. The proceeds from their exhibitions were used to help Czechoslovakian and Jewish refugees and they held shows promoting exiled, 'degenerate' artists. Under the auspices of the National Joint Committee for Spanish Relief it was decided to try to bring *Guernica* to Britain, with the support of several left-wing figures, including scientists, artists, writers and politicians. It was left to Roland, as Picasso's friend, to try to persuade him to lend the painting to Britain. In his biography of Picasso, Roland writes that he believed Picasso would be reluctant to send the painting to England at such an unpredictable time.

But he was wrong. He telephoned Picasso who was, according to Roland, emphatic in his wish for the painting to do its work, to show war.

Roland was a hedonist, dedicated to pleasure, to art and to gentle living. But he was also someone who got things done, made things happen. He was extremely wealthy, and wealth gave him freedom, to do and to buy what he wanted, to be what he wanted. He was passionate about working for peace and freedom. He'd inherited a puritanical strain from his family, but it was a strain that for him translated into hard work and dedication rather than religious zeal. In Lee's picnic photograph he's the odd one out, slightly awkward if amused, eyes to the heavens and radiating respectable Englishness.

Later in his life Roland admitted that he would never have been such a passionate surrealist if he hadn't first been a Quaker. It seems paradoxical, and yet he claimed that Quakerism armed him with the ability to honour his own views while maintaining respect for those who disagreed. A civilized dissent. He would carry that paradox throughout his life. He believed that surrealism wasn't so very far from Quakerism. Both were international, both encouraged a constructive introspection. One focused on dreams and the subconscious, the other on the Inner Light, the guiding force central to Quaker practice.

Roland was born in 1900 in Watford, into a strict wealthy Quaker family. His father, originally from Ireland, was a portrait painter who had studied at the Royal Academy. His mother was the daughter of a rich Quaker banker. Roland lived a seemingly enchanted Edwardian childhood with his three brothers, moving between grand houses with lovely gardens, where summers were spent painting. At Bank House, the estate of his maternal grandfather, Lord Peckover, he pored over the antiquarian books in the library and its rooms full of mysterious treasures. Tucked away amongst them he'd discovered Edward Young's *Night Thoughts*, a long poem adorned with engraved illustrations by William Blake of dreamy, ethereal bodies, particularly female nudes, hovering and swooping about the text. This chance discovery would have a formative impression on the young Roland and would prefigure his fascination for surrealism. Blake's floating female figures would still be with him as he painted as an adult.

As a Quaker, and hence a pacifist, Roland was a conscientious objector in the First World War. Then in his teens, he became an ambulance driver and for a few months served in Italy with The Friends' Ambulance Unit. But this was at the end of the war and Roland was home within months and studying history at Cambridge. He later switched to architecture, which was the degree closest to art at that time. There he had a brief affair with George (Dadie) Rylands, who was later to become an academic and theatre director. Roland found the university dull but there he also met the much older painter and critic Roger Fry, who swept him into a redeemingly entertaining and inspiring Bloomsbury world of Woolfs and Bells, of Grant and Keynes.

Roland graduated with a first-class degree in architectural studies, but it was contemporary art that now filled his imagination, no doubt fuelled by his friendship with Fry, whose groundbreaking 1910 post-Impressionist exhibition was one of the foundations of the modernist era in Britain. On Fry's advice, and against his father's wishes, after graduating Roland left to study in Paris. He enrolled in the studio of the Cubist painter André Lhote, who was a generous teacher and a passionate advocate for the work of Picasso.

Roland moved south, to Cassis, where he bought a villa in 1923. There he spent his time painting. In 1925 he married Valentine Boué, a French poet from the south. Valentine was fascinated by mysticism and wrote unique visionary, erotic and entirely feminine poetry influenced by surrealism, whose members she knew well. It was Valentine who first introduced Roland to surrealism and to Max Ernst, with whom he became great friends and who he believed had the greatest influence on his own painting. Soon he would meet André Breton and the other painters, poets and intellectuals (though not yet Picasso). And it was Paul Éluard who swiftly became, and would always be, his closest friend amongst them. He was also introduced to David Gascoyne, the young English poet who was fast becoming surrealism's greatest English champion. Now Roland was painting surrealism into his canvases. And perhaps more significantly – inspired by Paul in particular – he was living by it too. An entirely new moral framework based on personal liberties, to replace – to demolish – the one he'd grown up with.

Roland and Gascoyne dreamed of bringing surrealism to the British public. With Breton and Éluard's encouragement, they started planning what would become the sensational 1936 International Surrealist Exhibition at the New Burlington Galleries in Piccadilly. Perhaps Roland envisioned it as the successor to Fry's post-Impressionists, and he probably hoped for the same success. He bought a house in North London at 21 Downshire Hill in Hampstead and from there set about planning the exhibition, heading the English organizing committee alongside Herbert Read.

Although at this stage they hadn't yet met, Roland was desperate to include Picasso in the exhibition, and he asked Paul to intervene on his behalf. After much negotiation he was able to acquire eleven of his works from private collectors and dealers. In all, the committee gathered almost four hundred pieces of surrealist painting and sculpture alongside indigenous Oceanic, African and American objects. These they considered a source of inspiration, their perceived primitivism linking them more closely to the workings of the subconscious in the eyes of the surrealists. It was hoped these pieces might shock or challenge the audience into a new way of seeing the world, their inclusion being an anti-colonial gesture (albeit a misguided one, as the works were systematically appropriated and misunderstood). But overall the exhibition was considered a great success and attended by more than twenty thousand people.

Perhaps one of the greatest pleasures of the experience for Roland was his burgeoning friendship with Paul and Nusch, with whom he spent time during the planning and the duration of the exhibition. In July 1936 Paul (who was beginning to fall out with Breton) wrote to Roland to tell him how happy he was that he had found in Roland a new friend and how much he had enjoyed being in London together. Paul and Nusch invited Roland and Valentine to join them with Picasso, Dora and other friends in Mougins that summer.

Roland's marriage had begun to break down several years earlier and that 1936 trip to Mougins only exacerbated the problem, as Valentine's letter to him despairing of the open arrangements had expressed. From the start their marriage was a complicated one. Valentine had an undersized vagina which made intercourse impossible. But it seems the problem was more than that. Their personalities and their interests didn't align. Even Roland's obsessive collecting, and the collection itself, irked Valentine. She told him how much his pictures had come to annoy her, and how she had the urge to scribble all over them with a piece of chalk. In the autumn of that year, they had travelled to Spain together with David Gascoyne and others to see for themselves the cultural impact the war there was having, to connect with leading Republicans and to gather material that would help increase support for the cause back at home. Valentine left Roland in 1936 for an ashram run by a Spanish guru where she developed her interest in Eastern thought and philosophy. She began to have lesbian relationships, and lesbianism became an important theme in her work.

Roland's acquisitive impulse – the love of the chase – consumed him. It would be given free rein after the death of his parents in the early 1930s, when he became an independently wealthy man. By the end of the decade he had built a substantial collection of contemporary European art and was giving huge financial support to British surrealists. In 1938 he acquired a large collection (more than a hundred pieces) of important surrealist work when Paul sold him his collection. Downshire Hill became a cabinet of curiosities, no doubt inspired by his childhood memories of his grandfather's collection at Bank House.

At Mougins in 1936 Roland had finally met the person who was arguably the love of his life: Picasso. He was captivated by the artist and for Roland that holiday was an indelibly enchanted memory.

More of a nightmare was the fact that he could have killed Picasso in a car accident while Roland was driving, an event which caused the Englishman the greatest anguish and mortification. Picasso was more hurt than the others in the car and had himself X-rayed. He was fine. And, evidently, Roland was forgiven. In the spring of 1937, Roland visited Picasso at the rue des Grands-Augustins studio, where he was then poised to begin work on *Guernica*.

Roland was on a mission to buy a painting of Picasso's, a female bather, which he'd spotted in *Cahiers d'Art*. Picasso summoned his chauffeur and whisked Roland, with the Éluards, Dora, Paul's daughter Cécile and Picasso's son Paolo, straight to his house in Normandy to see it. He agreed to let Roland buy it and Roland was in a dream as he returned to Paris with his first acquisition of Picasso's work.

Roland's adoration of Picasso was almost an obsession. Some thought he was passionately in love with the artist. Certainly his devotion eclipsed all his relationships with women. Whatever it was, it seems that the love was relatively one-sided. Picasso could be cruel as with so many of his friends. He would keep Roland waiting, vacillate with him, toy with his devotion, but he was clearly fond of him and valued his friendship.

At Mougins in the summer of 1937 Lee, even in those first weeks of her relationship with Roland, must have realized how things stood. Later she'd describe herself as a 'Picasso widow'. There's a photograph that she took of the two men standing by Picasso's car outside the Hôtel Vaste Horizon. They're behind the open car door, their heads and shoulders framed by the window. Picasso's looking at Lee, smiling a little. Roland, further back, his hand resting on the car, is smiling too, as he gazes deeply – the gaze of a lover – not at Lee and her camera, but at the back of Picasso's head.

For all his obsession with Picasso, Roland was deeply in love with Lee and he was devastated when, in the autumn after Mougins, she reluctantly returned to Egypt and her husband. He wrote simply, mournfully in his diary that she had left, drawing teardrops beside the note. In turn she wrote to him from a cold, noisy train en route to Marseille that now it was her tears and not his ties that held her (presumably a reference to the ties with which he bound her to the bed). She told him that she was in love with him and would return to him. And in another letter, she repeatedly called him darling. She lingered over the gifts he had given her and questioned how long she could bear being apart from him after three such blissful months. She wondered if perhaps she had imagined it.

Roland comforted himself by visiting Picasso's studio in Paris to see if he would let him buy the Arlésienne portrait of Lee that he had his eye on. For Roland the painting radiated happiness and Mougins and the Mediterranean. And Lee, of course. It was another triumphant purchase.

They continued writing to each other. Lee told Roland how she longed to see his house filled with all his new acquisitions and how she longed to fill the house with herself too. She told him of her desperate boredom and how her life had been entirely upturned by him. They shared stories of encounters with other lovers, having agreed that neither should be monogamous; a sharing which only increased their intimacy. For Roland, Paul was a role model in these matters. He loved Nusch, and was committed to her, but that co-existed with his openness to other sexual experience. He saw the two as different things. Roland filled the void created by Lee's absence by making art. He channelled his longing into his work, into collages and paintings. It was an intensely creative time.

They were together again the following summer of 1938, meeting in Athens and touring the Balkans – Greece, Bulgaria and Romania. As they travelled, they photographed – themselves, and the people they met, their traditions, their landscapes. All soon to be destroyed by war. Roland would later create a surrealist-inspired photobook, part love poem, part travel journal, *The Road is Wider than Long*, with the photographs from their trip, alongside text handwritten in coloured inks, drawings and frottage (rubbing a textured surface with a crayon or pencil to recreate that texture on the paper). The first printed copy he gave to the woman who'd inspired it, inscribing in it: 'For Lee, who caught me in her cup of gold'.

Though *Guernica* had made little impact on the people of Mayfair in the autumn of 1938, by the following January it was on display in the Whitechapel Gallery in the East End of London. Alongside it were sixty-seven of Picasso's preparatory sketches, studies and paintings (including *Weeping Woman*, which Roland had bought from Picasso in 1937). Nearby, three years earlier, Oswald Mosley's fascist Blackshirts had battled in the streets. In Spain, the Republicans were fast being defeated by the Nationalists and by April they had surrendered to Franco. The exhibition had been opened by Clement Atlee, Labour leader of the opposition and a passionate supporter of the Republican cause. During the fortnight it was on, the gallery held educational events and screenings of films about the Civil War for the local community. Entrance to the gallery was free but Picasso had asked that visitors might donate a pair of boots or shoes to send to Spain for refugees and for the volunteers of the International Brigades. Hundreds of pairs built up in front of the painting.

The exhibition was a huge success, attracting more than fifteen thousand visitors from the local area in those two weeks. Though it would prove too late to help the Republican cause, it must have been a terrifying image of war on a grand scale, which was increasingly seeming inevitable. At the end of the tour *Guernica* was sent to New York to be shown at the Museum of Modern Art in the largest Picasso retrospective to date. Two months later, in March 1939, Hitler occupied Czechoslovakia, making a mockery of the Munich Agreement. That month Britain pledged its support to Poland in the event of an invasion that now seemed certain.

Roland visited Lee in Cairo early in 1939 and by the summer, three years after their separation, he was divorced from Valentine. He had been longing for Lee to leave Aziz and join him in London. Roland and Lee travelled to the Continent, staying first with Max Ernst and Leonora Carrington near Avignon, and then with Picasso and Dora in Antibes, where they were spending time in Man Ray's apartment. There Lee and Roland had found Picasso working on a scene of men fishing at night. It was to be their last trip to France before the war.

As tourists started to leave, machine-gun posts began to appear along the coast. The French army was mobilized on 26 August and Roland and Lee left hurriedly for London. Picasso and Dora returned to Paris. It would be five years before the two couples met again.

In Britain, since the summer, everyone had been readying for war. In August the National Gallery had evacuated its paintings to Wales and barrage balloons began to appear in the sky above London and other cities. Hitler invaded Poland on 1 September. That day the evacuation of children from major cities began, a nationwide blackout was imposed, and the British army was mobilized. War was declared two days later.

DORA, PICASSO, ROLAND, NUSCH, PAUL, PAOLO PICASSO AND CÉCILE ÉLUARD

Boisgeloup, Picasso's château in Normandy, March 1937. They've gathered in the garden for Dora to take a photograph. Picasso's son Paulo, Paul's daughter Cécile and Nusch are slightly in the background. Standing front and centre, Picasso, in a jacket with a light scarf hanging around his neck. He's looking directly at Dora, smiling faintly, amused by something. Flanking him and slightly behind is Paul, a cigarette in his lips and smoke puffing from his mouth, a cloud of white in the cold air. He's turning aside and gesticulating at something. On the other side stands Roland, taller than the rest, a hand stuffed into the pocket of his overcoat and another holding a cigarette to his lips. He's looking rather pensive, or perhaps he's overwhelmed by the occasion, having just secured the acquisition of his first painting by Picasso. Perhaps the photograph is to mark the moment. They all hurtled back to Paris at great speed in Picasso's Hispano Suiza. Roland, as if in a dream, with the promise of his new purchase. Prophetic of the summer to come, the painting was of a nude woman lying in the sun on a beach.

ROLAND AND LEE

In reality she'd been wearing a simple dark blue evening dress the night he'd met her at the costume ball in Paris earlier in 1937. It was that simplicity and her radiant beauty which set her apart, which beguiled him so entirely. But in a letter to her that autumn he described an imaginary costume he'd have given her, and then painted *Night and Day* to illustrate his idea. She is without clothes, but her legs are red-brick towers and her torso is a blue sky scudding with fluffy white clouds. A girdle of moss encircles her hips. One hand is a black swallow (migrating from Egypt) and the other a white dove (representing peace and the promise of return). Her face and hair are yellow like the flames of the sun. She is both monumental and elemental. She is light. And she is shade.

PICASSO

Night Fishing at Antibes. A deceptively innocuous title. It's a spiky, disquieting, claustrophobic vision of the bay. Two fishermen are spearing fish from a little boat. As in a nightmare, space diminishes, scale is warped, perspective buckles. The emerald sea has shrunk to the size of a pond, overcrowded with violence and dying. The anxiety of the moment disrupting the bliss of the south, flipping day and light into night and darkness. The bright yellow coil of a decoy lamp, like a false sun now the sun has gone, lures the fish to their deaths. Stars that could be shells explode in the sky. Olga (possibly) a green and white spectre haunts the sea wall. Beside her, Dora, a bicycle standing next to her, contentedly licking an ice cream as she looks out on death. The apocalypse has come to the Riviera.

II

Occupations

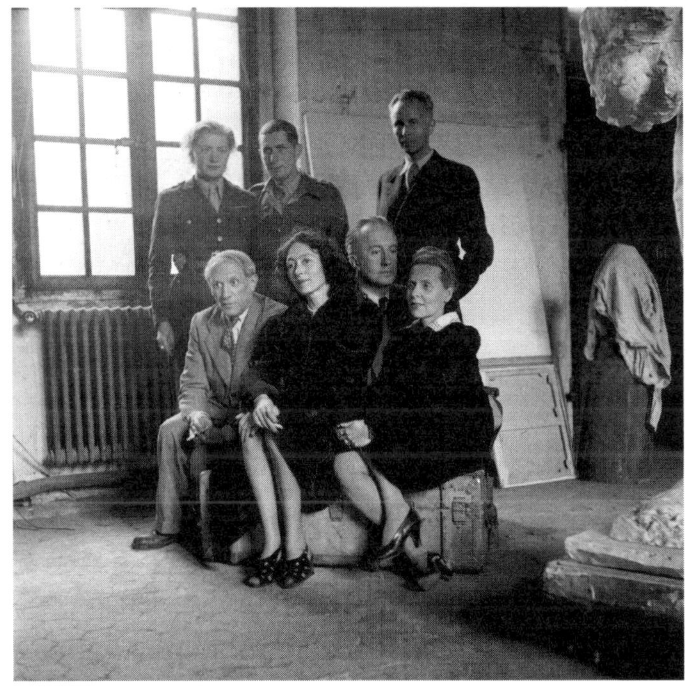

In the dark times
Will there also be singing?
Yes, there will also be singing
About the dark times.

Man Ray wrote to his sister from Paris in April 1938, telling her not to worry about him or the coming war. He reassured her that he would be able to leave France before it was too late. He was in denial and determined to stay, and perhaps in 1938 it was just about possible to believe that he could. When his friend the Hungarian photographer André Kertész announced he was leaving for New York, Man Ray told him that he shouldn't, that as an American he knew that it wasn't where an artist should be. He didn't want to be forced back there.

By the following year he was painting war into his work as a premonitory gesture in a work called *Le Beau Temps* (*Fair Weather*). There's a photograph of Ady in front of the huge canvas. She's smiling at Man Ray and has a paintbrush in her hand, looking as though she's helping to paint it. For Man Ray at least, the recent years had been fair weather – he had been happy with Ady, with the pace of his life, living between Paris and Saint-Germain-en-Laye and Antibes, and prolific with his work – and so they seemed to continue even after the war began in September 1939. Though he was Jewish and a pacifist, Man Ray wasn't politically engaged in the way that Paul and many of his other friends were. He was happy to try to see out the war in France as long as it didn't get too close. He drove to Antibes and back, having organized for his canvases from the apartment there to be transferred to his house at Saint-Germain-en-Laye for safekeeping.

In his memoirs Man Ray observes the rationing of food, tobacco, petrol, how people began to hoard them, and how lines appeared outside shops. Inevitably a black market soon sprang up. He describes taping up his windows to stop them from shattering in the event of an invasion, and how it made him miserable to do it. And he writes of the paradise that is Paris in its spring glory, sitting securely behind the fortifications of the Maginot Line in those early months of 1940, the chestnut trees in blossom, gardeners tending to the parks. Spring and the beauty of the city offered Man Ray a false hope. But then in May the German army pushed north-west through the Low Countries, bypassing the Maginot Line, and raced down towards Paris. The British Expeditionary Force dashed for Dunkirk. There had been frantic efforts to defend the capital – trenches were dug, barrage balloons erected and a smoke screen sent up. But the panic started, and Parisians had begun to flee the city by 5 June, aware of what was coming. The government left the capital on 10 June. The following day it declared Paris an open city, a signal to the Germans that the city was undefended, that it was essentially surrendering, and therefore need not be attacked.

Man Ray and Ady held out for a few more days before filling up the boot of their car with petrol cans, having new tyres fitted and plunging themselves into the exodus in Man Ray's Peugeot 402. They joined the rivers of people and vehicles and bicycles and prams and carts flowing south, with a vague idea to head to Spain.

Around two million Parisians fled the city, about two-thirds of the population. From time to time German aeroplanes bombed the columns of cars or flew low, strafing them with machine guns; Man Ray writes in *Self-Portrait* that it felt biblical. He was fascinated by the things people were taking with them and their strange priorities. Characteristically it was the oddities he noticed, the bird cages and the goldfish bowls teetering on top of mattresses. He was in despair at leaving his studio, filled with his paintings and photographs and equipment and books and things he'd collected over the years. He packed only some clothes, a coat and walking shoes. He writes that Ady had to be dissuaded from packing her loveliest clothes and that they filled a basket with some food and a bottle of champagne, which he acknowledges was equally as frivolous as any of the weird and wonderful treasures carried by his fellow fugitives.

If his memoirs are a true reflection of the time, then Man Ray –

with typical sangfroid – didn't seem to be in a rush. They travelled out to Saint-Germain to close up the house there and were stopped en route by a policeman who told them that the German army was heading in that direction. But they sped on, regardless, stopping for lunch and a decent bottle of wine. Having locked and shuttered the house, they drove on. That night they pulled into woods and slept in the car. They continued through Tours and slept another night in the car. Man Ray writes of Ady, and how wonderful it was to travel with her; how she was amiable and uncomplaining, and that her light-heartedness rubbed off on him too. They drove on, breakfasted, found a hotel, lingered for a week.

They heard General Pétain on the radio announcing the Armistice, signed at Hitler's request in the Compiègne Forest, the location of Germany's humiliation in defeat at the Armistice of 1918. It declared that the war in France was over and that there was to be a demarcation line that ran between the northern and western zone and the southern and eastern zone, the former under German occupation, the latter nominally 'free' under Pétain and his government. The announcement was followed by 'La Marseillaise'. Man Ray and Ady planned to go further south to Arcachon, below Bordeaux, from where Marcel Duchamp was hoping to get a ship to New York. But then the German tanks rolled in. Seeing the Paris address on his passport, Man Ray was told to turn back and that he couldn't pass into the unoccupied zone as he'd planned.

And so they returned, at one point passing a Nazi truck playing Wagner's *Twilight of the Gods* from its loudspeaker. At Saint-Germain they found the house untouched, except the garage from which Ady's beloved bicycle had been stolen. Man Ray writes that she was devastated and he consoled her, playfully, with the promise of a gold bicycle that would be decorated with mink. He describes in *Self-Portrait* how that amused her, softened the blow, and how she admitted that the stress of the past days was wearing her down. Man Ray claims she'd shown no sign of anxiety until that point.

He visited the American Embassy to try to organize his repatriation. Nearby, at the luxurious Hôtel de Crillon, a huge swastika flag had been hung from the balcony. He observed posters stuck on to walls urging Parisians to see their new occupiers as friends. One day, according to Man Ray, Ady rushed into their apartment having been followed by two Nazi officers in a black convertible. They tried to persuade her into their car with the promise of money and gifts. She demurred, they persisted, and, so Man Ray's anecdote goes, she questioned their sense of racial superiority, pointing out that in their terms she was 'subhuman'. It was her exoticism they admired, one told her. She managed to escape and fled home.

The embassy told Man Ray that he could apply to the Germans for permission to board a train to Spain, from where he could travel to Lisbon and then sail to America. He duly applied, asking for passes for himself and his 'wife', as he described Ady. The German officer knew of him, he writes in his memoirs, and suggested he should stay and work for the occupier. Man Ray replied that he was under contract to work in America, and needed to return to honour that. The fabricated story worked and he received the passes.

He drove his car out to the house at Saint-Germain and left it in the garage. He rolled up his canvases and organized the care of his house. At the last moment Ady decided to stay in Paris to be with her family. This angered him but then he began to see that it might be better for her to stay behind. At least this is how Man Ray tells it in his autobiography. Perhaps it was her decision, an autonomous gesture. Perhaps it was his. He packed some suitcases, a few rayographs and other pieces of work, his dinner suit, patent-leather shoes and two cameras that he was to carry around his neck. He went for a last walk around his beloved Montparnasse before the train departed that evening.

Ady, feeling ill, was in bed and apparently too upset to see him off at the station. They said their farewells at the studio. He promised to write and told her to stay inside as much as possible. Her brother helped him to the station.

Man Ray arrived in Biarritz and applied for a visa. From there he eventually crossed into Spain and then took a sleeper train to Lisbon. The city, he told his sister, was like a Bedlam of European refugees. Writing to Roland from Lisbon on 27 July he tells a slightly different version of events from those in his autobiography, particularly concerning Ady. Perhaps he was saving face, justifying his apparent abandonment of her. He told Roland that he had left the majority of his belongings with Ady and her brother and that he hoped it wouldn't be long before he could return for them. He told Roland that he couldn't get a visa for her and that they hoped to meet in the Antilles if he couldn't get back to France. He wrote that he longed to be united with his friends and for happier times.

Eventually, on 6 August, he departed for New York on the *Excambion*. Gala and Dalí were also on board. Man Ray slept with his cameras under his pillow, but one day awoke to find they'd been stolen.

His biographer Neil Baldwin writes that it's not clear whether being Jewish was the principal reason for Man Ray's decision to leave Europe, because he didn't think of himself as Jewish. Of course that would have made no difference to the Germans. In October 1940 a Vichy law announced the creation of camps for the confinement of Jewish foreigners. Man Ray had left only two months earlier.

MAN RAY

He'd recently had a dream about a battle between mythological animals. And like any of his good dreams it couldn't be wasted, but must be recorded, reworked, on canvas. He called it *Le Beau Temps* (*Fair Weather*). The animals fight in the background on the roof of a house. Inside the house, in a warmly lit room, the silhouette of two lovers who are embracing beside what appears to be an easel. Perhaps they are oblivious to the battle that rages above their heads. To the left of the canvas a stone wall is partly destroyed. There's a robotic harlequin, posed like a mannequin, with a lantern for a head. (Breton called

Man Ray 'the man with the magic lantern head'.) And another figure (Roland Penrose writes that it's a woman), like a kaleidoscopic weathervane, stands opposite. The harlequin figure – is this a self-portrait? – has opened a door. Blood drips from its keyhole and pools on the ground. He's about to step from the light into the dark. Which way will the wind blow, in which direction will the weathervane spin, who will win the battle? It's more surreal nightmare than reverie, as if teetering on the threshold of terror. A portent, a premonition.

Home Front

By early 1939 Lee had resolved to leave Aziz and join Roland in London. Writing to her lover from Naples, she told him that she was returning to him and that she had left Egypt for good. Aziz and Lee would continue to write to each other, Aziz always telling Lee of his love for her. He had recognized that Roland made his wife happy and they remained friends until Aziz's death in 1976.

After their summer near Avignon with Max Ernst and Leonora Carrington, and later at Antibes with Picasso and Dora, Lee and Roland arrived in London on the first day of the Second World War. Drawing into Waterloo Station they could see barrage balloons in the sky, and they heard the false alarm of the first air-raid siren.

Lee moved in with Roland at 21 Downshire Hill. She'd considered a hotel for propriety, but that idea was quickly forgotten. After a few weeks she received a letter from the American Embassy telling her to join the next available ship home. But she'd made up her mind that she would see out the war in London. She told her brother, by way of explanation that she couldn't – wouldn't – leave. Europe was where she had battled to live as a young woman, and it was where her friends were.

For the next eight months, as nothing happened on British soil and everyone waited, lives were filled with planning for what was bound to come. Gas masks were reluctantly carried everywhere, more and more children were evacuated (and many soon returned), signs for air-raid shelters appeared in the streets, dugouts were carved into the grass in Hyde Park, Anderson shelters were constructed in gardens, sandbags shored up buildings and windows were taped to prevent glass shattering when the bombs that hadn't yet fallen eventually began to fall.

The London Gallery had closed in July and its collection moved to a depository in Pimlico. The depository was later bombed and everything destroyed, including a large amount of Roland's personal collection. Roland joined the Air Raid Precautions Corps (ARP) and spent his nights wandering around Hampstead, checking that his neighbours were abiding by the strict blackout rules, a job he quickly found tiresome – until the war began in earnest. His days were spent painting, negotiating with internecine squabbles amongst the English surrealists and trying to keep the movement alive, and relevant to the moment, in the revolutionary spirit of its foundational objectives. And he found a way to make himself useful. With several friends, including his near neighbour, the architect Ernŏ Goldfinger, Roland founded the Industrial Camouflage Research Unit, the plan for which was to give camouflage advice to companies (on contract) in order to help protect them from aerial bombing. There were wild and wonderful ideas. Roland – a surrealist at play. There were trees made of plaster, ruined houses, thatched cottages and cafes, and bodies in tanks made of rubber. And there were houses on wheels concealing pillboxes (small fortified structures with narrow windows from which weapons could be fired). All sham, decoys to lure German planes off course. Enthusiastic amateurs as far as camouflage was concerned, they only received one contract (which was never realized) and, after much internal disagreement, the unit disbanded in July 1940.

Roland, however, persevered and became a civilian lecturer in camouflage at the Home Guard school, which was housed at Osterley Park in West London. He went on to publish the *Home Guard Manual of Camouflage* in 1941. Later he would write (with typical self-deprecation) of this wartime work, claiming that it was like playing boy's games for two years. In 1943 he was discharged from the Home Guard, commissioned into the army and given responsibility for running the Eastern Command Camouflage School on the advice of General Montgomery, who had heard and been impressed by one of Roland's lectures.

Roland had practised his skills on Lee, covering her naked body in a camouflage net, foliage and paints as she lay on a lawn. He claimed that if the camouflage could conceal Lee's loveliness, it could conceal anything. He had a colour photograph of this experiment (in which she looks like a marooned mermaid caught in a net, her loveliness very much in evidence) and took great pleasure in adding it to the pile of slides during his lectures.

As a foreigner Lee couldn't work for the government as Roland was doing. Bored and cold in London, she was itching to do something. In the New Year as the male photographers at British *Vogue* began to leave the capital for more official roles related to the war, Lee joined the staff in New Bond Street and set to work. At first, she was photographing fashion. Fashion meant something different now. Though couture continued to thrive, women were donning the uniforms of the women's auxiliary forces, as well as slacks and siren suits. These were essentially adapted boiler suits, which could be flung on over nightwear or clothes when an air-raid siren sounded and a shelter needed to be reached quickly. (Winston Churchill famously loved wearing them – even at the White House.) Women were also being taught to bind up their hair in turbans while working machines. They were being encouraged to look their best; red lipstick and a snappy hat meant that all was well with the world, or at least it would be again one day. Later, when fabric was rationed, there was advice on how to make the best of the situation, to 'make do and mend', to streamline outfits, recycle, and enjoy the freedom of necessarily shorter skirts. It was Lee's job to convey these messages to the magazine's readers, which she did with aplomb – beautiful models looking elegant, happy and dynamic (rather than the cool and luxurious languor of old), ready to be useful, in their lipstick and work wear.

As France fell in a matter of weeks and generals of the German High Command were cosily ensconced in the Crillon by mid-June, all communication between Roland and Lee and their friends in France effectively ceased until the end of the Occupation. Having claimed France (and posing to illustrate the point on the terrace of the Palais de Chaillot in front of the Eiffel Tower on 23 June) Hitler turned his attention to Britain.

The first bombs fell on London on 2 August 1940. Late in the afternoon on 7 September the Blitz began in earnest, bombs raining down on the city, killing over four hundred people and injuring many more in just that one day. And so it continued for the next fifty-seven nights (and sometimes days) consecutively. But for one exception, captured and celebrated by Lee in a photograph of a blackboard in a street – perhaps propped beside a newsstand – declaring in chalked capitals: 'LONDONS NO NIGHT RAID – ONE NIGHT OF LOVE'.

That month's *Vogue* was the first issue under the editorship of Audrey Withers. Soon after her arrival the offices were damaged by incendiary bombs. Lee photographed the magazine's staff calmly going about their work at desks set up in the basement: the impervious British spirit. When the photographs were published in the November issue its headline declared that *Vogue* had survived. These gestures were symbolic of the magazine, which positioned itself as a bastion of fortitude and civilization, and was indicative of the editor's approach to her new job. Withers was an Oxford-educated socialist, and not remotely interested in fashion. As she admitted in her autobiography, *Lifespan,* she was the right woman for the time, but would have been wrong at any other moment in the magazine's history. During the war she would become one of Lee's closest allies.

Under Withers' editorship *Vogue* became a soft propaganda machine, which she believed was fundamental to the war effort, working hand in hand with the Ministry of Information. The magazine helped women negotiate wartime conditions and restrictions: how to deal with stress and headaches, how to keep fit, how to style the new shorter hair that they were encouraged to have, which red lipstick best suited khaki.

From up in Hampstead on its hill overlooking London, Roland and Lee watched the city's pummelling, the East End and the docks aglow and searchlights streaking across the night sky. At 21 Downshire Hill, as the years passed, the house filled with waifs and strays. There were wild parties with politicians (of all persuasions) and journalists and artists and spies and musicians who all pooled their rations. There were friends who stayed over and slept in the kitchen or wherever they could find space in a hallway. There were other friends who had been bombed out of their own houses and moved in. At some point Lee adopted two stray kittens and for a while she looked after a goose. In September 1940 Roland received a telephone call from his ex-wife Valentine to tell him that she was stranded in London. Returning from India to her parents in France, her ship had been re-routed to Southampton. She was immediately beguiled by Lee when they met and soon Valentine had moved into the house too. She stayed with them for a year and joined the Free French, the government-in-exile under General Charles de Gaulle, based in London.

Writing to her parents in the autumn of 1940, Lee described life at Downshire Hill. She told them how the house was often full of friends who had retreated to the perceived safety of Hampstead. She said she had friends who didn't want to be alone while their husbands were on night duty, just as Roland was doing, all night, three times a week. She told them she was starting to get used to living at war.

War is inherently surreal, transfiguring everything ordinary into something bizarre, macabre, ridiculous, dreamlike. Where once Lee had sought out such things to photograph in the world about her, now they were everywhere, a surfeit of strangeness. There was beauty to be found in the wreckage, incongruities, juxtapositions and new forms so beloved of the surrealists. As Lee went about her work, her eye was continually caught by scenes which she captured with her camera and invariably these photographs were given their own title, usually playful, pithy, and always enhancing, transposing reality into metaphor.

Rubble spews forth from the pedimented door of a building like vomit from an open mouth; *Nonconformist Chapel*, she called this. A shattered typewriter, its keys all askew, becomes *Remington Silent*. The statue of a woman lies amongst bomb debris, a brick on her breast and a metal bar across her neck. It has another witty title, *Revenge on Culture*, but it also conveys outrage, as if the bombing has given life to this stone woman and then taken it away. These and other photographs would be published in 1941 in a book called *Grim Glory: Pictures of Britain Under Fire*, its job primarily to help persuade America to join the war and, as the book declared, to show the Germans that their bombs couldn't destroy everything, especially the English spirit.

Though Lee was still shooting fashion photography (and running the photography studio at *Vogue*) and taking celebrity portraits, increasingly, towards the end of 1941, she was portraying women at work, often on the land. There's a softer, bucolic quality to these photographs, to reflect the shift to a rural focus – Land Girls in their gumboots and breeches, working on farms, thatching roofs and cutting down trees – a sense of self-sufficiency, of the nation's survival, heroic, romantic. And the images radiate a sense of liberation, of purpose, of women out of their homes and in the world. By 1943 almost ninety per cent of single women and eighty per cent of married women were engaged in professional war service.

As a woman shooting women, Lee was able to put her subjects at ease. There's an intimacy, an obvious rapport in these photographs. As Lee photographed these women, who had stepped with such ease into the roles vacated by men, she was drawn more and more to tell their stories, to capture their dedication and vitality, their quiet courage. The war had shaken Lee awake too.

Between 1940 and 1944 Lee produced over four hundred pages of fashion images, and that was just fashion. She began to feel a sense of purpose, a sense of ambition that outran the work she was doing. She was growing tired of photographing fashion; she wanted to get closer to the action. She was spending more time with her fellow Americans and was particularly drawn to men who had seen the war at close quarters. In December 1941, at a dinner party, Lee met David Scherman, a twenty-five-year-old *Life* photographer and war correspondent. Lee and Dave (as she called him) were soon great friends. He was a charismatic New Yorker who had already made a name for himself as a brilliant photographer. By the following February Scherman had moved into Downshire Hill, and soon Lee and Roland's relationship shifted to accommodate a third party. Roland was often away and Lee and Scherman became lovers. He was initially shocked by the openness, but they soon settled into a new domestic rhythm.

It was Scherman who suggested that Lee should apply for accreditation as a war correspondent with the United States Army, to give her official work and official access into the inner workings of the conflict. Certainly Scherman later took the credit for it, claiming that as an expat of twenty years Lee had never thought that she could exploit her nationality. But for Lee the impetus was already there. Eventually, with Audrey Wither's backing, on 30 December 1942 she became an official war correspondent for *Condé Nast*. She had a uniform made for herself on Savile Row and her first article was a feature on American army nurses in Oxford early the following year.

During the war the US War Department accredited only approximately one hundred and twenty-seven women as official war correspondents (as against the thousands of male correspondents). Four of these women, including Lee, were photographers. The job came with a lot of perks. Lee would get a jeep, food, accommodation. But she was also subject to military discipline, her photographs subject to censorship, and as a woman she was barred from the front line. At least for now.

DAVID SCHERMAN, LEE AND ROLAND

A cosy image: fireside, curtains closed against the night, a plant, a cabinet, a clock. Lee's in an armchair with a tray on her lap. She's playing cards. She's wearing a dress and coat (perhaps it's cold) although her legs and feet are bare and stretched out on a leopard-skin footstool. Either side of her, Scherman and Roland in their uniforms. Scherman's crouching awkwardly beside the chair in his shiny shoes – the guest. Roland's sitting on something, cigarette in hand, socks not shoes – at home. Both men lean into Lee, watching intently as she handles the cards: a queen and her attendants.

ANGEL OF ANARCHY

It could be a Catholic relic, or a jewel-encrusted baroque skull used as a memento mori, or something older still. Beneath, there is a plaster cast of a man's head; a copy of a sculpture Eileen made of Joseph. But the head is all but lost beneath swathes of material. The neck is encased in brown barkcloth with jagged, heavily stitched lines in places. The head itself is bound in embroidered black silk, on top of which a band of light blue Chinese embroidered silk is wrapped around the eye area and over the nose, like a blindfold. A diamanté-encrusted nose protrudes beneath this. To one side of the nose there's a strip of blue tape and on the other a pink feather fans down across the lower part of the face. Tufting out of the top of the head like hair are black ostrich feathers and other, more spiky, green feathers spray out at the sides. Falling down the back of the head is an African beaded fringe with cowrie shells dangling along the bottom.

Angel of Anarchy was the second and much altered version of a sculpture with the same name that Eileen had made in the mid-1930s, which was later sent to an exhibition in Amsterdam and never returned because the war had begun. She began this second one in 1940, shrouding the features so that it was no longer a portrait but a totem. And, as she would write in a note now in the Tate Archive, she wanted this one to be wholly unlike the previous one. It would be more dynamic, more potent, more malignant. Though the head beneath the fabrics is modelled on a man, the finished sculpture is entirely feminine, and the use, reappropriation and repurposing of textiles (which she'd bought in antique shops or taken from her mother's wardrobe) is aligned with the subtle subversion of woman's work – the expressivity of the Lady of Shalott weaving in her tower, the resistance of Penelope at her loom. And also an association with the feminist tradition of making things new, of giving things new meaning. In this way, a man's head, shrouded in silks and feathers and jewels, becomes a powerfully female avenging angel.

At the beginning of the war Eileen and Joseph hosted a farewell dinner for refugee artists who'd escaped from the Continent and were in London en route to America; amongst them Walter Gropius, Marcel Breuer and László Moholy-Nagy. They set up a ping-pong table in the studio adorned with curious objects and a fruit- and flowers-bedecked fretsaw as a centrepiece, for a surrealist-inspired evening. They ate stuffed goose and pink potatoes and other dishes of bizarre colours. Though she maintained she wasn't a surrealist, Eileen also met her surrealist comrades once a month for dinner in Soho at the Barcelona Restaurant in Beak Street. There were arguments and debates about intentions and convictions and loyalties, and they were asked to renounce all participation in non-surrealist group exhibitions that were considered to spring from a bourgeois spirit. Often Lee and Roland were at the dinners. Though Eileen admits in her memoirs that she never got on well with Lee, she thought her extraordinary, and marvelled at the work Lee was doing, and at her fearlessness. But Eileen considered Lee to be without sentiment and capable of ruthlessness. Perhaps a little at arm's length then, they talked of Picasso in Occupied Paris, of the rumours about him, and wondered what had become of him.

The war inspired Eileen to propose to Joseph and they were married on Leap Year Day in 1940. Nonetheless she continued her affair with Paul Nash, who occasionally came to London to steal moments alone with her. They met at the Natural History Museum, the Café Royal or at Paul's flat near Euston. Sometimes they walked in the park. Their relationship caused Nash's wife Margaret much pain, and Joseph grew increasingly intolerant.

In *A Look at My Life* Eileen admits that she was appalled by the (albeit unlikely) possibility that she could be called up to do official war work and sent off to some obscure, windswept corner of the British Isles. The idea made her feel miserable rather than heroic. She writes that she was not belligerent by nature, and she thought such a job would get in the way of her quest to become a better artist. She wanted to continue to live in her flat in London, to face the bombs which she thought less terrifying than a provincial exile. Though nature was her greatest inspiration, at heart she was cosmopolitan. She volunteered to work in a canteen on Savile Row which served hot meals to civil servants and Ministry of Information personnel. Peeling potatoes and mopping floors were, she felt, preferable to marching in military parades.

Mostly she was impatient for the war to be over, and the ennui is evident in her memoirs. Both Eileen and Joseph served as fire watchers on night duty – she was taught how to use a hatchet – and Joseph also served as an air-raid warden. Eileen recalls watching with excitement through a crack in her blackout curtains as bombs fell and destroyed buildings nearby. And yet life continued. They holidayed in the Lake District. Eileen attended the private view of a Magritte show at the London Gallery in 1940. There the reporter for *The Daily Sketch* observed her in cream gloves with scarlet cloth tips like fingernails. Eileen's own work was exhibited in several group shows, including one with Peggy Guggenheim in New York. And she had a solo show at the Redfern Gallery in Cork Street in 1942, for which Paul Nash wrote the foreword to the catalogue.

But Eileen struggled to make new work. She found herself disorientated, unmoored, paralysed by the war. It dominated her imagination and stifled all subtlety. In *A Look at My Life* she writes how she tried, and mostly failed, to make anything. There were exceptions, and these are filled with references to the natural world – the skies and the sea – and to ancient mythologies and love. Things the war couldn't touch.

The blindfolded head of *Angel of Anarchy* is sometimes associated with seduction and submission. At other times it's seen as a denial of the current moment. But for Eileen it's not a grand gesture, it's not a confrontation. It's an intimate, feminine gesture. It's a withdrawal, a turning inside herself, to a place where the power of the imagination, of womb magic, could still counter the deadening, dehumanizing and entirely masculine forces at work in the war. For Eileen this was a kind of internalized resistance, a defiant interiority, a retreat into the irrational in response to the cold, ordered, rationality of fascism. The same was true in her life: living well, and loving, nurturing her inner life, staying in London when many of her friends, and her two sisters, were escaping to America. For Eileen these were gestures of resistance.

Amongst the newspaper cuttings in Eileen's archive is a little undated quote from *The Daily Sketch*, written sometime during the war: 'There is one artist I know who is getting ready for a show to be held during the boom she believes will come when the war is over,' it says. 'She is Eileen Agar, famous woman Surrealist, who tells me that all her pictures will be light-hearted ones.' Eileen waited impatiently for that time to come.

Eileen

At the centre of the collage there's a black and white photograph of a nude woman demurely covering her breasts with her arms, her hands elegantly touching beside her head. The top half of her face

– her eyes and forehead and hair – has been cut off and in its place there's some kind of organic form in black and yellow, resembling the unopened head of a tulip. Her body is smooth and hairless like a classical sculpture. Beneath her crotch Eileen has added a tiny black spiky triangle as if to counter its purity. It's densely layered with organic shapes; a tree in a postcard lies horizontal in a corner and there's seaweed and swooping lines like waves and clusters of circles and something that could be an octopus with a red dot in its centre. A large brown fish swims along the bottom. Eileen called this collage *Erotic Landscape*. The headless woman echoes the blindfolded Angel of Anarchy in its denial of war and reassertion of sensation. This is an image of desire, not as an object to be looked at but as something felt, something private. It's a deeply feminine, deeply sensual image, its eroticism implied by the salty, slipperiness of the undulating marine forms that swirl around the woman's body.

DESIRE CAUGHT BY THE TAIL

Since the start of the war, Picasso and Dora had been living at the Hôtel du Tigre in Royan, a resort on the Atlantic coast. Frightened that the Germans would attack Paris, Picasso had decided that they should all flee the city. He was not an *étranger nondésirable* as a Spaniard, but as a 'degenerate' artist he was in a precarious position and rightly scared of what would happen to him if France fell.

Lodged nearby since the summer in a building where Picasso initially set up a studio, and at first unbeknown to Dora, were Marie-Thérèse, with her sister, mother and Maya. Later Jacqueline Lamba and her daughter Aube joined Picasso and Dora too; Breton, who had been called up and was working in the medical corps as he had in the previous war, was stationed a short distance away.

In Royan Picasso painted in the studio, and filled sketchbooks with drawings, ideas and poetry while he sat in cafes. That year there were many nudes, images of rape and violently distorted, abridged portraits of women inspired by Dora and the last of his weeping women. There were still lifes with skulls like memento mori, the raw redness of skinned lamb's heads and a painting of a cat eviscerating a bird.

He sometimes returned to Paris through the autumn and into the winter of 1939, to get supplies, to organize his papers and to attempt to apply for French citizenship, which would make his position more secure. His application was ultimately rejected because of his early anarchistic tendencies and a perceived over-enthusiasm for communism. He was also slowly moving his collection to a safety-deposit room at a bank. And he was selecting and preparing works for his first retrospective, *Picasso: 40 Years of his Art*, at the Museum of Modern Art in New York, which opened in December 1939.

German troops arrived in Royan in June 1940, the day after the Armistice was signed. Picasso had to make the decision whether to return to the now Occupied capital, or to stay put at the coast. But the idyll of Royan ended when a German sentry was shot in the town and the Germans imposed restrictions and banned dogs, Jewish people and French people from using the beach. The next day a bullet was fired and flew into the window of the room below Picasso's studio. It was probably this and Dora's unsurprising unhappiness that prompted him to make the decision to leave.

And so, Picasso and Dora and the piles of canvases and drawings they'd made in the past months had returned to Paris in August 1940, driven by Marcel the chauffeur (recently demobilized from the defeated French army) in the Hispano Suiza. Marie-Thérèse and Maya stayed on in Royan until December and then were housed by Picasso in a Parisian suburb.

In Paris he discovered that the German authorities had banned him from exhibiting in France, at the behest of Spanish fascists, although dealers found ways to sell his work discreetly and the ban only enhanced its value. Picasso's support of the Spanish Republic and the very public gesture that was *Guernica* would never be forgotten. He was vulnerable, but not cowed, and determined to carry on living his life in Paris despite the danger. Spanish and German cooperation meant that he could easily have been extradited to Spain, and there were offers of asylum from America and Mexico, where the artists Diego Rivera and José Clemente Orozco had organized a special visa for him. But Picasso turned them all down. Françoise Gilot writes that he wasn't actively courting risk but that he wasn't prepared to capitulate to intimidation either. It wasn't courage, he claimed, merely a kind of stubborn, passive resistance. Quite simply he didn't want to leave, and he would only do so if he suddenly felt like it.

Despite the sanctions imposed on his art he was mostly left in peace, and it was probably his celebrity that saved him. After he'd returned from Royan he went out of the city only once during the Occupation. The Gestapo searched his apartment and inspected the bank's safety-deposit room, and Nazis occasionally called on him to confront him about his work and his views, to pay homage to or to ogle at the famous artist. In his biography of Picasso, Roland recounts a possibly apocryphal but well-known anecdote about a Nazi officer, who, visiting the studio and noticing a photograph of *Guernica* lying on a table, asked Picasso if he had done it, to which Picasso answered, "No, you did!". Roland writes that the artist delighted in handing out postcards of *Guernica* as souvenirs to any Germans who called on him.

Paris was a changed world from the one he had left for Royan. A place of curfews, rationing, permits, food queues. There were reports of executions, there was propaganda and soon yellow stars began to appear on the coats of French Jews. There were disappearances, distrust, whirlpools of suspicion, shifting loyalties, betrayals. Swastikas adorned buildings and the streets were filled with the grey-green of German uniforms. As time went on there was cold and hunger, as fuel, produce and forced French labour leached to Germany.

Picasso moved out of his Right Bank apartment on the rue la Boétie, where he had once lived with his wife Olga, and instead created a living space next to his studio in his rooms at the rue des Grands-Augustins. Perhaps he felt safer, tucked away in its dark, cavernous depths, barely changed since it was built in the seventeenth century. It was heated by a vast iron stove that devoured fuel and offered little warmth. He converted his bathroom into a sculpture studio and there constructed assemblages made from whatever he could get his hands on. These were then sent away to be cast in bronze, despite a German ban on bronze casting. A discreet act of defiance.

During the Occupation Picasso's world reduced to the Left Bank and to the streets around his studio in Saint-Germain-des-Prés. He lived quietly, but would not go into hiding. He feared exile more than the Germans. Just a few doors down from his building was Le Catalan, his favourite restaurant, where he could hear Catalan spoken every day, and where he lunched, usually with Dora and often with Paul and Nusch, and sometimes Cocteau and other friends who would join him. Alan Riding, in *And the Show Went On*, writes that during the Occupation 'many family-run bistros stayed open, with some willing to risk fines or closure by offering two menus: one official, the other black market; one cheap, the other pricey'. He adds, '[At Le Catalan] on some days, it was possible to have oysters followed by *gigot d'agneau*.' Also nearby was Brasserie Lipp and the Café de Flore, with its wood-fired stove that was always warm in winter. There Picasso preferred to dine, and meet, talk, debate with friends, amongst them Jean-Paul Sartre and Simone de Beauvoir, who lived in a hotel nearby. Dora, who had never moved in with Picasso, still lived around the corner on the rue de Seine and, later, Marie-Thérèse and Maya moved to an apartment on the Île Saint-Louis, a short walk along the river.

That single time Picasso left the city was to visit the poet Max Jacob, his old friend and sometime roommate, who was living in a monastery in the Loiret. He was Jewish by birth but had converted to Catholicism many years earlier. He knew that conversion would not protect him from the Nazis and was waiting for his inevitable arrest. Picasso travelled to meet him, and they spent a day together, walking and talking. Jacob would be picked up by the Gestapo in early 1944. He managed to smuggle out a letter in which he begged his friends for help. Many tried. Picasso did not. Apparently he was advised by someone loyal to the Vichy government that his interference would do more harm than good. Perhaps that explains his behaviour. Or perhaps he was merely protecting himself. Picasso did later attend two memorial masses for Jacob, who died of pneumonia at Drancy before he could be transported to Auschwitz or Dachau.

Picasso had links to the Resistance; many of his close friends were members. But it is unclear how involved he was, if at all. Alan Riding writes that there was a young theatre teacher called Annie Ubersfeld, a *résistante*, who later claimed that Picasso took great risks to support the Resistance, that he had been giving them money since 1942, and at times hid people who were on the run.

Whatever Picasso's motives for staying in Paris during the Occupation, and however much or little he was directly involved in the Resistance, for many, especially young people, he became a symbol of endurance, of resilience, of bravery. He had stayed when he could have left. In the freezing January of early 1941, Picasso began writing a play in a notebook. He called it *Le Désire attrapé par la queue* (*Desire Caught by the Tail*). In a matter of days, he had finished it. On the first page he sketched a self-portrait from overhead, balding, bespectacled, in the act of writing about those desires his characters seek to catch by the tail. Above it he wrote 'Portrait of the Author'. The original text is interspersed with sketched illustrations of scenes from the play. There is a writer called Big-Foot who is in love with the Tart (the edible variety); there is Silence, Onion, Round Tip, Fat Anxiety and Thin Anxiety, both of whom are friends of the Tart and are in love with Big-Foot. There are two dogs called Bow-wows, and The Curtains. The play is mostly concerned with the cold and with hunger and desires. Their feet lament their chilblains. They long for money, warmth, food and sex. There is farting, pissing, embracing and conversations about shit.

The play is an orgiastic whirl of free association – nonsensical, surreal, absurd – almost absurdist. Existentialist in the manner of Samuel Beckett. Bernard Frechtman, who later translated the play into English, writes in his foreword: 'It says nothing of human destiny or of the human condition [. . .] It is gratifying to advise the reader that Picasso has nothing to say of man, nor of the universe. This in itself is a considerable achievement.' And this was probably the point for Picasso in those freezing months of early 1941. His own life, in a world turned upside down, had been reduced to desires: for warmth, for friendship, for food and sex and the all-powerful urge to create. Perhaps it's not about the play's text itself but the gesture of writing it: a burst of defiant, farcical nonsense in a world governed by order and restraint and inhuman logic.

Desire Caught by the Tail wouldn't be performed until 1944, a defiant gesture in the dangerous, heightened days before the Liberation. It was read in the apartment of Michel and Louise Leiris. Albert Camus directed, and the parts were played by Picasso, Dora Maar, Raymond Queneau, Simone de Beauvoir and Jean-Paul Sartre. Georges Bataille and Jacques Lacan were amongst the audience. 'Never were we freer than under the German occupation,' Jean-Paul Sartre would declare in an essay called 'The Republic of Silence' in 1944. He writes of the Germans silencing the French, insulting them, taking away their rights, deporting them, bombarding them with Nazi propaganda. And how in doing so each word spoken or written became a principled action. The more the Germans oppressed them, he writes, 'the more each one of our gestures took on the nature of an engagement'.

PICASSO

It was one of the paintings he kept all his life, one of those that meant the most to him. A memorial. It's charming, idyllic, a cafe in Royan, all light and candy-striped awnings and planes of washed pastel colours to represent windows and walls and streets. Beyond the cafe there are trees and the sweep of the bay in palest blue. The little cafe almost resembles a carousel. It feels as if there should be music, and laughter. But there is nothing – it is emptied of life. The Nazis had arrived and stifled all that. His refuge was no longer a refuge. Picasso returned to Paris just over a week after he'd painted this.

PRESERVATION

Man Ray tells Ady he's arrived in New York having slept for seven nights on the floor of a cabin with many others. He worries that her airmail letters are late, or that they never arrive. He feels guilty at having left her, tries to convince himself he's done the right thing. His life is on hold until they are together again. He's with his sister, he tells her, and he's been keeping busy. He walks and reads. He has no appetite, in spite of the plenitude in America. They must have patience. He loves her, he says, and tells her that they should try to feel only hope. She must be brave. He wonders how she spends her time in Paris, and about their house and their friends, whether she has utilities. He thinks of her day and night. Ady writes that she's sorry she hasn't heard from him and wonders whether he has arrived. She writes to him at his sister's address. She's at their house in Saint-Germain so that no one else can take it. She misses him, she loves him, she wants him to write and questions whether he's missing a little black girl he used to know. He wants to be alone with her; still wonders why she hasn't written. She must be patient, he tells her. It will all be well. He asks her again to write. He sees no one, thinks of nothing but her. He writes again, still having heard nothing from her. He hopes she has all she needs. He misses her, has nothing to tell her but that he loves her. He sends her kisses. He writes again, telling her that he has still heard nothing from her, and worries about her. He tells her he is hers for all time. Ady asks for money and for documents to prove ownership of the house. She hopes they might meet in South America or Guadeloupe. She asks him to think of her in his sleep. She tells him he has all of her heart.

Ady and Man Ray wrote to each other for several months and then their correspondence tailed off, ending abruptly in the autumn of 1940. Her later letters were not received as the war began to affect the postal service; some were lost, and others returned to sender. Ady begins to retreat back into the shadows. We know very little about her life during the Occupation. Accounts are often hazy and conflicting. She had been left some money by Man Ray and for a while she continued to live in his apartment in Paris.

Man Ray's hurried departure meant that most of his belongings, including a large amount of his work – paintings, prints and negatives – were left in Paris with Ady. She dedicated herself to the task of looking after it all, squirrelling it away, moving it from place to place, keeping it safe. She sold some of the paintings and objects he owned to Paul Éluard, and then sent the money to Man Ray. She also sold some photographic equipment on his behalf.

In her *New York Times* article about Ady, Sala Elise Patterson quotes an interview with the art historian and Man Ray expert Francis M. Naumann and a conversation with Andrew Strauss, consultant at Sotheby's and chairman of the Man Ray Expert Committee. According to Naumann, Ady was responsible for the preservation of Man Ray's entire studio. And Strauss adds that if it wasn't for her, a great swathe of Dada and surrealist artwork (Man Ray's own pieces and his collection of others' work) would have been lost. This, and simply surviving, was Ady's war work.

For a woman like Ady, the racism of America would have been almost as challenging as life in Occupied France. Relationships between white and black people were still a crime in many states. Yet for the two hundred thousand or so men and women from the French colonies who lived in Paris during the Occupation, the German presence meant they were subjected to heightened racism and persecution. People of colour were 'to ride in the last carriage of the metro, to stay within the limits of the demarcation line, and to give up their professions in the arts', writes historian Ludivine Broch. According to The Wiener Holocaust Library, black people were imprisoned by the Nazis for their involvement in the French Resistance, or simply for their skin colour. And Broch corroborates this, adding that records from concentration camps show that race was a key motive for incarcerating people of colour. The Nazis closed Le Bal Blomet and other venues considered decadent that were associated with Caribbean music and African-American jazz. Many of the artists who had performed in those clubs, and many of those who had frequented them, fled Paris or went underground. Many black entertainers had to contend with both discrimination and unemployment.

Correspondence from after the war shows that as time went on, Ady began to struggle. She became ill and it was difficult to find work. A letter to Man Ray from one of his and Ady's mutual friends, called 'DD' in their correspondence, reveals that they had been forced to sell some of Man Ray's belongings during the Occupation. They tell Man Ray that Ady was desperate for money, that she was unable to work. Included in the letter is a list of things Ady had sold including his Peugeot 402 (which the friend claims would have otherwise been co-opted by the Nazis), several paintings and sketches by other surrealist artists in his collection, various African objects and some surrealist literature. A special edition of *Les Mains libres* was sold to Paul Éluard.

It's not known what Ady did to survive during the Occupation, but she did survive. Throughout, she hoped that she would be reunited with Man Ray after the war. Writing to him in April 1945, she questioned whether he had forgotten his 'little black sun', reminding him that that was what he had once called her. And in another letter that year, she writes that she loves him as her closest friend, that she wants to live with him again, that being with him had been the best time of her life.

FROM THE SKY

May and June 1943. RAF bombers fly over French cities – Paris, Lille, Rouen, Nantes, Caen, Orléans and Le Mans. It is not bombs they drop from their bellies, but words. Not death, but hope. Words falling from the sky, words hurriedly gathered, hidden away. And the potency, the potential of words, written and then carried off, they gain a kinetic energy, a life of their own. They are read and felt deeply, memorized and carried within or hurriedly written down, collapsed into tiny folds, passed on, or whispered, pocketed, replicated, circulated, broadcast, gaining momentum: a chain reaction. Words cannot be destroyed, defeated or occupied. Though the Nazis tried, and failed. Words are invincible, they are resistance.

At the start of the war, Paul, then aged forty-three, had been mobilized as a lieutenant and sent to work with supplies in the Loiret and later in the Tarn region in the south-west, where Nusch joined him. In the south Max Ernst had been arrested and put in a camp for foreigners. Though he'd lived in France for seventeen years and though the Nazis had branded him a 'degenerate', he was still a German on French soil, and therefore the enemy, an 'undesirable'. A desperate Leonora Carrington begged Paul to help him; his wrangling worked, and Ernst was released. Thanks to the young and incredibly brave American journalist Varian Fry and his Emergency Rescue Committee in Marseille, he escaped to America with Peggy Guggenheim, whom he married in 1941 (though they later divorced). Carrington was never reconciled with Ernst.

As the Germans occupied France, Paul was demobilized and made his way back to Paris. Unlike many of the surrealists, Nusch and Paul chose to stay in the capital. Before the war they'd lived for a while in the countryside in Le Pecq, to the west of the city, but at the end of 1940 they moved back into Paris, to an apartment in a modest part of the city, on rue de La Chapelle in the eighteenth arrondissement. They filled it with Paul's collection of books and paintings, painted the walls grey and beige and hung up a nude of Nusch painted by Picasso. With Picasso and Dora, they celebrated their new apartment and then stayed up all night with them on New Year's Eve. Friendships became more vital than ever.

In October 1940 the Vichy regime had begun imposing its widespread anti-Jewish laws, initiated not by the Germans but by the French government itself. These would be consolidated and extended the following summer. The laws defined who was considered Jewish and laid out all the civil liberties that they were to lose, as well as granting the state the right to arbitrarily imprison a Jewish person. Paris in the Occupation was a cyclone, everything in flux, everything unpredictable. As time went on no one could be trusted, desperate people were doing desperate things. Loyalties shifted, ideals withered in the face of restrictions, fear and, later, deprivation. Collaboration became a matter of survival. Nusch and Paul were in the minority who became *clandestins*.

Alan Riding writes that many French artists, writers and other professionals who felt paralysed by the Occupation remained politically inert, adopting a wait-and-see position or revelling in their impotence. This meant that they could carry on with life almost as normal, while waiting passively for France's allies to do the work of liberating the country from the grip of the Nazis. But this was not true of everyone. There were some who, from the first weeks after the Fall of France, began to find ways to cultivate a spirit of resistance, as a mindset, long before active insurgency could begin.

While they remained in Paris, Paul and Nusch's home became a haven of intellectual resistance activity. They transported secret and subversive leaflets and texts between neighbourhoods. It is said that Nusch hid them within a box of chocolates, while Paul carried them in a briefcase. And they helped with the printing and dissemination of clandestine publications. Nusch also worked with organizations that helped Parisian Jews who, by the summer of 1942, were being rounded up in their thousands, to be interned and ultimately deported to Auschwitz and other camps in the east. Paul and Nusch risked arrest at every turn. 'I saw him grow pale, pale, pale in the rue de Dragon one morning in 1944, while waiting for the cyclist from a clandestine printer who did not always come,' his friend, fellow poet and *résistant*, Claude Roy, would recall in *Paul Éluard: Selected Writings*. 'He did everything: action against the Germans, dangerous things or simply boring things; envelopes to glue shut, tracts to fold . . .'

Once Paul had joined the Resistance, he began to put his poems in the service of the Resistance too, the first of which were published in 1941. He often used *noms de plume* or, rather, *noms de guerre*. Paul put much thought into how his poems should be printed, that they should be small and slim volumes, and therefore easy to pass from hand to hand, to slide into a pocket, to do their work.

In 1936, at the International Surrealist Exhibition in London, Paul had lectured on the concept of *poésie engagée*, of committed poetry, and its moral purpose and of the responsibility, the agency and the responsiveness of the poet in dark times. 'The time has come for poets to proclaim their right and duty to maintain that they are deeply involved in the life of other men, in communal life [. . .]' he had said. 'Poetry must be made by all. Not by one.'

The Spanish Civil War had inspired Paul to even greater political engagement, to greater protest. In *Donner à voir* (*Given to See*), published in 1939, he wrote about the duty embedded within all creative endeavours. Having left the French Communist Party (PCF) in 1933, and though he had been firmly anti-Stalinist, he was now drawing back towards communism, believing that it was the only viable force in the battle against fascism. In doing so Paul increasingly questioned his relationship with surrealism and the value of the movement itself. He believed it was decadent and increasingly irrelevant. A rift developed between Paul and Breton, who had always doubted his commitment to the movement. While Paul published work in a Stalinist publication, Breton had been spending time with Trotsky in Mexico and the surrealist movement was openly critical of the PCF and how Soviet communism was evolving under Stalin.

Their conflicting political allegiances were cleaving them apart. By 1938 this had come to a head and they parted ways in a definitive split, which became known as 'the rupture'. Breton insisted that the surrealists should also break with Paul and sabotage his poetry. Picasso, Roland, Man Ray and Max Ernst all refused.

This shift in Paul's thinking was reflected in his poetry: it would be plain speaking, it would communicate with the ordinary man, it would be direct. And it would not only have meaning, it would have purpose: it would counter inertia, isolation, introspection. It would bear witness. It would be an attempt at intervention; a voice of dissent, of change, of engagement, of action.

As a poet, Paul could have retreated from the world into an ivory tower, as many of his fellow artists did. And many chose the alternative, to collaborate or to create passive, unprovocative work that would pass censorship. Alan Riding writes that for many people who worked in creative industries – in film, music, the visual arts – it was easier to maintain a political neutrality, one that allowed them to go about their business in relative safety. But writers in France were used to engaging publicly in politics. Their audience expected it. And it was writers who put themselves in the greatest danger as they established and expressed their allegiances.

In 1942 Paul re-joined the PCF, which was banned by the Nazis. He was compelled to do so by his feeling about Spain, by his experiences in the Resistance, by his repulsion for Nazi oppression, and by his passionate belief in fraternity and solidarity with his fellow man. He also believed in the promise of a new way of life founded on equality and respect for his fellow man. He joined the literary arm of the PCF, the Comité national des écrivains (CNE), and soon afterwards wrote 'Courage' for *Les Lettres Françaises*, a publication founded in 1942 as part of the Resistance movement. A homage to Paris, the German Institute denounced the work as a dangerous tract.

During the Occupation, Paul wrote of love and desire that engendered connection, a connection that countered fear and offered the promise of longed-for freedom. He wrote of the daily oppression, of the hardships and horrors, and of hope and the need for resistance. That year, 1942, as his poems became more explicitly hostile to the Nazi Occupation, he was marked as a public enemy. He and Nusch began to change address every few weeks to evade the Gestapo and the police. For some time they stayed with the writer, publisher and antiquarian bookseller Lucien Scheler at his shop near the Luxembourg Gardens. Eventually they moved to Vézelay, a hill town in Burgundy, to hide in the house of their friends Christian and Yvonne Zervos, the founders of the journal *Cahiers d'Art* who were publishing much of his clandestine poetry.

In April 1943 Paul prepared a poetry anthology, *L'Honneur des poètes* (*The Honour of Poets*), for Éditions de Minuit, a clandestine publishing house founded by Jean Bruller and others during the Occupation; Scheler's shop was their distribution centre. *The Honour of Poets* included work by Paul's communist comrade Louis Aragon and by others, as well as his own. He would compile a second anthology called *Europe* while in hiding in May 1944. In the unsigned foreword to *The Honour of Poets*, Paul wrote that the writers within its pages, from across France, had gathered in an effort to counter the danger facing humanity. Poetry, he declared, had new purpose, new power, to speak out. In his foreword, poetry becomes a slippery and dangerous and invincible force that lurks, lies in wait, in the shadows.

In 1941 Paul had written a poem dedicated to Nusch, which he had called 'Une seule pensée' ('A Single Thought'). The following summer he changed the final word of the poem from 'Nusch' to 'Liberté' (Liberty). It would also become the title of the poem, and it is possible to see the original handwritten text with its erasure and new title at the Paul Éluard Museum in Saint-Denis. In Paris, in 1942, Paul met with Max-Pol Fouchet of the literary magazine *Fontaine*. Fouchet, who was scouting for Resistance texts to publish, would later write about their meeting, which took place in public, in a restaurant. Paul was carrying his briefcase stuffed with his Resistance texts and, as he left, he forgot to take it with him. He returned, picked up the briefcase and pulled out a copy of his poems, which included 'Liberty', and which he handed to Fouchet, in full view of the other diners.

Fouchet secreted them out of the Occupied zone and they were published in *Fontaine* in Algiers. The Vichy censors had not read the whole of 'Liberty', dismissing it as a love poem, and Fouchet used its original title, 'Une seule pensée'. The French poet Louis Parrot read it aloud to a meeting of the leaders of the Resistance in the Auvergne. It was read in public in Marseille by the poet Gabriel Audisio. Three months later it was published in secret with its new and provocative title by the clandestine surrealist collective La Main à plume in a collection of Paul's work called *Poésie et verité* (Poetry and Truth). In Paris Paul gave a copy of this collection to Cicero Dias, a Brazilian diplomat and artist, who carried it across Spain and into Portugal. According to Antony Penrose, his wife, a seamstress, had sewn the pages into the lining of his coat. From Portugal, he posted the poems to Roland in England. They were then translated by Roland and E. L. T. Mesens. 'Liberty' was published in *La France Libre* to be circulated in Britain, and Roland and Mesens would print it under the London Gallery Editions banner in 1944. While emphasizing that Paul was categorically not a patriotic poet, they were appalled that his writing had been co-opted as propaganda. Roland worried too that this increased attention would put Paul in greater danger. Laurence Olivier recited the poem in French on the BBC. In the early 1980s, when Antony Penrose was researching Lee's war work, he asked Roland if he regretted having put Paul and Nusch in increased danger, by publishing the poem. 'He told me', recalls Penrose, 'that was something that had tormented him at the time, but during his visit to Paris at the Liberation he had the opportunity to ask Paul and Nusch if he had done the right thing.' Roland told his son that Paul and Nusch had reassured him that he had, and that their lives were insignificant compared to their desire to return liberty to France.

The Ministry of Information acquired the poem and in April 1943 it was included in issue four of the *Revue du Monde Libre*, a literary magazine written in French and published by the British government explicitly for the purposes of spreading propaganda in France. The magazine was printed in a very small format and included work by British and French authors such as Vita Sackville-West, E. M. Forster, T. S. Eliot, Michael Foot, Rebecca West (who wrote about the Nazi attitude to women), Louis Aragon and Vercors, the *nom de plume* of Jean Bruller, previously a children's writer, now a *résistant* involved in planning escape routes for British prisoners of war. Bruller's 1941 novella, *Le Silence de la mer* (*The Silence of the Sea*), was perhaps the other most famous text of the Resistance. An extract was published in the same issue of the *Revue* as Paul's poem. Hundreds of thousands of copies were dropped by RAF bombers over Occupied France, and similar publications were dropped over other Occupied countries and Germany.

The editors included a message to their readers in France living in the 'dark night of total German occupation', to whom they dedicated the review. They vowed to maintain a 'skylight' to the outside world, a conversation, an exchange of ideas, between occupied countries and those that were free. They reminded their readers that men and women were risking their lives to deliver these little books, and that it was vital they reached the right people, those who could make use of them. The review was for the people of France, it said, and urged them to read it, and to persuade others to read it too.

Towards the end of the war, Cyril Connolly wrote in his magazine *Horizon* that the literary arm of the Resistance had triumphed by engaging in humanism rather than hatred. He marvelled that the authors, being such lyrical lovers of life, were so willing to put those lives in jeopardy. But Paul's poem is all about love. It was a love poem first. At the time Nusch had been ill and was hospitalized, and the poem was written in celebration of her recovery. The following year as Paul changed the poem's name, and therefore its emphasis, his love for Nusch became irrevocably intertwined with his love of freedom. Nusch, as ever, sacrificed to the service of the community.

'Poetry makes nothing happen,' W. H. Auden wrote in early 1939.

It doesn't fire bullets, or drop bombs. And yet 'Liberty' became a powerful weapon of war. The Occupation was an ideological battleground, the fight for public opinion was carried out with words and images – in books, clandestine literature, posters, newspapers, at gatherings, and on the radio, in the cinema. 'Liberty' is about the power of language, something the Nazis understood, with their terrifyingly efficient and euphemistic terms like 'living space' and the 'Final Solution'. The Vichy government had replaced the French revolutionary motto 'Liberté, Egalité, Fraternité' (Liberty, Equality, Fraternity) with the altogether more German, more submissive 'Travail, Famille, Patrie' (Work, Family, Fatherland). Paul's poem claims back that absent freedom.

In war, words become potent, in gossip, careless talk, whispers, denunciations, speeches. In war, poetry means freedom, the uncontrollable, irrepressible imagination. And it means consolation, a defiantly transcendent beauty. Poetry has a way of insinuating itself into the psyche in a way that other words, or images, can't. 'Liberty' became the rallying cry of the French Resistance; it brought hope to a people in despair.

In 1943 the poem inspired a drawing by Jean Lurçat, an artist and Resistance fighter, which was then secretly woven into a tapestry in the attics of the workshop of Suzanne Goubely-Gatien in Aubusson. That same year the poem was reworked as a cantata by Francis Poulenc as part of his masterpiece *Figure humaine* (*Human Figure*), and was premiered in London in English by the BBC in 1945. Sung unaccompanied, it relies only on human voices. After years of the poem being whispered – a secret recitation, or passed discreetly from hand to hand – this was perhaps its natural evolution, a groundswell, becoming a loud, insistent polyphonic hymn that crescendos in triumph, in celebration of the victory of freedom.

Auden qualifies his statement that 'poetry makes nothing happen' by adding that 'it survives / A way of happening, a mouth'. 'Liberty' became a prayer, and its listeners, its readers, a clandestine community held together by the invisible bond of the hope it offered. And it survives. Its words are still being whispered in places where people are still not free.

PAUL (AND NUSCH)

Love and freedom. Love of freedom. An ode to love and a paean to freedom. It is incredibly simple, deceptively so – and the Vichy censors were deceived. As if to emphasize its theme there's no punctuation, but for the final, emphatic, definitive full stop at the end. The poem is composed of twenty-one quatrains, all of the same length, and all but the last stanza starts with the same word 'on' and ends with the same line: 'I write your name.' And that name – freedom – is written onto an inventory of things, tangible and intimate and quotidian: schoolbooks, trees, nests, his home. And also intangible, yet palpable things – the pleasures of life, the wonders of the world, the elements, the weather, nature. Paul's entire and very personal world. It is both specific and universal. As he would later write of the poem, freedom is all he could think of, his single thought.

By inscribing freedom on everything around him Paul seeks to reclaim those things that have become tainted. Naming it becomes a ritual, almost an exorcism. And in the process those things are transfigured into something sacred, numinous. And with the unrelenting repetition of the poem, it becomes a chant or a litany invoking freedom. The word is only revealed in the last line of the poem, a dazzling gesture, a battle cry.

SELF-PORTRAIT CUT IN TWO BY A RAZOR

Dora cut the paper in half with a razor so that she could make two pieces from one and on each she drew a still life. But on the reverse of the paper there was already a drawing, a delicate self-portrait she'd made in pencil. It's only her head, and not even that. It's positioned at the very bottom of the paper, which cuts off her chin as if she is falling out of the frame. Her hair is lightly sketched, a suggestion. There's more emphasis, heavier markings, on the face, particularly her finely wrought eyes that gaze off into the distance and the outline of one side of her face, a high curved cheekbone arching down into the hollow of her cheek. But running down the centre of her face like a faultline is the razor cut, a violent gesture at odds with the delicacy of the drawing, the fragility of the face. Someone reassembled the drawing and framed it with the two sides pulled just slightly apart, to emphasize the jagged cut and Dora's act of self-destruction.

In Royan in 1940 Dora had written to Picasso telling him that she was going out of her way to stop him loving her; that she believed that he didn't love her. She begged him to forgive her. She was madly in love with him, she told him. She said that she didn't know how to write letters but that it made her feel better to tell him how much she loved and admired him. Dora had entirely given herself to Picasso, and it tortured her that he had another life, a family life, with Marie-Thérèse and Maya. With them he was domesticated, paternal, gentle, but with Dora he was humiliating, domineering, brutalizing. His neglect and the extraordinary ease with which he could hurt her made Dora miserable and they fought daily, often physically. In Royan he painted her with tears like two streams pouring from her eyes and then drew a sketch of her with an X over her mouth. Picasso told Françoise Gilot that women fell into one of two categories, goddesses or doormats. In his imagination Dora had now shifted from one to the other.

Returning to Paris did little to improve the situation. During the Occupation Picasso used Dora's likeness in paintings of ever-increasing violence and cruelty, reflecting the world outside and perhaps the world within. How did Dora perceive this use of her image? How did she feel about the humiliation her likeness received on canvas? In the gifts Picasso gave her we see glimpses of his tenderness. Little paper dogs he whittled at supper when her own dog had disappeared, and she was grieving. A tiny portrait of her with dried leaves for a hat and starburst eyes. And that tenderness, and their understanding of each other, is evident in photographs she took of him in her apartment in 1942, as he lounges in a chair, a cigarette in his hand, gazing at her gently. Between the portraits Picasso painted of Dora, the 'weeping woman' motif and the legend of Picasso as Minotaur, it is easy to lose sight of the complicity and the complexity of their relationship, the nuanced intelligence and paradoxical nature of Dora herself, and her strength, her fragility. James Lord, in *Picasso and Dora*, writes that she told him that when she was in a relationship with Picasso it was as if she existed at the centre of things, that it had been exciting and terrifying, that it made her feel simultaneously revered and demeaned.

And he thrived on the power that he had over her. Cocteau in his journal recounts an incident in 1942 when Picasso had invited him to Dora's apartment. While he was there Cocteau drew a portrait of Dora he thought was charming and a good likeness. Later Picasso found it and painted over it with his version of Dora, an act of erasure, of reclamation, of domination. But such was Dora's devotion to him that she remained entirely at his mercy, and at his beck and call. She was summoned by telephone when Picasso wanted to meet up with her, perhaps for lunch or for dinner, she would never know until the last moment. She made herself perpetually ready in her apartment and liked to be by the phone in case he called her or appeared at her door. He would have been angered if she made other plans, so she rarely did. She wrote a poem in early 1942 about her despair, her silent isolation, and how she was immobilized within it.

That year she had acquired a new studio, which marked a fresh direction in her work as she began painting still lifes (like Picasso) and landscapes of the Seine. Later in 1945 she would have an exhibition of the still lifes at the Jeanne Bucher gallery in Montparnasse.

Dora's life became a web of complications in those years. In 1940 her father returned to South America for work and Mrs Markovitch was left alone in Occupied Paris. From that point she relied upon Dora for emotional support, which Dora struggled to provide. In mid-July 1942 more than thirteen thousand Jewish people were rounded up by the French police and confined to the Vélodrome d'Hiver in the suburbs, before being sent to internment camps and thence, from December, to Auschwitz, Dachau and other concentration camps. The city was stricken with terror. It is sometimes suggested that Dora's father was Jewish, which explains his departure from France in 1940. But this is not clear. Dora, however, became paranoid that her Croatian surname would be mistaken for a Jewish name. Her having changed it to Maar was perhaps even more suspicious.

And yet as Picasso refused to leave Paris, so did Dora. Instead she lived in constant, enervating fear. Late in 1942 her friend and model the surrealist artist Sonia Mossé, who had Jewish origins, disappeared. She would be murdered at Sobibor in 1943 but no one knew that until after the war. Dora's mother was arrested in 1942 and imprisoned for five weeks before being released. One night, weeks afterwards, Dora was arguing over the phone with her mother. In the middle of the conversation her mother stopped talking and Dora heard the receiver drop to the floor. Because it was late and after curfew Dora couldn't get to her until the following morning and, when she did, she found her dead on the floor beside the phone, having suffered a cerebral haemorrhage.

The act of making the cut through her self-portrait could have been coincidental. Paper was in short supply and perhaps she was merely recycling. Perhaps it was an accident and she was unaware that her own likeness was on the reverse. But then the surrealists didn't believe in accidents. Dora enjoyed the power of a gesture, particularly one that involved blades and violence and self-harm. And it was not the first time she'd broken up her face in a self-portrait. Whatever the reason, she evidently kept the two halves, and kept them together. Perhaps she felt it perfectly expressed her acute anxiety, her increasingly fractured sense of self in the years of the Occupation, and her years with Picasso.

DORA

The interiority of the years of the German Occupation, the retreat inside,
a distillation of the claustrophobia. The objects in Dora's still lifes, rendered in muted greys, browns and creamy yellows, are entirely isolated, their isolation undoubtedly echoing her own. And yet they have a
soft, lambent quality entirely different to those Picasso was painting at
the time. The light from a candle or from a bulb or that falls on a jug is
not harsh, but glows. The objects are still but they have an intrinsic energy that radiates through her brushstrokes across the canvas.

EXILE

Man Ray's ship arrived in New York on 16 August 1940. His sister
and niece were waiting at the pier, alongside scores of journalists and
photographers, keen to catch a glimpse of the notorious Salvador
Dalí with Gala by his side. Man Ray slipped quietly through the
crowd, determined to avoid publicity, disapproving of the way Dalí
shamelessly courted it. He went to stay at his sister's home in Jersey
City and was there for five weeks, depressed that, almost twenty years
later, he had to return to the scene of his early humiliations. He had
no desire to be in America. Though he was a famous photographer,
with the promise of work and a new start, America meant commerce.
He knew he'd need to plunge into that world in order to survive.
New York, which he had left all those years ago vowing never to
return on any permanent basis, was a place of miserable memories,
of feelings of failure, the place he'd left for his beloved Paris.

He thought he could hide, wait the time out until he could return
to Europe. Paris, he believed, allowed for a gentler life, a more pleasurable working life, and there, art had greater permanence. Until
then he wanted to disappear and lie low, escape to Tahiti, perhaps,
as Paul had done back in 1924 when his complicated ménage with
Gala and Max Ernst had begun to overwhelm him.

His biographer Neil Baldwin writes that Man Ray's return might have felt like a regression to Emmanuel Radnitsky of Brooklyn, a version of himself he'd worked so hard to move away from. The surrealist ideal was always to venture towards new horizons, in search of the marvellous. Man Ray was instinctively a seeker. Instead he was retreating in the face of danger. Writing to Ady in those first weeks in America, he told her how he was living like a recluse, how he ventured very little into New York, made almost no effort to contact old friends and actively avoided the art scene.

One night when he had gone into the city, he met a travelling necktie salesman at a party who was planning to drive to Los Angeles. Man Ray decided to join him. They set off in late September. He took no photographs on the journey. They arrived in Los Angeles at night and, driving into Hollywood, he felt he was entering a frontier town. Europe, the war, Ady and his friends in Paris must have felt very distant. They stopped at a Mission-Revival-style hotel, which amused Man Ray; he expected to see people walking around in costume, he writes in *Self-Portrait*. Later he realized that it was the anachronisms that made Hollywood; its strangeness out-surrealled surrealism. But the next morning he found new resolve and set off to explore the city, soon feeling that it was not so very different to the South of France with its streets lined with palm trees and its bright sunshine, but somehow more businesslike. He felt that it was a place where he could live and work discreetly, that there was no need to go any further.

Someone at the party in New York had suggested he look up an old friend of theirs, a twenty-eight-year-old dancer and artist's model called Juliet Browner who had left for the west coast in the previous year. She had trained with the celebrated dancer and choreographer Martha Graham and had had a fling with the young Willem de Kooning. Her friend told Man Ray, giving him Juliet's phone number, that she was desperate for work. Might he like to pay her to model for him? The morning after he arrived in Los Angeles he phoned the number.

He was enchanted by Juliet, her delicate face and oval eyes, by the exoticism he perceived in her. She also knew about art. More importantly, she knew about Man Ray and his work. They had dinner, then went to a club and danced to jazz. He marvelled at how light she felt in his arms. Soon they had moved into a residential hotel, albeit in separate rooms. Early in the following year they rented a large, peaceful apartment together on Vine Street in Hollywood. It had a courtyard with hibiscus, palm trees, hummingbirds, and Man Ray created a studio and a darkroom. He bought a fast car. All communication between Man Ray and Ady soon stopped. Had the postal service failed, or had his sister stopped forwarding Ady's letters to him, knowing that he now had a new life? It seems that perhaps that was the case. Ady had been forgotten along with all thoughts of reuniting in the Antilles, as he'd suggested to Roland. And all so swiftly. 'Well, now I had everything again, a woman, a studio, a car,' he writes. He was settling in.

Man Ray was still living on his savings from the years of commercial and fashion photography, and money was tight in the first years in Hollywood. Even so, he remained dedicated to painting, to being a painter, believing that photography was inherently a second-rate art form.

It was a brave decision. It would have been easier in New York, because in Los Angeles there was little commercial value to his work. Initially, rather than painting new work he sought to recreate the paintings he'd left in Paris; he was convinced he'd never see the originals again. And perhaps it was as if he was resurrecting some old part of himself that he'd had to leave behind. But ultimately, in the ten years he would live in Los Angeles, Man Ray produced more work than he had in the previous thirty – photographs, paintings, rayographs, objects. He made chess sets (in lucrative editions), paintings inspired by Shakespeare and new assemblages. And he took many photographs, many of Juliet, even though he was insisting that he was no longer a photographer.

Perhaps it was his distance, his exile from the art worlds of Paris and New York, that gave him a freedom he'd never felt before. He often referred though to the theme of *Le Beau Temps*, of the journey from lightness into dark, his passage from Europe to America. Although he was happy in Los Angeles, at ease, there was always a rope pulling him back towards his spiritual home.

He began to put out feelers in the art world and eventually Los Angeles became more than a haven: it provided Man Ray with new opportunities. There was great wealth in the city, and wealth meant patronage. He reconnected with Walter Arensberg, the wealthy poet, who he'd known since his New York days, and had first introduced him to Duchamp. Arensberg and his wife Louise were art patrons and collectors with a brilliant eye for radical European art. He met gallerists and was offered exhibitions, the first of which was held in February 1941. He showed, amongst other pieces, *Noire et blanche* and a first edition of *Les Mains libres*. Nothing sold and according to his biographer Neil Baldwin it would be the same at many subsequent exhibitions in California. And he was continually frustrated in his desire to prove himself a painter, and maddened when he was referred to as a photographer or if his photographs were requested for an exhibition. He resented his designation as chief chronicler of the Roaring Twenties, as surrealism's staff photographer. He didn't want to be seen as modernism's mirror, iconifying the great and the good of the art world. He wanted to be seen as one of them.

For many exiled European artists, particularly the surrealists, like Man Ray's old friend Marcel Duchamp, and also André Breton, Yves Tanguy and Salvador Dalí, the journey ended in and around New York, which was soon to become the new epicentre of the art world and eclipse Paris after the war, thanks in great part to the European influx. Many artists, including Breton, his wife Jacqueline Lamba and their daughter Aube, had been helped to escape by Varian Fry's Emergency Rescue Committee. But Man Ray wasn't alone in Los Angeles, fellow exiles included Thomas Mann, Igor Stravinsky, Arnold Schoenberg, Christopher Isherwood and Theodor Adorno. He played chess with Bertolt Brecht. He became great friends with Henry Miller, whose transgressive, rule-breaking and erotic writing shared so much of the spirit of Man Ray's art. Miller in turn admired Man Ray's extraordinary memory and that his home was an unpretentious and welcome haven in Hollywood.

He lived a contented, domesticated life with the devoted, acquiescent Juliet, who would go every morning to buy fresh food from the store opposite their apartment. They went to jazz clubs, entertained friends at home and played charades or chess into the early hours of the morning. Eventually they would marry in 1946 in a double wedding with Max Ernst and Dorothea Tanning in Beverly Hills. Man Ray lectured, he gave private tuition, he resisted invitations to become part of the local art community, and the surrealist disputes that were happening in New York as the exiles settled into their new world did not interest him. He was happy to live peacefully with Juliet, and his imagination, and to paint.

Hollywood, the dream factory, would seem like the perfect fit for Man Ray – and lucrative too – but he was never to have much involvement with the film world. Though he'd made his own short films in Europe and did become involved in some avant-garde projects in Los Angeles, the Hollywood studios were a different matter. When he was offered work in film (and there were many offers to recruit the famous Man Ray) it almost never worked out. As ever, he wanted to be master of everything – to art-direct, to design the sets, to do the lighting. And while he'd enjoyed collaborating on projects with his friends over the years, the idea of working in a huge team, and on something bigger than himself, was anathema to him.

He did become involved in the film world, albeit indirectly, by photographing portraits of its stars, writers, composers – Igor Stravinsky, Ava Gardner, Jennifer Jones, Jean Renoir, Leslie Caron and others. And the Man Ray magic that the film studios had hoped to employ is all there, imbued in the photographs – the chiaroscuro, the oblique glance, mystery, drama. But that was as close as he would get.

In the autumn of 1944 Man Ray had his first ever retrospective, at the Pasadena Art Institute. The show covered thirty-six years of his career as an artist, including photographs of paintings he'd had to leave behind in France. As the war in Europe came to an end many of his friends assumed he'd return as soon as he could. But he didn't. Susan Sontag, in her 2003 Friedenspreis Acceptance Speech 'Literature is Freedom', describes the United States as 'a profoundly conservative country in ways that Europeans find difficult to fathom [. . .] it is also radical, even revolutionary, in ways that Europeans find equally difficult to fathom.' Perhaps Man Ray had found an unexpected contentment, an unexpected freedom. And yet he would write to his sister that he thought of California as 'a beautiful prison'.

MAN RAY

He glowers out of the frame, piercing eyes beneath heavy black brows. He's confronting the viewer, or perhaps he's confronting himself. It seems he's undecided about who to be, which story to tell, which guise to present to the world – one side of his face is bearded, and the other is clean-shaven. The beard that creeps across his upper lip and chin comes to an abrupt end beneath his nose. 'Who am I?' he seems to ask himself with the ferocious look of a man in need of an answer. Ever in exile in his home country, at home abroad – this Russian, Jewish, American, almost Frenchman, photographer, filmmaker, sculptor, painter, bohemian, socialite. And more. The construction of the self, himself, his life's work.

FRONT LINE

Lee's official accreditation as a war correspondent gave her the freedom to get closer to the action. But she could never get close enough. Few obstacles were insurmountable, she felt, and this compulsion, with her fierce determination and recalcitrance, propelled her ever forward, ever closer during the last years of the war. And her photographs testify to this. As with Paul in his wartime poetry, she bears witness. She is in the thick of the action and she wants others to bear witness too; whether it's an operating theatre, or in the intimacy of a nurses' billet, the women's underwear drying in the window or, later, standing on a bank looking down at the burning Berghof on the Obersalzburg. We can almost smell the blood, the laundry soap, the smoke. And yet there's always beauty and poetry in Lee's pictures, always her painterly eye for composition. And there is always compassion, the pity of war, a reminder that behind the cold mechanical eye of the camera there is empathy at work.

Now she was able to get inside military sites, shooting Wrens and WAAFs and ATS gunners. One article for British *Vogue*, its subheading 'Night Life Now', shows the women at work at night-time. Lesley Blanch wrote the copy and Lee took the photographs with David Scherman. One image is of a row of ATS searchlight operators, the bright beam of the huge light glowing up into the night sky from behind them. The women in the foreground, in boots and trousers and thick tunics and tin hats, are arm in arm, laughing together. Just after the photograph was taken, they would come under fire from German planes.

In the spring of 1944 Lee asked Audrey Withers if she could photograph and profile Ed Murrow, the American radio broadcaster. Sending the finished draft to Audrey, she worried that she'd made a mistake trying to write something when she'd spent so many years perfecting her photography. But her fears were misplaced. Audrey was delighted with the copy, telling her that it illustrated how the observations of the photographer's eye converted effortlessly into the words of a journalist. Lee was drawn to the honesty of Murrow's writing, which, as her biographer Carolyn Burke notes, entirely reflects what Lee would try, and succeed to achieve, with her own.

In those months before the Allied invasion of France, which everyone knew was coming but few knew when, Lee continued with her work for *Vogue* – fashion and portraits of film stars and socialites and women at work. She started experimenting with colour film which, with her technical know-how, she mastered quickly. She was spending most of her time with David Scherman, with whom she had an easy affinity. They were kindred spirits, shared an eye for things, a similar American humour, and they had the same references. He and the other *Life* photographers – including Robert Capa, David 'Chim' Seymour and Ralph Morse – were champing at the bit to get to a warzone. As was Lee. Writing to her parents at the end of May she tells them that Aziz has been ill, and says that she should go to him, but admits that she doesn't want to, that she is so entirely focused on the work that she is doing and that work sustains her life.

Her chance came in the coming weeks. On 6 June 1944, D-Day, the Allies landed in Normandy. David Scherman joined a US Navy ship to photograph the action, but Lee and the other female photographers and journalists had to make the most of what they witnessed from the south of England. In July the rules were slightly relaxed, and women were allowed to go to France and Italy, but not to report on the front line or to witness combat. Audrey sent Lee to report on American nurses working in the wake of the invasion in Normandy. As she flew over France, she writes that she almost had to hold back tears as she returned to the beloved country. In the distance she could see the front with its columns of smoke. As soon as she landed, she set to work, clutching a notebook, her camera slung around her neck. She was driven through Norman villages to the 44th Evacuation Hospital, at Bricqueville behind Omaha Beach, and later to another hospital closer to the front.

And then she was in the thick of it. In the operating theatre, almost as close to the patient as the team working around him, their heads leaning in and over him, shrouded in surgical gear and masks, a circle of care and acute concentration, a strange intimacy with the anaesthetized man. Another photograph is of a makeshift operating theatre in a flimsy tent. It's taken at night and the fabric of the tent is rendered transparent, inside a medical team are operating on a man beneath lamps that illuminate the scene. She noticed a man badly burned and entirely wrapped in bandages. He asked her to take his photograph, which she did, although not clearly, she says, as he looked in such a bad way. In the photograph he looks as if he's grinning. He died soon after. She photographed a nurse emerging from a tent, perhaps after an operation or at the end of her shift. She's carrying her jacket, and another hand is at her brow. Her utter exhaustion radiates from the image. As she photographed, Lee must have been making notes, or at least mental notes.

Her writing, like her photographs, takes us there to the heart of the matter. She's telling the truth. Reading it we're there with her, registering everything with her, feeling the urgency with which she writes, in amongst the chaos, the damaged bodies, the tired medics and the blood-stained bandages. Her eye missed nothing and her attention was with both the wounded and those trying to keep them alive.

Lee's photographs and writing would be published by *Vogue* that September in an article entitled 'Unarmed Warriors'. They would also be published in American *Vogue*. Audrey would later admit that publishing Lee's work was the highlight of her war in journalistic terms. She delighted in the incongruity of the type of articles Lee produced appearing in the pages of a glossy fashion magazine.

After a brief return to London, in August Lee managed to get assigned back to France, where she was sent to Saint-Malo in Brittany. It had been announced that the city was liberated, and Lee's job was to report on how the US Army was establishing order. The job was meant to be a behind-the-front-line assignment, but when she arrived it quickly became clear that the city was still under siege and the Germans, under Colonel Von Aulock, were holding their own. The fighting raged, tanks trundled in and infantry troopers followed under heavy sniper fire. Not having authorization to report on the front line into which she'd accidentally stumbled, Lee should have retreated. Instead, delighted, disobedient, she launched herself into the fray with only the clothes on her back, a blanket and about twenty or so rolls of film. She was the only photographer on the scene and she had her scoop: 'now I owned a private war,' she wrote.

She was billeted with the Civil Affairs Team and became friendly with the 83rd Division, who helped her with work, showing her where to get the best views, telling her when there was incoming fire. She photographed, and would later write about, the damaged city, its literally shellshocked inhabitants and its women, the so-called 'horizontal collaborators', whose heads were being shaved as punishment for having sex and sometimes relationships with German soldiers. She witnessed the fighting and described it with extraordinary immediacy: machine-gun fire, soldiers crawling about like ants, the noise – yelling, gunfire, the smoke, the fire, the explosions and the deadly silence. Her work gives the reader not just a general sense of the atmosphere but a comprehension of what was unfolding around her, a narrative.

David Scherman arrived in Saint-Malo on 17 August and found Lee. She was unwashed and bedraggled, and so he photographed her, in the midst of the action, squinting, mid-conversation, a bag and her camera and goggles hanging around her neck, the sleeves of her uniform rolled up above her elbows and what looks like a water canteen in her hand. GIs are scurrying about behind her, two are looking up at her, one is grinning. She had made herself one of the men at Saint-Malo, toughened, smoking, wisecracking, drinking requisitioned champagne with them. She tried to make herself look as inconspicuous as possible, wearing loose-fitting clothes to avoid unwanted attention. Attention she still received by men asking her for a kiss or pointing her out as a woman in a very masculine world.

Though she'd witnessed the chaos of the Blitz, in a few short weeks Lee had been propelled into another level of horror, of pain and destruction, of shamed women and broken bodies and death. The alcohol she drank, the cigarettes she smoked, the camaraderie of the men she worked alongside all helped, but the things she witnessed and the things she was yet to witness would prove indelible. She despaired that she was not impervious, that what she saw affected her. It angered her that the sight of a wounded German could soften her heart just as much as an Allied soldier. Later, as she pushed on into Germany, it is that impartial humanity that most marks her photographs.

Lee photographed the bombing of the fortress at Saint-Malo before the Allied soldiers were to storm it. In one image, with characteristically perfect timing, Lee captures the blast from an aerial bombardment – a dense grey cloud expanding on the horizon, beyond the rooftops of the town. Lee was photographing through the open window of an upstairs room. The light contrast of the camera renders the interior a flat black around the window – a perfect foil that draws the eye in to the scene unfolding in the light outside. The window with its wrought-iron balcony at the bottom and the tattered remnants of (presumably battle-torn) curtains along the top creates an ornate, seemingly incidental frame. Lee's extraordinary ability to frame an image in action. And the surreal serendipity of her eye.

She also inadvertently photographed one of the American army's first uses of napalm, and the negatives would be hurriedly confiscated by the Ministry of Information when she returned to London. Scherman wrote to Audrey to ask whether *Life* could publish some of Lee's photographs, pointing out that not only was Lee the only woman amongst the Allies to witness the battle, but that she was the only photographer and the only reporter, and that she'd stayed with the infantry through all manner of gunfire and the bombing carried out by the Americans.

Lee recorded the eventual surrender of von Aulock, jaw gritted, arrogant in defeat, with his monocle and his Knight's Cross of the Iron Cross with Oak Leaves pinned to his chest, surrounded by GIs and German troops. She describes how he covered his face when he noticed her camera. She heard him muttering something about the fact that she was a woman, and she noticed his cheeks turning red in shame as he tried to avoid her lens, her presence clearly adding to his humiliation.

The battle over, the Public Relations Office caught up with Lee and she was placed under house arrest for exceeding the terms of her accreditation. She was sent to Rennes and spent a week at a hotel, mostly writing, but she must have been allowed out because there are more photographs of women having their heads shaved. She applied to continue with the 83rd Division, but her application was rejected. She despaired. She still had every intention of re-joining them as soon as she could but, for now, she was to head to Paris, which had just been liberated, to report on how the fashion industry was going to recover. She wrote sorely to Audrey Withers that she was in trouble for her scoop at Saint-Malo. She resented going to Paris now that she knew the thrill of battle.

LEE

A fleeting calm in Saint-Malo. Spotting a mirror in an open doorway, perhaps as she walked down a street, she stopped, stepped inside, looked closer at herself – her new self – and photographed what she saw. The mirror is smeared and possibly scratched; we don't see her clearly. She's some way away, a dark figure against the bright sunlight reflected on the buildings behind her. She has one foot on a step, the other down, she's leaning against a wall, her head looking down towards the camera in her hands. She's a silhouette, a soldier in fatigues and helmet – faceless and genderless. A reflection. A moment of reflection.

LEE

Fellow photographers Robert Doisneau and Henri-Cartier Bresson refused to take photographs of the shaved women, 'les femmes tondues', those victims of the people. But Lee did the opposite: she moved closer and set to work. In just a few images we see glimpses of a nation's an-

ger and impotence being projected upon these women, and the defem-
inizing violence of the gesture. Two of the women are standing in a
room. One of them is in the foreground, perhaps beside a window, the
light falls on her face with its shiny nose and on her freshly shaved
scalp. Her head is cowed, vulnerable, perhaps in submission, or fear,
or both. She is wearing a short-sleeved blouse with a filigree brooch
clasping its collar, these little humanizing details possible because Lee
got close enough. She is a woman, a person, Lee's photograph says.
She stood right beside the woman, and she saw the woman too.

ASYLUM

Two photographs. In the first, Paul is sprawling on the ground, apparently asleep, although he is smiling. He's wearing a thick wool overcoat. One arm is outstretched in the long grass, and the other lies
across his body. The bright sun picks out each blade of grass, bathes
his coat in light and almost obscures his face. Scribbled onto the print
in pen is 'St Alban 1943 JM'. This was Jacques Matarasso, the photographer. In the second, Paul and Nusch, also taken by Matarasso.
It must be night-time. Their heads are illuminated, almost as if floating
in a sea of darkness. Their faces are looking towards each other.
Paul's head is framed somehow, it's unclear; perhaps he's behind a
window and looking out. He's smiling and wearing a hat. Nusch is
grinning, her eyes closed, likely against the flash of the camera, or
perhaps in pleasure as she laughs. A wool scarf is wrapped around
her head. It's a lovely moment of happiness, of intimacy, enhanced
by the darkness that engulfs them, isolates them, holds them.

November 1943. Paul and Nusch are still in hiding. They have had to
go deeper underground, to find somewhere yet more remote, where
the Gestapo and the Vichy police cannot find them. In the months
since 'Liberty' was first published in Paris, and then scattered over

cities by the RAF, Paul has become a hero, and a wanted man. The poem is doing its work. They are at Saint-Alban, a psychiatric hospital set within a sixteenth-century castle at Saint-Alban-sur-Limagnole in Lozère, high on the Margeride, a granite plateau in the mountains of the Massif Central. It is freezing. Snow covers the hard earth, and icy winds batter the high pink granite walls of the castle. And yet they have found sanctuary – asylum, in its original sense of the word.

The castle had become a sanatorium in the early nineteenth century and was a typical mental asylum, with all the usual misery that term implies. But in the twentieth century it was gradually transformed into a haven of progressive psychiatry and its patients treated as humans rather than as animals. During the Nazi Occupation and the Vichy regime about forty thousand people with mental health conditions were either murdered or left to die in French institutions. But Saint-Alban was an exception, being tucked away in the depths of the countryside and never running out of food because it grew its own. Its survival was also because of the care of its director, Lucien Bonnafé, communist, résistant and visionary psychiatrist, and his colleague, a Catalan refugee and psychiatrist called Francesc Tosquelles, who had provided therapy to traumatized fighters in the Spanish Civil War before escaping over the Pyrenees to France.

Their approach to the administration of a psychiatric hospital was entirely avant-garde, pioneering, experimental and innovative. Tosquelles sought to revolutionize how psychiatric institutions were run and how their patients were treated, a movement that would later become known as 'institutional psychotherapy'. Tosquelles introduced many ideas that are now used in modern psychotherapy, such as artistic practices. The patients' artworks were exhibited on the outside of the asylum gate and, later, with the intervention of Paul and other famous visitors, were swept into the art world, labelled as 'art brut', or outsider art, monetized and ended up (contentiously) in international collections. He encouraged social connection amongst the patients and with the outside world; a sense of community was at the heart of the project. They were allowed to come and go, to work in the fields beyond the castle walls. They were exposed to culture and provided with occupational therapy workshops. Staff received proper training, and their wellbeing was also provided for. Everyone dressed the same. Walls were knocked down. Hierarchies were done away with. In 1942, he created the 'Société du Gévaudan', which he called 'the Club', a cooperative system which gave his patients a feeling of autonomy. And they produced things – artwork, craft, fresh food – which could then be sold or exchanged.

Tosquelles believed that psychiatric disorder was alienation, meaning both an inner state and an external separation imposed by capitalism. His approach was therefore one of disalienation, seeking to cure his patients, to 'cure' the institutions that held them, and ultimately society itself. Lofty ideals, but ideals that make sense, that are entirely humane and are still heroically aspirational today.

Bonnafé had long been associated with the surrealists, and greatly admired their work. Under his directorship Saint-Alban became a refuge for the Resistance and other dissidents, and for Jewish people fleeing persecution. All were blended in with patients and nursing staff. The seriously injured were hidden in the attics and cellars and cared for by nuns from a nearby community. It was whispered about in Resistance circles like the castle of the Grail, a mysterious and inviolable haven, its location remote and unknown, a place of safety and of sanity. During the Occupation it became a clandestine community of outliers, a melting pot of communism, surrealism and progressive psychotherapy.

For Paul and Nusch, Saint-Alban offered freedom in its confinement, and solace amongst people with mental health problems when the world outside its walls had gone mad. Nusch, exploiting her background as a performer, set to work providing theatre workshops for a group of children with schizophrenia. And Paul – registered under his real name, Grindel, and listed as having 'mild neurosis' – did not slink into the shadows either. He lived and worked amongst the patients, getting to know them, as people, as individuals. He talked with them, read with them, ate with them. He took a Rorschach test with Bonnafé and made gouache paintings inspired by the process, reproductions of which would later be published alongside the poems he was writing. Paul and Nusch lived with Bonnafé in his lodgings, and they lived happily, peacefully, as Jacques Matarasso's photographs of the couple illustrate.

Paul spent much of his time writing. He'd long been interested in states of insanity, ideas about which had been incorporated into his work since the 1920s. And, as a surrealist, he had associated it with the absolute manifestation of convulsive beauty – Breton's term for the explosive, transgressive, disruptive beauty they perceived in the disturbing, the violent, the bizarre aspects of life. But that must have seemed an abstract, obsolete concept, once he'd experienced the reality of mental health conditions. His work had long since evolved into simpler, truer, less contrived poetry. He was deeply moved and inspired by the patients he was living amongst, by what he perceived as their tragedy, their melancholy, their resilience and their individuality. He observed their delusions and moments of clarity and while there he wrote a long poem with several individual portraits of patients he had encountered, and then an epilogue about the cemetery outside the castle wall containing the asylum's dead. He wrote of the patients' fears and desires, of their habits and their mannerisms, of spirits lost and occasionally found.

The collection would become *Souvenirs de la maison des fous* (*Souvenirs from the Madhouse*) and was published after the war. When Paul and Nusch later returned to Paris it was with armfuls of art made by Saint-Alban's patients, with pages of poems and with stories of the castle tucked away in the mountains, and the compassion and humanity they had found within it.

PAUL

Paul's poem about the cemetery at Saint-Alban is now engraved on a stone tablet in the place that inspired it. The poem is simple, plaintive, elegiac, as austere and elemental as the landscape it evokes. It tells of a place 'born of the moon / between two waves of black sky', an 'archipelago of memory' that 'lives on mad winds and ruined spirits'. He writes of the hundreds of unnamed bodies, first exiles from the world and then from life, liberated in death from their prison into the bare earth.

STILL LIFE

The horizontals and verticals of the window frame and the large espagnolette lock holding them together are painted in heavy lines of black and grey like a monochrome grid. We see nothing from the window, just a grey light, warmed with pale yellow in places; perhaps it is morning. It is painted from within and there is a sense of being locked inside, the outside irrelevant. This is not a prison but a stronghold. On the sill stands a tomato plant in what may be a Cubist rendition of a terracotta pot, painted in warm amber, sitting on what looks like a white saucer. The plant is bound to a thick supporting stake. The leaves are spiky, and the vines look like dancing arms reaching for the light at the window. The plant, its stalks and its unripened tomatoes are the true, uncomplicated green of tomato plants, outlined in black. The tomatoes are pendulous; one has turned a primary red. Colour and organic life are set against the black rigidity of the window frame.

In the spring of 1943 Picasso (who was then sixty-one) was dining at Le Catalan with Dora when he noticed a beautiful young woman with green eyes at a table across the room. He walked over to offer her a bowl of cherries. This was Françoise Gilot, a twenty-one-year-old artist and reluctant law student, who was dining with her best friend Geneviève Aliquot and Alain Cuny, a famous actor who Geneviève was attracted to at the time. He asked Françoise what she did, and when she told him she was an artist he laughed, telling her that girls who looked like her couldn't possibly be painters. As he was wont to do, the (attempt) at reassignation – to deny her as an artist, and the weaving of a chrysalis of myth around her – was already beginning. Picasso and Françoise's meeting marked the start of a slow-burning relationship, and it marked the beginning of the end of Picasso's relationship with Dora.

In the last year of the Occupation, Picasso spent less and less time outside the sanctuary of his Grands-Augustins studio. In the summer of 1943, in the garden of the Jeu de Paume, the Nazis burned between five and six hundred paintings by artists they considered degenerate: Ernst, Léger and others. A number of Picasso's works were amongst them. It was safer for him to keep a low profile, to sequester himself away and to work. For Picasso, continuing to live, continuing to paint, was an act of defiance, of resistance.

Françoise was invited to visit him at the studio, to enter the Minotaur's labyrinth, so that she could see his work and so that he could try to seduce her. Soon she was visiting him almost daily, watching him at work, learning from him and, like Dora before her, learning how to please him, to seduce him in turn. After several months Françoise arrived at the studio in a black velvet dress with a high white lace collar, and her hair tied up like a Velazquez. And so their affair began.

Later Françoise would publish a book about her time with Picasso, an act for which he would never forgive her. *Life with Picasso* is full of observations about his routines and his habits, insights into his work and his appalling treatment of the women in his life. Françoise's friends had warned her off him, but she seems to have seen him as a challenge. She was as fascinated by him as he was by her.

She describes how Picasso liked to get up late, and then that people (like Françoise) were allowed to visit him between late morning and early afternoon. He'd have a modest lunch and then work for the rest of the day, with a light dinner in the evening. His meals were cooked by Inès Sassier, a young woman he'd admired in Mougins and who had arrived some years before to work as his housekeeper and cook. Inès had gone back to Mougins at the beginning of the war and got married, but had since returned to Paris with her husband. Picasso made a small apartment for them amongst his rooms. She was loyal and devoted to her employer and in turn he trusted her entirely. Mostly they ate vegetables during the years of the Occupation, whatever she could find – swedes, rhubarb, Jerusalem artichokes and cabbage – but with her southern cooking skills they always ate well.

Food was on Picasso's mind and in his paintings. Spending his days tucked away in his studio, alongside the increasingly violent, tormented portraits he was making of Dora, and the many sculptures he was making from junk and plaster and bronze (somehow acquired), he was also painting still lifes. Inspiration came from within the radius, the diminished limits of his world – his introspective gaze. One morning, on one of her first visits to his studio, Picasso showed Françoise his recent work. She found cockerels, skinned rabbits, pigeons, sausages, a scene from Le Catalan (with cherries), still lifes with lemons, glasses and other receptacles. There were portraits of women in hats adorned with food and cutlery. And there were portraits inspired by Dora that he'd been producing for the past two years, which Françoise thought some of the best he'd ever painted.

The still life is often associated with mortality, a vanitas. It marks the passage of time and the inevitability of decay, of death. All is in vain, it says, earthly pleasures – wine, music, literature – are fleeting, and food rots just as we do. Perhaps Picasso, in the bleak years of the Occupation, was turning what was to hand into signifiers of death. He greatly admired the work of Francisco de Zurbarán and other Spanish still-life painters and Picasso's own works have something of his strangely isolated, illuminated forms. But although he used many objects that are traditionally associated with the iconography of the genre, there is nothing of Zurbarán's smoothness or his harmony of composition in Picasso's still lifes of this period. All is jagged, sombre, serrated, barbed, dissonant – a return to the unsettling visual complexity of Cubism. There are skulls and jugs and dripping candles and limp-looking vegetables, often painted at night. There are sea urchins that look like mines and fish laid out on a table with startled eyes and bodies coiled as if in their death throes. He told an American journalist after the Liberation that although he had not painted the war (not being an artist, who, like a photographer, goes out in search of a subject), the war was certainly present in the paintings he'd been working on.

But the tomato plants that he painted between the third and twelfth of August, days before the Liberation, show a shift. Something is changing. Picasso had been lovingly nurturing a tomato plant on a radiator in his studio since the spring, probably given to him by Marie-Thérèse, who was growing several in her own apartment on the Île Saint-Louis. There are nine pictures, all of the same size, some portrait, others landscape. Within them, not the implication of death but the promise of new life burgeoning in the secret space of the studio, just as a new life was beginning for him with Françoise, and for the world beyond his walls. As for Paul in 'Liberty', in the microcosm of the visible world around Picasso, ordinary, tangible things become imbued with the potential of hope, of freedom. And as spring turned into summer and the tomatoes slowly, silently began to ripen into fruit, he began to paint them.

PICASSO

Into portraits inspired by Dora, Picasso was pouring all the tensions of the war, tensions he tethered in his imagination with Dora's own anguished state of mind. They're often set in cramped, oppressive spaces, scored with lines both horizontal and vertical, as if imprisoned by them. The woman is usually wearing a hat and an elegant outfit, usually pinioned to a black metal chair, her body and the chair fusing into one complex geometric form. Her face is abbreviated to a shape resembling a hatchet, with a long nose, a mouth in profile reduced to a zigzag and sometimes just a single black line. Her eyes are wide open, alert, terrified. The portraits become more and more distorted, grotesque, the bodies more ossified. The repeated motifs of hat, chair, hatchet head and popping eyes become a kind of simplified short-hand until the woman in the paintings starts to resemble the inanimate forms of the still lifes he was painting, as if she too is becoming inani-mate. No longer a portrait but a still life herself.

REUNION

Around midnight on 24 August the bells of Notre-Dame began to sound the freedom of the city. It was a little premature, there was still fighting, but a small group of French soldiers had fought their way to the Hôtel de Ville and the Liberation was hours away. Earlier in the month, it had not been certain that Paris would yet be freed. The supreme Allied commander General Eisenhower had wanted to push towards the northeast and bypass Paris. But General von Choltitz, the German commander of Paris, had ordered the retreat of thousands of soldiers from the city. And from London de Gaulle emphasized the symbolic importance of liberating Paris, in order to establish a new government.

At the sight of the retreating German army, the Resistance stepped up its activities and Parisian defiance began to stir. There were strikes; the railway workers, the police force (which until only days before had been collaborating in the arrests of *résistants* and Jews) and then the *Métro* stopped working. The forces of the Free French began to ready for action. The Germans that remained entrenched themselves in key areas around the city. *Résistants* were still being executed, Jewish deportees were still sent in trains to the east and the Germans tried and failed to send a train-full of art from the Jeu de Paume to Berlin. But the fight soon began, Parisians unearthing their revolutionary spirit, throwing up barricades built from cobble-stones, and the Free French fighting from street to street with German snipers. Françoise, in *Life with Picasso*, observed that even children were helping to build the barricades. She writes that there was heavy fighting near the Senate, close to where Picasso lived in the sixth arrondissement, and that it was difficult to get there.

Many buildings burned. Many are still pockmarked from the shelling. Lives were lost in the fight. Some questioned the point of this last-minute insurrection, when the advancing Allied forces could do the job with far more efficiency. But then there were many for whom this was an imperative, an ineluctable gesture, after years of oppression. Hitler had ordered von Choltitz to leave the city in ruins, an order he disobeyed (perhaps seeing the gratuitous pointlessness of such destruction and that it had no strategic value) before surrendering on 25 August. The French General Leclerc's Second Armoured Division entered the city, followed by American, British and Canadian forces.

That afternoon de Gaulle arrived in Paris and gave a speech at the Hôtel de Ville in which he acclaimed Parisians as victors, as the liberators of their own city. He was rewriting history, laying the foundations of a Liberation myth it would take years to dismantle. To the assembled crowds he asked: 'Why should we hide the emotion which seizes us all, men and women, who are here, at home, in Paris that stood up to liberate itself and that succeeded in doing so with its own hands?' In answer to his own rhetorical question he continued that, no, this emotion should not be hidden. 'Paris! Paris outraged! Paris broken! Paris martyred! But Paris liberated!' That liberation, he emphasized, was carried out by the city itself and by all of France, with only a nod to the continuing efforts of the Allies.

News of the Liberation spread to Rennes, where Lee was waiting for her travel orders. She was angry to be sent to Paris, away from the fighting, but if she must go she particularly wanted to avoid arriving in the city in her scruffy battle fatigues. She ordered for her new uniform to be sent from her tailor's in London and evidently decided to make the best of it, writing to Audrey that, although she wouldn't be the first female journalist in the city, she'd be 'the first dame photographer', unless someone was parachuted in before her.

Lee found a city in a frenzy of joy. Her description of it evokes the madness of the streets, the chaos of shouting, kissing, cycling, cheering, drinking, the flag-waving crowds pumped with the adrenaline of still being alive. She describes lovely, happy faces. And all this alongside battered buildings, shattered windows and barbed wire, tanks in flames and children playing amongst abandoned German vehicles.

Lee and Scherman established themselves in adjacent rooms at the Hôtel Scribe near the Opéra, which the Allied journalists were using as their headquarters and where the atmosphere at the bar was festive. Lee and Scherman celebrated with Capa, Seymour, Cartier-Bresson and others, as well as Hemingway and Lee's fellow female correspondent, Mary Welsh, who'd set up camp together at the Ritz.

David Scherman took a photograph of Lee's room at the Scribe, which she would use as a base from which she came and went for the next year or so. The room is a chaos of piled books and scattered papers, overflowing boxes, a dressing table arrayed with bottles and jars of presumably beauty products. We see Lee's reflection in the mirror; her camera bag slung over the door handle, and in the foreground a desk piled with papers and paraphernalia, her typewriter and beside it a bottle of whisky, two of her trusty companions. Her life reduced to equipment. A few months later Lee would take a similar self-portrait-by-proxy, this time of champagne bottles and jerry cans nestling in thick snow on the balcony of her hotel room. Both photographs insightful portraits of Lee's current way of living, her current state of mind, her current priorities.

One day just before the Liberation, while Picasso was looking out of the window of his studio, a bullet passed just inches from his head and embedded itself into the wall. As the battle had drawn closer, he'd moved to Marie-Thérèse's apartment on the Île Saint-Louis (where the fighting was particularly intense) to be with her and Maya. He'd spent the next days painting furiously and singing at the top of his voice to drown out the clamour of gunfire. After the Liberation he returned to his studio with two paintings he had made during those days based on a print of Poussin's *The Triumph of*

Pan. The wild, anarchic freedom and eroticism of Poussin's bacchanalian scene is Picasso's response to the fighting below.

Visitors flocked to his studio – old friends and enthusiastic strangers – to see the famous artist who, they perceived, had heroically painted through the Occupation. Hemingway, finding that Picasso wasn't home, was asked by the concierge if he wanted to leave a note for the artist. He returned from his jeep with a box of hand grenades and signed it 'to Picasso from Hemingway'.

In October Picasso declared himself a communist, joining the party at an event alongside Paul and Louis Aragon. The next day it was announced in *L'Humanité* with a text written by Paul, who was overjoyed that Picasso was joining the cause. No doubt this was inspired by personal conviction and Paul's influence, but it was also an expedient gesture in the face of critics who wondered how he'd managed to survive the Occupation essentially untroubled. Later in the year he told a journalist that although he'd always been a revolutionary – a freedom fighter, in his painting, he had come to realize that that was not enough. Even so, his post-war ventures into political art would represent a certain lack of conviction. His art dealer, Daniel-Henry Kahnweiler, called him a sentimental communist.

Picasso was one of the first people Lee went to see. Finding him in his studio, they were overjoyed to see each other and Picasso told her he found it wonderful that she was the first Allied soldier he had encountered. He offered Lee coffee, soap and cigarettes. They laughed and cried together, and he pinched her bottom and messed her hair, she would later recall. There's a photograph of their reunion, Lee, in her uniform, towering above Picasso and his arm slung about his old friend's neck. They look delighted to be together again. Lee took many photographs, with Picasso dressed in a suit and tie for the occasion, standing proudly beside his beloved tomato plant, now weighed down with fruit and, at his feet, one of the paintings it had inspired. This image was published in British *Vogue* in October that year, and the caption described the tomato as his model and mentioned how he had kept painting in spite of the fighting in the streets below his studio. Lee ate one of the tomatoes which she joked was starting to rot but that she thought it would be amusing to eat an artwork. He told her that he wanted to paint her again, that the Arlésienne portrait from the summer of 1937 didn't reflect the soldier standing in front of him. He had hot water and encouraged her to wash, making her promise to return for a bath. With Dora they went to a bistro nearby to celebrate their reunion; they ate chicken and drank wine and brandy.

Lee sought out Michel de Brunhoff, the former editor of French *Vogue*, whose twenty-year-old son Pascal had been murdered by the Gestapo. Having suspended the magazine for the period of the Occupation, instead using the office to aid the Resistance, Brunhoff was hoping to relaunch it and asked for Lee's help. She also went to visit Solange d'Ayen, the magazine's fashion editor, who had been in prison and whose husband was in a German concentration camp. She photographed her surrealist friends hanging out of a window, Dora amongst them. And she photographed the legendary novelist Colette, with her shock of hair and kohl-rimmed eyes, demonstratively holding court from her bed. She had seen out the Occupation with her Jewish husband, who had survived thanks to much string-pulling on Colette's part, in her apartment in the Palais-Royal. She also took portraits of her old friend Cocteau, who was trying to redeem himself after flirting with fascism during the Occupation. Perhaps because he was homosexual and associated with pre-war decadence, he had understandably sought to protect himself from the right-wing press and the Nazis. And there was Marlene Dietrich (glamorous in Schiaparelli), Fred Astaire, Bob Hope and others who represented the new Paris or had come to perform for the troops.

Officially Lee's job was to cover the rebirth of haute couture, and she dutifully set about darting between fashion houses and shooting models. Arriving in Paris she had marvelled at the appearance of the women she saw in the crowds, their perfectly painted faces, terribly thin bodies dressed in yards and yards of fabric and large hats worn as an act of defiant frivolity (a French instinct that Lee's British readership would probably have found difficult to comprehend). She observed how the spirit of resistance had pervaded fashion, how French women had grown their hair in contrast to the short styles of German women, and how they used as much material for dresses as they could. Saving fabric and the work that went into making clothes helped the German war effort, so dutiful profligacy was the order of the day. She was fascinated by the way French women had tried to maintain their standards during the war, and admired how the fashion industry was trying to rehabilitate itself. She did some of her best fashion photography in Paris in those months, improvising as she went and shooting in daylight as there was limited power. Edna Woolman Chase, the editor of American *Vogue*, was not impressed, however, and complained that the women Lee had recruited as mannequins were not 'well-bred'. Lee replied that Edna needed to be reminded that there was still a war going on.

In the wake of the Germans, the Communists and the right-wing Gaullists jostled to fill the power vacuum. As the city quickly settled into its new normality, and as the initial elation of the Liberation started to dissipate, so the retributions and recriminations began. The '*épuration sauvage*' ('savage purge') was mostly instigated by the Resistance, with its questionings and tribunals and executions and people scurrying to justify their actions of the last four years. Women accused of sleeping with the enemy, as Lee had photographed at Rennes, had their heads shaved, some were stripped naked and spat on in the streets. Simone de Beauvoir described their treatment as medieval and sadistic. That year Paul wrote a poem, 'Understand Who Will', about their abuse. Though he was a champion of the Resistance he makes it very clear that he neither condemns the women who slept with Germans nor approves of their subsequent humiliation. He describes it as a way to absolve those who were guilty and the words of his poem closely echo the humanizing spirit of these abused women as captured in Lee's photographs. Very soon the balance of power shifted again, as de Gaulle established a right-wing government which included men who had been Vichy collaborators, giving other collaborators amnesty while former Resistance members were prosecuted for their perceived Communist ties.

After reuniting with Picasso, Lee went to find Paul and Nusch. She tracked Paul down to the back of a bookshop where he was talking on the phone. He instinctively recoiled at the sight of the uniform. Now his hands were prone to shaking. Lee found that they had little to say to each other, that the conversation that they could muster – about the weather and how she'd found him – seemed trite. The author of 'Liberty' was now hailed a hero of the Resistance and the poem would be read in public at a theatre in the presence of General de Gaulle in October.

Paul took Lee back to meet Nusch at the Zervos' apartment where they'd been hiding until recently. Nusch rushed to embrace her old friend. Lee took photographs of the couple – one of Paul sitting at a table with Nusch standing behind him, her chin resting tenderly on the top of his head. The years of living in hiding and hunger and in fear had taken their toll. They look older, thinner, Nusch especially, her beautiful eyes tired, though still sparkling, in her now gaunt face. In another image (later published in British *Vogue*), they're in front of Picasso's *Night Fishing at Antibes*, which he'd been painting the last time Lee and Roland saw him before the war. It had been bought by Christian and Yvonne Zervos and was now a vast unframed, unstretched canvas adorning a wall in their apartment.

During the war Picasso had painted Nusch, a tiny, luminously pale – almost white – torso and breasts, a waif, a woman-child, against a grey-green background. Flesh tone and background almost indistinguishable from one another. A long thin neck, a face in shadow, unsmiling, downturned eyes with their long lashes, narrow black arches of her brows and a blue ribbon holding back her frizzy dark hair. Vulnerable, introspective, she's a spectre. Or haunted herself, fragile, ethereal. Lee wrote about Nusch after their reunion; how she was still the same lovely Nusch in spirit, grinning her wide, toothy grin with her halo of frizzy hair, but that she was a shadow of her former self, almost emaciated from ill-health and hunger. She describes how large her elbows looked compared to her arms, and that her pelvic bones showed through her now loose-fitting skirt. She thought it odd that they were in such an exquisite apartment but that they had almost no food, adding that only a few days earlier the building had been searched, and Paul had lain under the roof of the building next door to evade discovery.

Back in London, Roland wrote delightedly to Picasso the day after de Gaulle had entered Paris. He was desperate for news of his friend, of Dora and the others. He was trepidatious, after so long and such dangerous times. He wrote that the war had destroyed all that was important to them and that now it was time to live again. Roland received a letter from Paul, telling him that Picasso was increasingly painting 'like God or the Devil' and that he had behaved admirably during the Occupation and continued to do so.

Lee's adventures had left Roland feeling inadequate and guilty that he had been ensconced in comparative safety. This was compounded by envy at the news that Lee had hunted down Picasso on the day of the Liberation – he needed to be there too. In a few days he had managed to hitch a lift in a supply plane to Le Bourget and David Scherman was temporarily replaced by Roland in Lee's bed at the Scribe. Lee had declared that it was time for her to take a bath to honour his arrival. She took a photograph of Roland looking out of the balcony of her room onto the street below, handsome, pensive, in his uniform.

He joyfully reunited with his friends, and they posed for a group photograph. Nusch in a fur coat, Paul, Picasso in his suit and the Russian-born writer Elsa Triolet are sitting on a trunk on the dusty floor of Picasso's studio. Triolet was married to Louis Aragon, and it was she who had first encouraged him to join the Communist Party. They had been in a relationship since the 1920s and married in 1939. During the Occupation she had worked with Aragon in the Resistance. Behind Nusch, Paul, Picasso and Triolet stand Lee and Roland, both in uniform, alongside Aragon. In spite of the joy, no one is smiling. According to Antony Penrose, his father Roland told him that they had heard news that day confirming the existence of the death camps.

This time Dora did not join them. But it was a reunion of sorts, of the friends who had gathered in Mougins back in 1937. 'They were all in tremendously high spirits, their enthusiasm hid at first glance the signs of strain they had been through,' Roland would later write. 'My surprise was that any should have survived.' But so much had changed. Though some friendships from that summer would be rekindled in the future, others never met again. Man Ray was still far away in Los Angeles, Eileen and Joseph in London. Ady, it seems, was not invited, and it's possible that by then no one knew where she lived. Did anyone wonder about what had happened to her?

HENRI CARTIER-BRESSON, LEE, NUSCH AND PAUL

Another gathering with Lee, Nusch and Paul. Sunlight pours into the room. Lee's in her dress uniform (which had evidently arrived from her tailor in London), metal buttons glinting in the sunlight. She's sitting on Paul's knee, her arm around his shoulder, his hand tightly clasping her arm. She's turned to talk to Nusch who is beaming back at her, the light limning the fuzzy halo of her hair. This subsequent reunion was captured by their friend Cartier-Bresson. So we see Lee too this time, with her beloved friends. Their ease, their love, their happiness at seeing each other again. At having survived.

III

Time Overflows

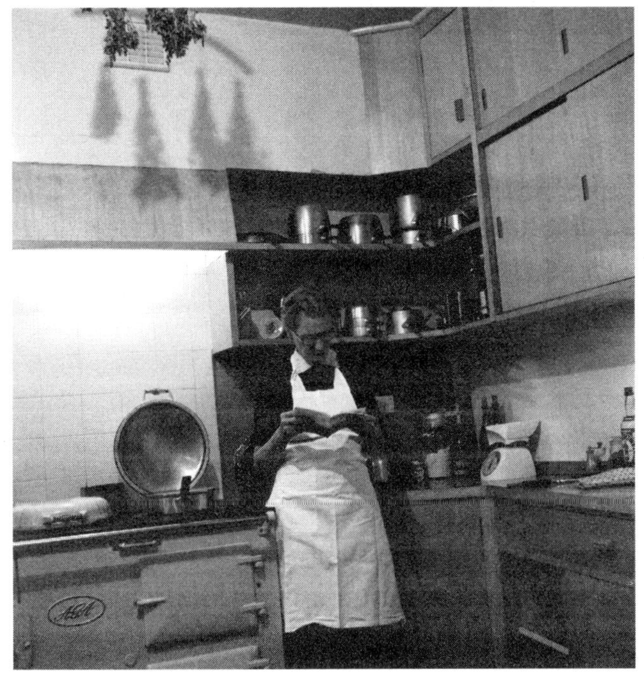

LEE MILLER IN HER KITCHEN AT FARLEY FARM, C.1955.

'Nothing is simple or singular'

PAUL ÉLUARD, 'DEATH, LOVE, LIFE', 1951

Lee grew tired of Paris, of its return to life and its old frivolity, of haute couture and portraits of celebrities, and where a new order was being established. The years of the Occupation seemed swiftly forgotten. For many French people there was a feeling of collective amnesia, the guilt and the shame of the war years, of collaboration, brushed under the carpet of memory in what would later be called 'Vichy syndrome' by the writer Henry Rousso.

In December 1944 Lee wrote to Audrey Withers that she would enthuse about the Liberation if she approved of the way that it was unfolding, but she did not. She was happier, she told Audrey, writing about damage that she could see – damaged towns and damaged people – than with the unseen damage of a disenchanted, disillusioned populace. She felt the war rumbling on. The western Allied forces were then fighting in freezing conditions in the Vosges, and she longed to flee the city and be a part of it.

In Paris, David Scherman took a photograph of her in the passenger seat of a jeep, screwing her eyes up against the sun, eager to be on her way, in her thick army overcoat, a peaked cap and driving goggles pushed up on her forehead. The elegant model standing in a dainty hat and fur coat looks entirely incongruous beside her, or perhaps vice versa. Lee went briefly to Luxembourg where she was delighted to reunite with her much-loved 83rd Division from Saint-Malo; they had declared her AWOL when she had been forced to leave them. And in mid-March she plunged east to Germany, having received her authorization to travel. She had with her a hipflask, a knuckleduster, and K rations – boxed ready meals provided for military personnel on the move. She was also carrying maps, her typewriter and photographic equipment, as well as her mess tin and cutlery. And she was wearing a fleece-lined coat.

From Paris, Roland urged Lee to come home. But she could not.

Each photograph she took, each damaged person she met, each story of injustice and horror she heard and relayed to her readers convinced her that she was doing something of value, of service. It would become her life's work, but in doing it she would destroy her life. She compulsively moved onwards, capturing everything she saw with her camera and in her writing, which was then dispatched back to Audrey Withers in London.

Writing to her editor in April, she told her how swiftly everything was moving, and she with it. She told Audrey that she was still wearing the same trousers she was in when she left Paris six weeks earlier and that she'd lost her only other shirt. She could only keep going, she said. Lee missed nothing: everything was swept up into her work – politics, personalities, injustices, ironies. The details – little, incidental, sometimes poignant or shocking or bizarre – that few would notice and even less would use created an impression of a battle-bruised world. These things make Lee's photographs, and perhaps even more so her writing, so compelling, persuasive, immersive, unique. Audrey Withers was to write in her memoirs that Lee's involvement with *Vogue* was the magazine's 'greatest publishing excitement of the war'. 'Lee's features', she writes, 'gave *Vogue* a validity in wartime it would not otherwise have had'.

On her journey east Lee captured ruined cities, heaps of dead bodies, just-about-living tortured bodies, shrunken civilians with war-weary faces attempting to rebuild their lives, and others blinkered in defeat, in furs and in denial, carrying their responsibility lightly, as if there had been no wrong done and the world had not stopped.

In Germany a kernel of hate and repulsion burned within Lee. The more she saw, the greater it grew, and it fuelled the writing she was sending to Audrey. She was torn between that hatred and an inherent empathy that informed how she framed and composed her photographs, and which her photographs entice from those that look at them. In the highly charged theatre of war, we are her complicit audience. The body of an SS prison guard floats in the canal where he's been dumped, sunlight catching on the ripples of the water and on his face, gentle in death, submerged beneath the surface. It's a disturbingly beautiful image, almost pre-Raphaelite. And yet this is Dachau, and the dead man will have undoubtedly committed the greatest brutalities.

Looking at her photographs we, at times, become voyeurs. In Leipzig, Lee and fellow photographer Margaret Bourke-White were told that the city bürgermeister had committed suicide with his family. Bourke-White photographed them from above, at a distance. Lee photographed standing beside them, at their level. Crouching down, she took a picture of the bürgermeister's daughter reclining on the arm of the sofa as if asleep, her head tipped back, her arms resting gently across her body. Her face in the light is like smoothly wrought marble, a Bernini sculpture in death.

Lee's writing, though much admired, gave her great pain. It reads as the spontaneous outpouring of everything she was seeing, but she found the process laborious, 'stone-wringing' she called it. And the multiple drafts she wrote of every piece are testament to her perfecting process. Back in Paris, at the Scribe, David Scherman had supported her with encouragement, sex and cognac. And increasingly she drank heavily, no doubt to steel her nerves and to try to untether herself from the scenes she was witnessing and capturing and remembering. She photographed too closely, too personally, too subjectively. It was not long before she was taking both benzedrine (a US Army-approved amphetamine) and sleeping pills.

And then the rumours began to reveal themselves as realities, as the Allies swept slowly across Germany and discovered the camps. Lee arrived at Ohrdruf in the Thuringian Forest in the weeks after its liberation. Her reaction was to put down her camera, telling Audrey that she knew that she wouldn't be able to publish the pictures anyway. She told her to read about it in the papers, and to believe what she read. For a moment Lee was at a loss for words and for how to make sense of what she saw there. But she knew she needed to use her photography and her writing to show the world what had been happening, and to persuade people to believe it was true.

Buchenwald followed with its all-pervading stench of death. There were burned bodies, stacked bodies, people barely alive. Lee photographed the piles of the dead, getting as close as she could so that we can see their faces, and know that they were once living people before they were heaps of decaying flesh. She photographed the prison guards, the bruises and bloody noses they received at the hands of survivors. And she photographed those survivors. One image is of a released prisoner's legs. We see the striped trousers of his camp uniform tucked into socks made into makeshift shoes. One foot is raised, its toe pointing down as if the man is dancing, as if defiantly alive, the air of commedia dell'arte countered by the terror the trousers immediately evoke. And then Dachau, which Lee and Scherman reached at the end of April, as it was being liberated and where a train of about forty carriages was parked outside the camp filled with thousands of dead bodies covered in blood and excrement.

Once inside the camp she photographed the brutalized, skeletal survivors as she walked amongst them, and the bodies of those who were dead, all close-ups of their faces, as if searching for her Jewish friends that she knew were missing. She photographed the GIs who were uncovering the horrors, and the medics who were doing their best to help survivors. The images are confrontational, unavoidable.

She cabled Audrey with the news of what she had seen, begging her to believe the veracity of the images and accounts, but by this time British *Vogue*'s tone was one of jubilation. In the June 'Victory' issue just one of Lee's photographs was published alongside an article about what she had witnessed. Several of her photographs, including one of a pile of dead bodies, a tangled heap of emaciated legs and gaunt faces and open, lifeless eyes, opposite one of the swollen, battered face and torso of a lynched guard hanging from a hook, were published in American *Vogue* in June with the title 'BELIEVE IT', as if to echo Lee's emphatic entreaty to Audrey.

She told Audrey that Dachau was as awful as one could imagine. There she had imagined the thousands of pained, exhausted, freezing feet of the inmates, and how many of them eventually ended at the gas chamber. She said in comparison to the shattered bodies and bestiality she'd witnessed in the camps, that the front line, where she and Scherman were heading for after Dachau, seemed human and pristine. She was looking forward to seeing the fall of Munich, she told Audrey, as it had been the crucible of the nightmare she was witnessing.

Lee and Scherman persuaded their way into Hitler's apartment (which was occupied by American signallers) as a billet for the night, eager to see inside the epicentre of evil. They found a modest apartment, with dull art and commonplace interiors, and cupboards filled with monogrammed china, silver and table linen: ordinary middle-class pretensions, an extraordinary capacity for evil. They also discovered that, miraculously, the apartment had running hot water. That night Lee took her first bath in weeks. She also took what is perhaps her most famous photograph.

And then on she went, from Munich to Berchtesgaden to witness the burning of Hitler's symbolic heartland, and later to newly liberated Denmark. For a while she returned home to London but then she went back to France for the trial of Pétain, the puppet head of the collaborationist Vichy government. From there she went on to Austria, where she watched and described, bitterly, the death of a malnourished baby. And then to Hungary, Romania. When the war ended, she could not stop but kept going. She wanted to go further east to witness the aftermath of the war there. To keep revealing.

At some point David Scherman returned to London and would later go to New York. Though he loved Lee, he now sought to distance himself from her, and by then was seeing someone else. Lee and David's was a wartime relationship, one of action, of shared adventure, not one that could survive in peacetime. Lee had stopped writing to Roland or to anyone else – there was no room in her life for a relationship or even for friendships. She was suffering from nervous exhaustion, relying on alcohol and benzedrine. Her gums bled, and her skin was covered in rashes.

After seven months of silence Roland sent her a long letter by way of an ultimatum, imploring her to return to him. He tells her that he's been trying to make sense of her silence, as have her parents and Aziz, that she's become a phantom. He talks of honouring their heartfelt agreement to give Lee her freedom and how she had given him such happiness. Before she had left, Lee had asked Roland if there was someone he loved as much as her; now there is, he tells her. Someone who is tangible, present. He tells her he won't beg again and that if she doesn't reply he shall take that as her answer. But if she does answer, he tells her, it would shatter his anguish. His love for her is great, he says. And at the end of the letter: 'Lee – my darling – answer Roland.'

From New York David Scherman sent her a cable with two words: 'GO HOME'. She replied 'OK'. And, finally, she did what everyone was begging her to do. She went home.

LEE AND DAVID SCHERMAN

It was the dust of Dachau that she trampled into Hitler's bathmat that night as she took off her heavy, mud-caked combat boots and parked them beside his bath, before climbing in to wash herself clean of the day's misery. The bath was necessary, a luxury neither Lee nor Scherman had enjoyed in weeks. But it was also a gesture, to be photographed, memorialized. Undoubtedly for Lee it was also an echo of the bathhouse she had seen that day, into which people had innocently trudged to their deaths.

Before getting into the water, Lee stage-managed the scene for maximum impact, placing a framed photograph of Hitler on the rim of the bath. A calculated gesture. And on a dressing table at the other side of the room she positioned a classical statue of a naked woman, cut off at the knees, its elbow pointing towards the bath. She then staged herself, bathing, scrubbing her bare skin with a cloth and looking up and away from Scherman's camera, weary, unreadable. She sits between Hitler and the Aryan ideal of the statue – a real woman, mud-stained – once more using her naked body as a tool, but here, subversively. It carries all the atrocities that she has witnessed and, as with her boots, she inserts herself into and besmirches the purity of Hitler's most intimate of spaces. The following morning they heard on the BBC that Hitler and Eva Braun had committed suicide in Berlin the day before. And so the photograph became an insult to his memory.

A collaboration with Scherman who worked the camera, this image of Lee became her most famous photograph. Beside the visceral realities of her photographs from the camps it's perhaps strange that a photograph of a woman having a bath in a bathroom should hold such power. But, as ever with Lee's photographs, it's the context that gives meaning. That she set the scene, rearranging the space, invites questions about authenticity and artifice, but perhaps it helps us to see things circuitously, makes images more powerful, easier to comprehend. In the 1860s, during the American Civil War, Emily Dickinson suggested that veracity was more affective, more affecting, if told indirectly. It was important to tell the truth, but to 'tell it slant', she wrote: the truth must be gradually illuminated or the sudden brightness of it would be blinding. Therein lies the potency of the subtle obliquity of Lee's bath photograph.

TWENTY-EIGHTH OF NOVEMBER,
NINETEEN HUNDRED AND FORTY-SIX

In Paris, Nusch has been delivering food to her mother-in-law and collapses in the street. She has suffered a massive brain haemorrhage and dies several hours later. Only that morning she had been chatting for hours on the phone with Dora. A distraught Dora tells Brassaï that Nusch had been happy and that they had made plans to lunch together that day.

Nusch was forty. Her health had always been vulnerable, but the stress and deprivation of the war years had shattered her fragile body. Having been forced into hiding and suffering after the publication of 'Liberty', she had died in the service of Paul's pursuit of freedom. Or perhaps, more simply, she had given her life for the hope the poem engendered. She was buried in early December at the Père Lachaise cemetery in the east of the city. And although in life she'd inspired such lyricism, her gravestone was simple, and engraved with only her name.

THE PHOENIX

In November 1946 Paul was ill and convalescing in Switzerland as he had in his youth and several times since. From there, in a letter to Gala, he wrote dismissively of his old ally André Breton's return from America – they had been estranged for years – and of his continuing commitment to communism. He told her that he was dedicated to the party, which expected nothing inappropriate from him, and that he was entirely in accord with its politics. Paul also told Gala of a great task he had committed to: starting his poetic life over, using a pseudonym, Didier Desroches. Apart from Nusch he had told no one else of his plans. That year he had refused the Légion d'honneur. By then the poet of freedom was tired of his celebrity, though it had helped him to survive. In his memoirs the filmmaker Claude Lanzmann writes about helping Paul to sell signed copies of the manuscript of 'Liberty' with its crossings out and corrections. He recalls watching Paul in his apartment diligently recreating all the original gestures with his pen on page after page of paper and then taking them away to be sold to the poem's adoring fans.

Three days after writing to Gala he received the news from

Paris that Nusch was dead. Dora telegraphed Paul in Switzerland and he dashed back to Paris on the night train and the poet René Char sat with him for three days as he mourned beside Nusch's body. Speaking with Brassaï on the day that Nusch died, Dora told him that her friend had been all to her husband: wife, companion, assistant, protector. Paul had told Dora in the previous year that he couldn't fathom life without Nusch, that he wouldn't survive without her. She worried deeply for her old friend.

Paul was devastated. Months later he would write to Gala that though the initial pain had diminished, his life was now empty, but for the huge presence of death. In another letter he told Gala that the blow was too great, and repeated that his life was entirely empty without Nusch. He felt profound guilt too, for the openness he had insisted upon in their marriage. Paul later told Gala that he had contemplated suicide at this time, but had been saved by the support of two young friends, Alain and Jacqueline Trutat, who were devoted to him, lived intimately with him, and saw him through the worst months after Nusch's death. He wrote that they gave him the will to live. And so instead of killing himself, he proceeded with his plan to write under the pseudonym Didier Desroches, and to kill Paul Éluard the poet, the husband.

This was Paul's way of escaping the reality of his life, just as he had done when he'd disappeared for months during his unhappiness with Gala years before. Brassaï wrote that Nusch's death had caused Paul to lose faith in everything – in hope and the belief in life, and even in poetry. He added that Paul's friends, including Picasso and Dora, could do nothing but look on at Paul's misery. As his biographer Jean-Charles Gateau writes in *Paul Éluard, ou, Le Frère voyant*, 'Orpheus had lost his Eurydice'. Roland told his son, Antony Penrose, that when he met Paul soon after Nusch's death Paul told him: 'Je dors dans un lit moitie éventré par la mort' ('I sleep in a bed half gouged out by death').

In the following year Paul published a book of poems called *Le Temps déborde* (*Time Overflows*) using the Desroches pseudonym, published by Zervos. It was dedicated to Alain and Jacqueline Trutat – 'who did everything to dispel the night which invaded me'. To many of its readers it was clear who had written the poems, and the gesture of the pseudonym was understood. The book was illustrated with several of the most beautiful photographs of Nusch, taken by Dora and Man Ray. The poems are filled with love and despair. For Paul they represented a final work. He did not want to write any more. He wanted only silence as his past life melted away, as he writes emphatically, definitively, at the end of 'Our Life'.

There are fourteen poems in two groups of seven. Between the two groups, the date of Nusch's death, spelt out in words, has a line to itself. A stark and plangent lament, it stands alone, a demarcation between his old life and happiness and his new life of grief:

> Twenty-eighth of November, nineteen hundred and forty-six
> We will not grow old together.
> Here is the day
> Too many: time overflows.
> My love so light takes on the weight of torment.

Later in 1947 Paul published (with his own name) *Corps mem-orable* (*Memorable Body*), which he dedicated to Jacqueline Trutat and which celebrates the power of eroticism to give back life. He mourned Nusch, deeply, for a year and a half or so after her death and then began to re-engage with his political commitment. In *Poèmes politiques* (*Political Poems*) he writes of being reborn, how he had moved from suicidal despair to a political being, and how this had been brought about through the solidarity of his friends who had nurtured him with food, companionship and passion. He defied moralizers to judge him for the way he had come to life again.

Over the next years Paul travelled widely, to Britain, Mexico, Czechoslovakia, Russia and elsewhere, for the communist cause and in the name of world peace, as a passionate and vocal ambassador at congresses and rallies, sometimes in the company of Picasso.

Together they attended the World Congress of Intellectuals in Defence of Peace in Wrocław, Poland, in 1948. Both continued in a shared belief in the power of art to bring about revolution. To the end of his life Paul's belief in communism – in the solidarity, the fraternity, the generosity it appeared to offer – was publicly unwavering.

On his return to Paris after the war, Man Ray was surprised by the change in his old friend. He writes in *Self-Portrait* that he contacted Paul as soon as he arrived, having been on such close terms before the war. He had always esteemed the simplicity and humanity of his poetry and in California had received and admired his passionate writing about love and freedom that was disseminated by the Resistance networks. He writes that Nusch's death had changed Paul entirely. For the most part he was melancholy and irritable. Though they didn't discuss politics directly, Man Ray adds, Paul made it clear that he was determined to continue to act as spokesman for the Communist Party, he felt that he was needed and that he was making the world a better place. 'Poor Paul, I thought,' writes Man Ray, 'enmeshed in the cog-wheels of ruthless intrigue. Only a simple nature could have been so misled.'

In 1950 Breton wrote an open letter to Paul asking him to intervene in the fate of his Czech friend, the surrealist and historian Záviš Kalandra, who had been arrested, accused of being a Trotskyist and attempting to overthrow the new Communist Czech government. Paul refused. He replied to Breton, publicly, with extraordinary and hitherto uncharacteristic froideur, that he was too busy with the innocent to engage with the guilty. Kalandra, who had been tortured into a false confession, was hanged in June of that year. Presumably Paul knew nothing of the torture that had led to the confession. Perhaps blinkered, he accepted it as truth. But for Paul the personal had always been political, and the political personal. And it is hard to reconcile this forsaking of humanity, this silence, with the man who had written so many words about love, of the love for his fellow man and of the profound responsibility of the poet to speak up. For a time his poetry, and the poet himself, had been put into the service of the party. He had slipped into didactic, rhetoric, become orthodox and blinkered by the cause, refusing to acknowledge the reality of life in the Soviet Union and other communist countries.

That same year he wrote 'Ode to Stalin', which was later published in a collection called *Thank You, Comrade Stalin!*. In his 1978 novel, *The Book of Laughter and Forgetting*, the Czech writer Milan Kundera imagines Paul singing, dancing, weightless and guiltless as he soars up into the air above Wenceslas Square with his fellow communists as Kalandra is hanged below him. Kundera believes that Paul, whom he had long admired, was responsible for Kalandra's death, that he 'forgot' his friendship and his true conscience in the name of communism. Paul, he says in an interview with the writer Philip Roth published in 'Conversations in London and Connecticut with Milan Kundera', became the greatest champion of what he describes as the 'poesy of totalitarianism', describing how 'the hangman killed while the poet sang'.

Was it naive idealism or was Paul under pressure to conform? Either way he toed the party line until his death. When he fell in love with and wanted to marry Jacqueline Duhême, an illustrator and Matisse's assistant just over thirty years younger than him (according to Duhême), the party deemed her too young and not an appropriate choice of partner. Duhême thought this very bourgeois thinking, and once upon a time so would Paul. But Paul acquiesced. They remained friends, wrote many letters to each other and collaborated on a children's book, but the opportunity for a true partnership with Jacqueline was denied him. And while he also had an affair with Diane Deriaz, a trapeze artist, who he similarly considered marrying, again she was vetoed by the party.

Then at the World Congress for Peace in Mexico in 1950 Paul met Dominique Lemort, a thirty-five-year-old French woman. Dominique had been married twice before, she had a daughter, she was intellectual and independent and a passionate feminist. The Communist Party seemed to have approved of her or perhaps, as it's sometimes suggested, she was nudged in Paul's direction. In 1951, inspired by this new relationship, Paul wrote *Le Phénix* (*The Phoenix*), a collection of poems in which he celebrates being reborn, and his poetry is reborn too, by this new love, by passion and connection. Paul and Dominique married that year. Picasso gave them a huge vase painted with musicians and dancers tumbling around it, but it seems that he did not much care for his old friend's new wife, perhaps because he had loved Nusch so much, or perhaps because she was a strident woman with strident opinions. But it seems he wasn't alone. It appears Paul's daughter Cécile was not at their wedding, and many years later she revealed in an interview in *The Observer* that after Paul's death Dominique had managed to disinherit her, and that she had subsequently lost most of her father's collection of art and books to his third wife.

In 2016, when Cécile died, she chose to be buried not with either of her parents but with Nusch, whom she had loved dearly. Nusch's original gravestone was replaced, Cécile's name added, as well as lines from the poem that Paul wrote marking the date of Nusch's death, and the end of his life as he had known it, after which 'time overflows'.

Paul and Dominique moved from Paris to Charenton-le-Pont, a suburb to the south-east of the city on the edge of the Bois de Vincennes. But Paul's new-found happiness was short-lived. He died of a heart attack in his apartment on 18 November 1952. He was fifty-six. Like Nusch, his health, which had always been impaired, had been irrevocably damaged by the war years. As a communist he was denied a state funeral, but the French Communist Party arranged for it to be held at the Père Lachaise cemetery.

'Nothing is simple or singular', Paul had written in 'Death, Love, Life' the year before he died. In the last years of his life he fought within himself a creeping scepticism about Soviet Stalinism, particularly after travelling to the USSR and perhaps influenced by Dominique, who was increasingly critical after what she had seen of the harsh reality of life there. Years after his death Dominique acknowledged that the posthumous revelations about Stalin would have appalled Paul, and that he would have relinquished his party membership. In his late writing, Paul sometimes hints at a nostalgia for the simple moral binary of the war years. When he wrote of love it was still with some of the same lyricism and eroticism as before, and in the last decade of his life he was writing with less of a tunnel vision, allowing the complexity, the ambiguity back in, and also re-engaging with surrealism. But, for the most part, the lover and fighter who had unshackled himself from surrealism and had offered the promise of liberty to a desperate nation had died a servant to dogma.

Despite this, to the many thousands who gathered in the streets to follow his coffin, Paul remained a hero and a humanist, a symbol of resistance, of commitment, of hope and freedom, and of love.

LEE, PAUL, DOMINIQUE, PICASSO AND FRANÇOISE

June 1951. Saint-Tropez. Picasso is signing documents in a room at the town hall, as witness to Paul and Dominique's wedding. He's sitting at a table beside the newlyweds with Françoise, his fellow witness. It's a serious moment, no one is smiling, everyone is watching – the bureaucracy of marriage. Lee and Roland are guests, and Lee is the unofficial photographer of the occasion. Afterwards they celebrate at a restaurant. They're outside under a vine-covered pergola, the dappled sunlight falling on their faces and on the table, which is cluttered with jugs and plates and glasses. Paul – the white-haired bridegroom, with his tired, animated face. Old friends, new loves, fleeting happiness.

CARTIER–BRESSON, DOMINIQUE, PICASSO, CÉCILE AND OTHERS

November 1952. The sky is resolutely grey, trees bare, autumn in Paris. A crowd, and countless faces. Picasso, grief stricken, bundled against the cold in a huge coat and a scarf bound around his neck.

Beside him Dominique in black, looking directly at Cartier-Bresson's camera. Louis Aragon and Elsa Triolet stand alongside them. The mournful face of Paul's daughter Cécile appears behind Dominique and Picasso.

They and many of his friends had joined the procession through the streets, following Paul's coffin. In other photographs there are crowds carrying flags and banners, and there's a giant photograph of Paul's face. He wasn't to be buried beside Nusch, but amongst politicians and communists, Resistance fighters and victims of the Nazi concentration camps. She was eclipsed in death, as in life, by his purpose, his politics. There were speeches at the cemetery gates by Louis Aragon, Jean Bruller (Vercors) and others. Cocteau was there too. And, somewhere, his mother, who had outlived him. There is no sign of Dora, Lee, Eileen or Roland (who was devasted by the death of one of his dearest friends). Perhaps some of them were there, lost in the crowd. But perhaps not. According to Antony Penrose, Valentine Penrose attended, and wrote movingly about the event to Lee and Roland. Man Ray, though he'd loved Paul and was equally saddened by his death, refused to attend a communist funeral. Picasso stood watch over the grave. At Vallauris, on the day of Paul's death, he had painted a dove taking flight, inscribing it 'pour mon cher Paul Éluard'.

LA JOIE DE VIVRE

A naked woman dances and seems to lift into the air at the centre of the painting, her arms aloft with a tambourine in her hands. Her skin is translucent palest blue, almost pearlescent. Her long brown hair swirls about her head. She has giant, buoyant breasts that dwarf her long narrow torso, which leads into the voluptuous curves of her buttocks and twisted, dancing legs. Beside her two goats are prancing;

a faun and a centaur are playing flutes. A Bacchanalia. They're all dancing on what looks like a stretch of golden sand. Behind them, a bright white sky above a blue sea on which a boat with a yellow sail is drifting past. The colours are chalky, clean, sun-bleached, diaphanous. All is simple, sensuous, sinuous.

This was happiness, outside, freedom. Picasso painted *La Joie de Vivre* in 1946, the vital, weightless nymph at the centre of the painting inspired by Françoise Gilot. And with her, inevitably, came a whole new phase in his work. It was a slow evolution, with nothing of the intensity of passion and the drama of previous periods and previous relationships. Françoise had only just agreed to live with him. She became his '*femme fleur*', a flower ready to be plucked; flora rather than fauna was a new identification for Picasso to use for the women in his life. And he painted her that same year with her oval face as a flower (palest blue once more) surrounded by deep green leaves in place of hair, her body a long thin stem from which two breasts cling like perfectly round buds that are bigger than her head. Leaf-like arms emerge from below. One is clutching another ball-bud, as if for good measure. For Picasso, Françoise was nature, represented by that deep green, and by fluid, spontaneous lines – all bubbling circles and ovals. He adored her face with its asymmetric green eyes, strong nose, full mouth and thick, arched eyebrows. And he loved her breasts. For Picasso, who was then sixty-five, Françoise represented youth, vitality, fecundity and plenitude. Cherry ripe. A return to life.

That year, having extricated himself from Dora, Picasso had moved south with Françoise to the Mediterranean. They stayed with a friend of hers at Golfe-Juan and Picasso was offered a studio in the attic rooms of the Grimaldi Castle, built into the sea wall at Antibes, with huge windows that look out to, and frame, the sea – planes of blue, only water and sky, like a Rothko. There he painted *La Joie de Vivre*.

The Mediterranean had always represented a mythological playground for Picasso. It was where he was born, where he felt he belonged. He had always interwoven his personal myths with those of the South and antiquity. His return, coupled with his feeling of revitalization, of new love, inspired a whole wave of works with mythological and bucolic themes. The rapacious Minotaur was for the most part kept at bay. Now all was mostly Arcadian. Mostly – there would always be death in his work, as in Arcadia – but playing at death. When death appeared, it was now in the form of little impish devils and sirens and heroes and fights between centaurs and fauns, often with naive, charming faces – two dots and a smile – like a child's drawing. Antibes was built on the foundations of the Greek town Antipolis, the Grimaldi Castle was built over the ancient acropolis. Picasso mused to Roland that he never drew these creatures in Paris but that they seemed to live amongst him in the South.

Picasso wanted to have a baby, no doubt to prove the virility he felt was reborn in him and also, Françoise claims in *Life with Picasso*, that he wanted to make her into a mother, what he thought a real woman should be, and perhaps it was to claim her, to stop her from leaving him. Perhaps he was unsettled by her inherent independence and by her ambitions as an artist in her own right. He wanted to rein her back in, to shoehorn her into the woman he thought she should be. Soon Françoise was pregnant, and their son Claude was born in 1947, followed by a daughter, Paloma, in 1949.

In photographs their life looks idyllic, a blissful, sun-soaked domesticity. In Robert Capa's famous image of them both, Françoise is smiling, striding along a beach and swinging her arms in a sundress and straw hat and a necklace that Picasso has made for her. He, in shorts and an unbuttoned shirt, walks behind her, shielding her from the sun with a parasol like a devoted servant. Lee and Roland visited them in 1948 and Lee took photographs of them frolicking with the children in the sea. Paul, his daughter Cécile and his granddaughter joined them and there's a photograph of Paul, Roland and Picasso standing together on the beach, an ageing echo of many images from Mougins just over ten years earlier.

Picasso and Françoise bought a house, La Gaulloise, at Vallauris, near Cannes. It was an ordinary, modest sort of house to reflect his commitment to communism (somewhat at odds with the ever-increasing fortune he was making for his work, although he was donating a lot of paintings to benefit various communist charities). That commitment would never resemble Paul's deeply felt dedication. Picasso revered nothing as highly as himself, and never liked to give himself to anything entirely. Rather, there were creative gestures. The lithograph of a white dove he offered for the poster of the 1949 Peace Congress in Paris would have an enormous and lasting impact as a symbol of peace. For this emblem, this powerful propaganda, Picasso was awarded the Stalin Prize in 1950. There were some who believed he should adhere to the optimism, overt political messaging and literalism of the official socialist realism that was expected of communist artists. But he had so far got away with it.

In 1953 when Stalin died, Louis Aragon asked Picasso for a drawing of him, to publish in the communist journal *Les Lettres françaises*. Picasso, claiming not to know what Stalin looked like, studied old newspaper pictures and drew a young man, black hair swept back from his head, dark, soulful eyes, bushy eyebrows and a thick crescent of bushy moustache that hangs down over his mouth. The drawing has an unconvinced urgency about it, and it caused outrage. There was no gravitas, no uniform, no medals; just a young, romantic idealist with pretty eyes and lots of hair.

Gertje R. Utley writes in *Picasso: The Communist Years* that it was the dreamer rather than the dictator who Picasso found more palatable. But many thought it mocked the great leader, and the ensuing scandal unnerved Picasso, but he didn't apologize, didn't disparage the movement, and neither did he adopt socialist realism. To Cocteau (according to Cocteau's diaries) Picasso acknowledged that he had joined a family and that like any family, it was full of shit. He continued to produce work for them, to bankroll them, and doggedly remained a communist all his life, even after the stories of purges and terror began to emerge. Eventually his misdemeanour was forgotten if not forgiven, and he was welcomed back into the fold, although never with quite the same warmth. Picasso was too important as a celebrity champion to be rejected, or to expect him to alter his aesthetic. And he wouldn't have done. He was a communist in gesture, but an egoist in life.

Near La Gaulloise he found an old factory and converted it into a studio. His paintings during the years he lived with Françoise were of and for children. There were still lifes, of fish and shellfish on plates – sea urchins, slices of lemon, squid, fruit, limes, red mullet, octopus – and fishermen, and his owl Ubu, which he had found injured in a corner of his studio at the Grimaldi Castle and decided to keep. And there were many portraits of a blooming Françoise. Picasso had stumbled upon the Madoura Pottery at Vallauris, not far from his home, in 1946 and, intrigued with the alchemical process, had begun to make ceramics of his own. Back in 1937, while staying at the Hôtel Vaste Horizon, Paul and Picasso had visited Vallauris together, and Paul had then urged Picasso to help revive the ceramics industry there, objects that would be within reach of ordinary people. Just as he had begun to write poetry that he hoped would resonate with them too. Perhaps the memory of that visit had stayed with Picasso. Of course, as with everything in his work, he first had to destroy the formal conventions of ceramics, to disconnect the form from function, to create new forms, to master the medium and make it his own. There was no Sèvres sterility, perfection; in his mind were the ceramics of Greek antiquity with their sensual forms – from the earth, hewn by hands – and of the stories they tell on their flanks. There were ingeniously dynamic sculptures, often vibrantly painted, and there were moulded plates with faces and fauns and fish and other food that seem to pop out of the surface of the plates.

But the domestic idyll did not last long. Unlike Dora, Françoise was not scuttled by a devotion to Picasso, and she was not afraid of him. Though she was the mother of his children, she refused to sublimate her work and her liberty for his sake. She began to tire of his mood swings, his taunting, his mercurial unpredictability, his sudden flashes of anger and violence. And also, his return to infidelity. Picasso believed his behaviour to her, and presumably to himself, was a mark of the courageous, open, honest way he had chosen to live his life. The damage it caused was an inevitable by-product. Eventually in 1953 Françoise left him and took the children to Paris. Picasso, who was the serial leaver, not the one left behind, never forgave her.

The following year Picasso invited Françoise to open the bullfight at Vallauris. In the Picasso lexicon of symbols and gestures and bull-fight-as-autobiography, this event was a formal acknowledgement of their separation, a kind of honourable discharge that masked the fact she'd left him. It's often seen as a gesture of reconciliation on Picasso's part, but perhaps it was his way of implying that he could still control her, and that her departure hadn't maddened him. There are photographs taken by the Irish photographer Edward Quinn of that day. Françoise, in high-waisted trousers, a white shirt, a sash at her waist and a flat, wide-brimmed fedora on her head, rides straight-backed, leading the matadors into the ring. She circles the ring, rides over to Picasso in the grandstand and doffs her hat at him – a final gesture of obeisance. He stands to applaud and then they shake hands. She looks radiant, triumphant. Later, when he discovered that she was planning to publish a book about their life together he, along with many of his friends and even the French Communist Party, tried to suppress it. Picasso attempted three lawsuits against the book. All their efforts were unsuccessful. Instead they slandered her and began a smear campaign against her and the publication. Picasso entirely cut his ex-lover and their children, Claude and Paloma, out of his life. Françoise's book became an international bestseller when it was published in 1964 and she had a long and successful career as an artist.

In the years after the war Picasso slowly turned into a sacred monster in the eyes of the public. It was a role he relished and was happy to live up to. He enjoyed the notoriety – the priapic, prolific, genius-brute: somehow it aligned with and elevated his own myths. Gradually it became him.

Soon Françoise was replaced by Jacqueline Roque, a young woman with a six-year-old daughter, who worked as a saleswoman at the pottery in Vallauris. He liked Jacqueline's face, and she was devoted to him. They would marry in 1961 (his wife Olga having died in 1955). For a few years they lived, and Picasso worked, at a villa in Cannes and there are many photographs of the rooms filled to the brim with his work – stacks of paintings, groups of sculptures and arrangements of ceramics, along with his enormous collection of found objects and African art, dotted about amongst the furniture in a seemingly haphazard, chaotic, beautiful, living installation. Eventually they moved to Mougins, with all its memories, and to a house called Notre-Dame-de-Vie, which was far less modest, and where he hung his work and created a studio.

In 1965 Picasso had a stomach operation after which he needed a year to recuperate. But illness and surgery did not stop him, and he continued to work for the rest of his life. Working, like breathing, instinctive and necessary. Protean. There were continual transformations, evolutions, new forms, new and strange colour combinations, new challenges to unpick and overcome. He painted, sculpted, wrote texts and continued to craft jewellery and trinkets and tiny sculptures out of whatever was to hand. He often worked serially as if ferociously trying again and again to figure something out, a nut to crack. And he was drawn back to Spain in his imagination, and to the Old Masters he'd always admired, to Goya, Delacroix and Velazquez, to rework their paintings and, as with everything, to take them apart and remake them in his own image.

As he grew older, Picasso began to paint himself, his ageing, to confront and perhaps to challenge his inevitable mortality. And he thought a lot about sex, relentlessly it seems, drawing and painting crude, carnal images of rapacious men and women with big breasts, and nipples and bellies, and open legs and vulvas and hanging testicles and swinging penises with a spiky crop of pubic hair. There were memories of brothels in his youth and drawings of sex at the circus and people watching other people having sex. There were giant penises with erotic scenes sketched inside them like the phallus sculptures of Ancient Rome that offered protection and good fortune. There were bodies, and life. The old waltz of sex and death, but with the music growing ever faster, ever more keenly felt. These libidinous drawings were like offerings to the gods to prove his youth, his virility, to prove that it wasn't yet his time. To beg for more.

Everything was becoming more urgent. To Roland he wrote of that time in Mougins, so many years before, with Dora and Paul and Nusch and Lee and the others, and of how time had felt infinite. There had been time to bathe and eat and dance in nightclubs together, to work and saunter and talk with one another. Now, he lamented, there was so little time. And so he tried to fight it, working and working and working. And he was still working in the early hours of the day he died on 8 April 1973 at the age of ninety-one, at his house in Mougins.

Picasso's huge charisma and his extraordinary talent had inspired great devotion from many of the women in his life, and many friends. But in turn he mostly damaged them. He had spent his life in defence of total freedom, and he had managed to achieve it, both personally and artistically. But in doggedly defending that right he had caused catastrophic collateral damage in the lives of the people who loved him. And yet the myth still holds.

PICASSO

Finally he began to look at himself. A reckoning, perhaps. He admitted he'd never made anything like this before. It's a face which is like a skull which is like a mask. All hollow cheeks and sinking flesh and stubbled chin. There's a band of red that sweeps around the top of the head and down one side to the shoulder. It could be a scarf but perhaps it's just a foil to offset the pallor of the face – a queasy greeny blue with patches of purple and the occasional flash of red. He worked with pencil and coloured crayons on paper and, here, there's something childlike about that. Somehow it makes the drawing more vulnerable. More honest. And that honesty is in the stark black lines and the soft, smudgy colouring. Hard and delicate at the same time.

And it's not the skull of the ox he found at Mougins in the summer of 1937 and grasped in front of his head for Dora to photograph as if he was the Minotaur, all beast and balls. It's himself. An old man with shrunken shoulders and wiry hair on his chest trying on his death mask to see what it will look like. The eyes behind the mask are alive, and they're how we know it's him, but they're wide open – one pupil dilated, the other small – and fixed, as if in the moment of truth. He's seen it.

'DANS L'AMITIÉ'

Roland and Lee had experienced very different wars. Lee's questing had taken her across Europe and into battlefields and scenes of barbarity: an intensely lived, intensely felt, period of her life. Roland had mostly stayed at home. He had played his part and with much dedication, flair and hard work – camouflage, translating and promoting the poetry and writings of the Resistance, passionately supporting artists who had sought refuge in England. But Roland and Lee were two very different people by the time they reunited in early 1946, Lee finally accepting that she needed to go home.

Though they had both pursued other relationships during the war they were determined to set those aside and to move forward together. Lee discovered that she was pregnant. She divorced Aziz Eloui Bey, who had and would continue to be a supportive, loving presence in her life, and married Roland in May 1947. Their son Antony was born in September that year. They bought a property,

Farley Farm, in East Sussex, and spent their time between London and the country.

Roland's career began to take off. He had come to realize, to acknowledge to himself that although he loved painting, it was not his greatest talent. He knew that he should be doing what he did best. This was his ability to organize, to make and sustain associations and friendships, both personally and professionally. André Breton had dubbed Roland '*un surrealiste dans l'amitié*' (a surrealist in friendship).

Though he continued to make and exhibit his own work, his considerable energies now went into bringing people together. He made connections and sought to find common ground between those with conflicting opinions. It helped that he was charming and presented with an English reserve that cloaked his aims and ambitions. And he used this to promote the work of surrealist and other modern artists, the work that he believed in so passionately and wanted to haul into the mainstream consciousness, and to keep it there.

His archive at the Scottish National Gallery of Modern Art in Edinburgh is filled with copies of letters he wrote to his old friends and letters they wrote to him in return – Picasso (of course), Eileen, Dora, Paul and Man Ray. Though their lives had diverged, and they had only ever been a fleeting community at that pre-war Mougins summer, he carried that collaborative, collective spirit within himself. He believed friendship was an active thing that required – deserved – work. In 1951 Paul – with whom Roland remained friends until the poet's death – presented Roland with an early copy of a book of his writing that had been translated into English, inscribing it to a 'full moon augmented by solar Lee, for his birthday'. It continues, 'To Roland, whose birth blessed my idea of friendship.'

Since the war Roland had been imagining a platform on which to present the work of contemporary artists, one which stood outside the grandeur of the other art galleries. It was not to be a museum, like the Museum of Modern Art in New York, or a modest gallery, like his London Gallery (which Roland closed in 1950). He wanted it to be an institution, more official, bringing contemporary art to mainstream audiences. But it was to be a more elastic, adaptable, organic environment for the promotion of contemporary work. He wanted it to be groundbreaking, and it was.

In 1946 the Institute of Contemporary Arts was founded by Roland, along with Geoffrey Grigson, Herbert Read, Peter Gregory, E. L. T. Mesens and Peter Watson. And Roland remained a key player in the development of the Institute for the next thirty years. For one of the first exhibitions in 1948 he somehow managed to persuade the Museum of Modern Art to lend *Les Demoiselles d'Avignon*. As they had yet to find a permanent site for the Institute, this exhibition was held in a cinema they'd rented on Oxford Street next to a bomb site. The front door was too small, and a hole had to be knocked into a wall at the back of the building to get the vast canvas inside. Later he was responsible for moving the Institute to its current – far grander – location on The Mall, down the road from Buckingham Palace. It's an intriguing choice of location, its proximity to the palace lending it a grand, establishment air. And yet in spirit it was a crucible of modernity, of creative freedom. That duality is somehow a very Roland choice. He remained a director of the ICA until 1976, when he reluctantly resigned, believing that the Institute had lost sight of its original vision – his vision – bound in its own bureaucracy.

But it was Roland's devotion to Picasso that dominated much of his later life. Over the years it would be tested – like many of Picasso's relationships – by his changeable, frequently spiteful nature. The friendship endured probably thanks to Roland's perseverance and diplomacy, his love. As a mark of this devotion, in the 1950s he decided to ask Picasso's permission to write his biography. He'd been mulling over the project for some time, and he went to Picasso with the idea. He found him in Collioure, in the south-west of France, and waded out into the sea to speak with him. Permission was granted, and Roland spent the next four years or so researching the project, shuttling back and forth between England and France with Lee, who took many insightful photographs of their encounters. The book, *Picasso: His Life and His Work*, was published in 1958. Picasso was delighted with it. Researching and writing the biography had forced Roland to see his friend with a more objective eye – his treatment of women, his violence, his brutally-dominating narcissism. The book itself, of course, has nothing of this; gossip was vulgar, discretion esteemed. Roland's insight, his focus, was on the art, the charisma, the virtuoso, the mythos of Picasso.

In 1960 Roland was appointed a CBE and in 1966 he was knighted. He'd questioned whether to accept the knighthood; it didn't really suit a surrealist. He was ever a man of the establishment and a nonconformist, a doubleness that had informed the entirety of his adult life. When a French friend asked how he could still call himself a surrealist now that he was Sir Penrose, Roland replied, 'I am now a Sir-Realist,' which sounds like a good compromise.

Roland was also endlessly busy working on exhibitions, and the publication of the Picasso biography, which had been an intense process, freed him up for other projects. In 1959 he organized a major Picasso exhibition at the invitation of the Tate Gallery, which many claimed to be the show of the century. And in 1965, after five years of negotiation, he persuaded Picasso to sell his masterpiece *The Three Dancers* to the Tate. Picasso told Roland that it was because of him that he'd agreed to sell it to the English.

Inspired by the success of his Picasso biography, Roland wrote books about other artists and friends he admired, including Man Ray, Joan Miró and Antoni Tàpies. He became a trustee of the Tate Gallery and continued to collect work for his own collection, much of which is now in British public collections. That Britain holds one of the finest collections of surrealist art in the world is thanks to Roland's dedication to surrealism since the 1930s. He had championed the movement ever since, a tireless promoter of its work and of modern art in general, both British and international, and of the artists who made it.

Roland outlived his greatest friends – Picasso, Max Ernst, Man Ray. And each death in turn brought with it a great sadness, a heaviness. He was distracted and comforted by women who came into his life with their youth and intelligence and their interest in him. These relationships sustained him in the absence of those old friendships he'd worked so hard to maintain.

In a strange turn of events, Roland's ex-wife Valentine, who was ill, came to live with Roland and Lee in Sussex, she and Lee having become very close since their days living together during the Blitz. She died there, at Farley Farm, in 1978, a year after Lee. When Lee died Roland told Antony that he and his wife had never been unfaithful to one another, something which baffled his son. He'd been fully aware of his father's other relationships. Roland said that from the very beginning they had promised each other sexual freedom but monogamy in love. Roland spent the rest of his life with Diane Deriaz, the trapeze artist who had been Paul's lover for a while after Nusch's death. Roland and Diane had had a long on-and-off affair since the early 1950s, with Lee's knowledge. But that he had been monogamous in his love for Lee, he told his son, had never changed.

Roland died in 1984, with Antony beside him, several days before the opening of an exhibition of his work in Brighton. It was 23 April, Lee's birthday.

LEE, PICASSO AND ROLAND

La Californie, Picasso's house in Cannes, 1957. He's sitting in a chair in the foreground. We see only his head and shoulders and that he's reading a book. Roland stands behind him. He looks very much the English gentleman, bespectacled, donnish, in his slacks, tweed jacket, striped shirt and tie tucked inside a knitted pullover. He's peering down at the book as Picasso reads, an anxious hand to his mouth, the biographer waiting for the reaction of his subject. Ever careful, ever behind the great man, the humble admirer. And Lee, the photographer, resigned to her role as witness, sidelined. Her husband, and her friend who had made her a kind of widow.

Colour

Eileen believed that the end of the war would bring with it newness, and marvels. Instead, she was lethargic, demoralized, bored by the mundanity of her life. She felt cut off from artistic communities and believed that this isolation was making her ill.

Slowly, inevitably, she began to make work again, and it was as if she was restoring her faith in life. And that optimism, that restoration, radiates from *Dance of Peace*, a painted collage which she made in 1945. It's an oneiric, Arcadian scene, all soft and billowing and layered with sheer washes of gentle bright colours and organic textures. The dancing figures – almost a single, lyrical, nebulous mass of movement – seem to have floated up from the green at their feet. A blue face in profile appears in the centre of the group. Perhaps this is Eileen re-emerging from, what was for her, the enervating, etiolating gloom of the war years.

Soon she was re-engaging with friends, including Lee and Roland, and with the artistic world; she was exhibiting again, prolific again, making collages, paintings, assemblages, taking photographs. Surrealism, in its European pre-war guise, all but disappeared. In France it was eclipsed by existentialism, which seemed far more relevant to the post-war world. And it was the individual rather than the collective that now mattered. 'What is surrealism today and how does it justify itself historically when we know that it was absent from this war, absent from our hearts and from our activities during the Occupation?' the poet and essayist Tristan Tzara would wonder, having been both a Dadaist and a surrealist. And yet surrealism lingered, re-emerged, re-emerges still, on different continents, and in new forms, with new artists, particularly female artists who like Eileen take what they want from it and discard what they don't.

It was as colour and bright light seeped back into her world that Eileen truly felt alive again. In the years after the war and for many years she and Joseph travelled abroad, particularly to the south, to Italy and France. When she discovered Tenerife it marked a turning point in her life. There she was engulfed in the natural world, having been isolated from it by the war. The mountains, the strange lunar landscape of an island shaped by volcanic activity, the black sand, the thrumming earth and its kaleidoscope of colour, the blue sea and its horizons; these things reached inside her to draw out her dormant creativity.

Eileen and Joseph remained together, happily, until his death in 1975. Devastated, Eileen found that she couldn't paint, that she'd lost her impetus. Joseph had been her loving critic, telling her when he thought a work needed improvement, or when it didn't. When she finally returned to her canvases, she painted Cleopatra reclining opposite Antony, like Eros and Psyche, both figures fused as if one, and painted blue against green and a glimpsed map of the world, with glowing shapes like hearts or butterflies or wings fluttering at their fingertips, as if proffering them to each other. Legendary lovers: Eileen's tribute to Joseph, to their own love.

She worked with endless and urgent curiosity and invention for the rest of her life. In 1985 she began working on her memoirs, *A Look at My Life*, with Andrew Lambirth. Eileen continued to develop her own metaphysics and to look for meaning in the world, her world, that which she perceived and which inspired her. In her memoir, she writes that it is that universe which is the art, not the work of the artist themself. She described herself merely as a sleepwalker in that universe.

In later years Eileen often looked back, reworking old forms and ideas, as a re-engagement rather than a regression. Perhaps she was hauling her old inspirations, her old self, onward, into her present, her future, like a continuum. Her paintings are filled with her recurring themes, personal motifs and symbols – dreams, landscapes, dream landscapes, the sea and its depths and the life it holds, organic forms, heads and profiles, and mythology. Her later work is peopled with maenads, nymphs, poets, sorcerers. There's Orpheus, Demeter, the Minotaur, Cleopatra, Joseph Bard, herself. And she looked to the people of her past, painting a portrait of her long-dead mother, and one of Dylan Thomas, whom she'd met in the 1930s and sketched swiftly as he enchanted the room with a flow of bawdy limericks.

And she returned to her Ploumanac'h rocks photographs, prints of which she had sent to Paul Nash. This time she reworked the black and white images into a series of boldly bright, radiating landscapes, somehow more New Mexico than Brittany, less their literal forms and more the latent animistic energy she saw in them. Nash had died in his sleep of heart failure as a result of chronic and debilitating asthma in 1946. Eileen was in a shop on the Earl's Court Road when the shop assistant told her they'd just heard the news on the radio. Nash had remained devoted to Eileen and they had continued to see each other until his death. Perhaps these later-life paintings honoured that devotion, but perhaps more so their affinity, their shared view of the world and love of the natural world, which they had immortalized, collaboratively, all those years before.

But Eileen also looked to the present, with a productive restlessness, with improvisation, becoming interested in abstract expressionism and experimenting with new media, like felt tips and acrylic paint, which she loved, revelling in its versality and the increased freedom it gave to her practice. Eileen never lost her commitment to a life of freedom and joy. She believed that allowing space for delight was paramount. In the 1989 documentary about her, *Colour of Dreams*, she talks of joy in her life and her work, of how happy her life has been, and how that joy almost inadvertently radiates from her work 'like a transparent skirt', presumably recalling her dance of freedom in a sheer dress all those years before on a rooftop in Cannes. And her playfulness continued to be her guiding force. She believed it unlocked a window into a magical world of freedom.

Though in 1988 she was invited to join the Royal Academy, it wasn't a sign that she had become grand or serious or inelastic. She writes in her memoirs that she lived in active defiance of convention. She kept her wit, her lightness, her irreverence. In her work, in herself. Amused by this anointing by the establishment – she'd always thought the RA rather pompous – she marvelled that she could be both (considered) a surrealist and at the same time a Royal Academician. She thought it a mark of how much had changed – in society, not her.

To the end she lived surrounded by her work and her wonderful bounty of bricolage, collected over a career that had spanned seventy years. And to the end she was painting. Eileen died at the age of ninety-one in London in 1991 and is buried beside Joseph. In the final line of her memoir, she writes that she hoped to die as she had lived, 'in a sparkling moment'. It's easy to imagine that she did.

EILEEN AND JOSEPH

Memories of Joseph, and youth, and Mougins. The colour of memory – of summer and heat and ease and lust and love – suffusing what was once black and white with the hyper-colour of dreams. Joseph, who had been dead for eleven years. In place of a photograph, paper, and the urgent gestural back-and-forth of felt tips, with pastel and collage. Eileen recreated the photograph of Joseph, arms aloft, head turned aside – a reverse of the original – sitting naked in the wicker armchair on what had been Picasso's balcony at the Hôtel Vaste Horizon. Behind him a blue sky and brick-red pyramids. Glowing pink and red and purple geometric forms that seem to burst in the air to one side of him. To the other, dark arabesques of branches intertwine with undulating patches of green foliage and a swathe of bright yellow – the sunshine that poured onto the balcony and bathed his body, remembered as a wall of light.

Joseph is drawn in warm sunlit shades of yellow as if anointed, his hair and a part of his thigh a glowing vermilion, his upper arms, torso and thighs adorned with bands of a deeper red that follow the broad curves and muscles of the body she so admired. Where there had been the shadow of leaves playing across his groin and partly concealing his penis, in the drawing there has sprung a branch from between his legs, as if he is a part of the plant that grows at the balcony's edge. Plant and man are one: alive, organic, vigorous. The branch is thick, trunk-like, curved, unfurling, like a snake uncoiling itself. It is deepest brown, topped with a burst of emerald-green leaves. This is not a playful nod to fig-leaf modesty as in the photograph, this is joyful immodesty: Joseph the lover, the pleasure-giver.

A memory captured, a resurrection, desire resurrected.

EILEEN

Two profiles of one head facing in opposite directions, like Janus. A doubleness, a liminality, a looking back and a looking forward, a beginning and an ending, a long-recurring motif in her work. They're pea-soup green, open-mouthed, overlaid with striated patches of yellow and darker green and darkest turquoise. Behind the head, a glimpse of sapphire sea and black suggestions of fish. A black hand from the centre between the two profiles outstretched as if reaching for something or emerging from the sea. Over the left profile she painted the elegant curve of a ram's horn like an Arabic crescent moon. Perhaps this was the horn she'd found while at Mougins. Over the head, sensual, blue, undulating lines like the transparency of swirling seawater allow these glimpses of the head beneath the surface. The sea and its depths, which she plumbed in her imagination, forever drew her, held her, like a life-force – amniotic, protective, eternal, enigmatic. Like a goddess, born of the sea, but this one horned, perhaps more animal than Olympian. The horn with its priapic, thrusting, virile or Dionysian implications, but reappropriated, feminized. Its power, its erotic potential claimed for herself, for womankind and her latent power, her strength. Her womb magic. 'The Horned Woman'. Woman as warrior, as survivor.

LANDSCAPES

After the Liberation, when friends met Picasso for meals in restaurants they would never know whether it was Dora or Françoise who would be with him. And those friends feared for Dora's well-being. Rather than abruptly ejecting Dora from his life when he met Françoise, Picasso continued to see her, to spend time with her, to toy with her. Sometimes he would visit her after work with gifts, engraved stones or whittled cardboard cutouts. Her capricious, inconstant lover. Their break was not finalized until 1946; he preferred his women to overlap. Picasso and Françoise were at the Café de Flore when Dora arrived. Picasso asked Dora to tell Françoise that it was over between them, and therefore that Françoise should not hesitate in living with him. Dora agreed that this was true. To Picasso she said that he was incapable of love and that he had never loved anyone. In *Life with Picasso*, Françoise writes that all the tales and exploits with the women in his life, and the fact that they were still just out of sight, hovering in the wings, convinced her that he liked to decapitate his women but retain their heads for his own private delectation. She adds that he didn't want to kill them entirely, because he wanted to have the pleasure of hearing their noises, their signs of life, life that he had granted and that he could take away. Any subsequent dramas in their lives entertained him greatly.

In May 1946 Dora wrote an untitled poem expressing her loneliness and despair. She writes of finding herself in the solitude of a wide open landscape, where, though the weather was pleasant, for her the sun was absent. Time was absent. She laments that she has seen no friend; she walks and talks alone. When her beloved friend Nusch died at the end of the year it only compounded her grief.

By then Dora was experiencing a nervous breakdown and friends observed her acting strangely. She claimed to have been attacked and that her bicycle had been stolen, though it was where she had left it. She was found naked on the stairs of her building. She forced Picasso and Paul onto their knees so that they could repent their sins. Arriving late for lunch at Le Catalan with Picasso, Paul and others, she rushed in and then quickly rushed out, declaring that she couldn't stay. Picasso told Françoise Gilot that Paul was so upset by his friend's state of mind that he smashed a chair to pieces and blamed Picasso. It was Paul who had first observed the intimations of Picasso's shifting desire in his paintings. Picasso exclaimed that she had always been mad and blamed it on surrealism.

Dora was taken to a psychiatric hospital and received electric-shock therapy. It was Paul who intervened most forcefully in her care, asking for help from Jacques Lacan, the psychiatrist and friend of the surrealists. Lacan moved Dora to a private clinic for three weeks, after which she returned home. She continued to undergo analysis with him for the next two years. He encouraged Dora's interest in mysticism, and after forays into the Kabbalah and Buddhism she alighted on Catholicism, which perhaps, with its redemptive hope, gave her comfort and to which she became devoted as the years went by. She believed that after Picasso, there was only God.

In 1945 Picasso had given Dora a house in Ménerbes in the Luberon, albeit damp and riddled with scorpions when she first moved in, and where he would later insist on taking Françoise Gilot for a holiday. For years after their relationship had ended he continued to humiliate Dora and to send her strange gifts, things that were simultaneously amusing and offensive, presumably to remind her of how they had been together, and to claw his way back into her consciousness, in case he had slipped from it. There was a chair very similar to one in which he had immobilized her likeness during the war, and there was a toilet seat (who was defecating on whom?). Another gift he had made for her but never sent was a silver signet ring engraved with P and D, with a spike on the inside; a sadistic gift for the masochist he saw in her. She responded to these gifts by sending him religious books.

Lee photographed Dora in the 1950s in her apartment, sitting reflectively in an armchair by the fireplace, beneath Picasso's portrait of her with green fingernails from 1936, the early days of their relationship. Dora visited Roland and Lee in England. Lee and Dora would sit and talk for hours, perhaps more at ease together than they had ever been, both older, both scarred. But over time Dora stopped communicating with Lee and Roland. In time her circle of friends shrank, or perhaps she shrank from many of her old friends. She saw less of Paul after Nusch's death, the grief from which absorbed him so entirely there was no room for her own. Though it seems she had no more lovers, Dora had a few close friendships, including the artist Nicolas de Staël, her neighbour in Ménerbes, and James Lord, a young gay American man who had been working for American military intelligence and was in Paris just after the Liberation. And she spent her time between Ménerbes and Paris, living more and more reclusively.

Throughout the years of Dora and Picasso's protracted breakup Dora had continued to paint and to exhibit. And she continued to work and to experiment throughout her life. Later, in Provence, she would paint the barren terrain of the Luberon, unpeopled swathes of layered colour beneath blue skies and buffeting clouds. An attainable horizon. Soft, romantic, gestural, the paintings look like peace, and freedom, and benign solitude.

In the 1980s she turned back to photography. She bought a Polaroid camera, which she loved. And as she had done in the 1930s, she made photograms, darkroom experiments with amorphous shapes and X-rayed, fragmented bodies. It was a return to the inventiveness, the strangeness that had driven her before she had been encouraged away from it. Picasso would have hated it. Painting and photography were central to her recuperation and the retrieval of her life, her exiled self.

There is a Dora that James Lord knew, and adored, and later wrote about in *Picasso and Dora: A Memoir*, published in 1993. A Dora who privately, discreetly, wriggled out of her old skin, and in her new skin regained happiness, vivacity and companionship (when she wanted it). Lord was entirely enchanted by Dora, by the rhythmical cadence of her voice, her radiant smile, her elegant hands with their painted nails, her eyes that sparkled and the stillness of her demeanour. He was fascinated by her moods and intransigence, by her eccentricities and perversities, her capacity for sudden happiness, and her volatility and unpredictability. Dora the spectacle, the idol, the human link to divinity, but also Dora the person, the artist. Lord's tone is adulatory, his observations intriguing in their detail: the way she captured her gold cigarette holder between her teeth, the way she could hold her own with Picasso by adopting a kind of stubborn immovability.

There's a photograph of Dora on the steps of her house in Ménerbes, taken by Lord. She's obviously just opened the door. She's wearing an elegant, fitted summer dress and espadrilles that are tied around her ankles. Her arm, draped with a shawl, is raised in greeting. She is beaming at Lord, and this image of the broad, evidently spontaneous smile as she opens the door to her friend is almost shocking in its rarity, and wonderful in the context of the received narrative of her life.

Later, she found a steadiness that she had lacked for so much of it. With meditation, and faith, and in her elective isolation, she unfettered herself, found peace. Her political stance, which had been so passionately left wing as a young woman, shifted to the right. In old age Dora would talk with more reflective and perhaps more ambivalent candour about her relationship with Picasso and the overwhelming impact he'd had on her life. She told Roland that she thought Picasso was a repressed homosexual and that this had had a profound influence on his creativity, for example. She was only thirty-eight when her separation from Picasso became permanent. When she died in 1997, twenty-four years after Picasso, her apartment in Paris was still crammed with paintings and trinkets that he had given her; the ephemera, the relics of their time together, things he had crafted for her, jewellery, paper burned or folded or painted with wine or lipstick, painted matchboxes and torn table-cloths, even the little insects he had drawn to animate the cracks in her walls. Yet, years earlier, when James Lord had pointed out that her likeness adorned the walls of some of the world's greatest museums and that, thanks to Picasso, she would never be forgotten, she replied: 'Do you think I care? Does Madame Cézanne care? Does Saskia Rembrandt care? Remember that I, too, am an artist.'

DORA

A series of four tiny prints with photographs of Dora taken by an anonymous photographer. Perhaps they're self-portraits; they may have been taken for her passport. In all but one she looks directly at the camera; in the other she looks away, her head slightly turned. They're undated, but could have been taken in the 1960s. She's wearing a dark jacket and a dark blouse with a neat, round neckline. In place of her long dark hair she has a chic, gamine, grey crop. Her lipsticked mouth is set, unsmiling, and slightly twisted to one side. Dora unadorned, unmediated. Dora, after.

DORA, AND DORA

A negative from 1935, when she was a Photographer and not some-one who takes photographs. It's of a naked woman standing with her arms up, her hands in her hair, her head tipped back, her eyes look-ing upward and away from the camera. It was probably taken as an advert, but it looks like freedom. The negative bestowing upon the white skin and blonde hair an uncanny sheen of burnished pewter, with mysterious lights and dark shadows. Smooth contours. Her eyes and eyelashes are white in a black face. A reversal.

1980. Dora now seventy-two or seventy-three. She returns to this negative. And she keeps of it what she wants, the rest she scratches out. A new work is made. The head and the body are glimpsed, but not all of it, because where she's scratched is now a startling white void all around her body, as if it's in thick cloud or a bath of milk. And her groin and inner thighs are blanked out in white because perhaps she's had enough of that, or perhaps it's now privately hers and not a public thing.

A palimpsest. That tells of the past and the present. A bridge between the two. An act of destruction, an erasure. And a woman emerging. A positive, a rebirth.

2 BIS RUE FÉROU

For Man Ray, Los Angeles was losing its lustre by the end of the 1940s. In 1947 he'd visited Paris with Juliet to seek out the work and books and equipment he'd left behind in the care of Ady, and other friends, in 1940. He organized the sale of his country house in Saint-Germain-en-Laye and showed Juliet around Paris. Like any tourists, they'd visited the Louvre, gone up the Eiffel Tower, eaten at expensive restaurants and climbed the steps to see the view from the Sacré-Cœur. It reminded him of what he'd been missing, and he was determined to live there again. As a final, symbolic gesture as he left Los Angeles, he sold his car, the car which he had bought with such pride and pleasure to mark his arrival, and his arrival in the city.

Man Ray and Juliet sailed from New York, where he hesitated for a moment, wondering if perhaps he should stay. But he felt that as a photographer-turned-painter he would be viewed with suspicion in the city's art world. Paris meant freedom and peace and a different pace. Juliet hadn't wanted to leave Los Angeles – her world, her friends. She couldn't speak French and until 1947 had never been to France. But she agreed to it, as it seems she always agreed to his desires. Having been unreliable in his previous relationships, Man

Ray would stay with Juliet, happily so. Happily for both of them, so it seems.

Marcel Duchamp was waiting in their cabin to see them off, with a plaster cast of female genitals as a farewell gift for Man Ray, a gesture of friendship and of their mutual understanding. Arriving in Paris, Man Ray and Juliet dined at La Coupole, drank champagne given to them by the owner, in honour of Man Ray's return, and danced in the club below it until closing time.

They found a studio on the Left Bank, not in his beloved Montparnasse, but not far from it, at 2 bis rue Férou, a high-walled, narrow street between the Luxembourg Gardens and the Place Saint-Sulpice with its charming cafes, its lively fountain and its elegant, neoclassical church (the third largest in the city). The building had originally been a garage and still retained its wooden garage doors onto the street. The interior was a roomy, whitewashed space with walls twenty feet high, skylights and large windows high up, through which the light streamed in. Man Ray thought it would be perfect for a sculptor of large-scale pieces. Perfect for him. He could see that it wasn't ideal as a space in which to live. And yet despite his and Juliet's reservations (which were quickly dismissed), he was smitten and decided to take it anyway. From there he could hear the bells of Saint-Sulpice sounding the hours. And there he could create his own, contained, private world, happily immured, with a view only to the sky above. Man Ray would live there for the rest of his life.

They emptied the space of almost all the old furniture that had been left, and Man Ray began to redesign the interior, to build new furniture from scratch, as well as creating a basic kitchen, a bathroom, a bedroom and a darkroom. He hung up *Le Beau Temps*, which Ady had helped him with, and he stretched a parachute below the ceiling to protect his art (as well as himself and Juliet) from the rainwater which leaked through the roof. The studio was heated by a giant stove. Together they used lighting to create a warm, intimate atmosphere and soon he had lined the walls with paintings and photographs, while objects jostled for space on all the surfaces, slowly making their way up the walls towards a balcony, where he worked. Others hung from the ceiling on a system of pulleys. Paintings were hung and re-hung, objects positioned and then repositioned, to suit his whim. Everything was provisional, improvised, elastic. There were boxes of postcards and negatives and index cards. Over the years, the studio filled not only with his old work but with new pieces: readymades, paintings, photographs, sculptures. There was little of his friends' work on view; it was almost all his own. It became a temple to the life he had forged for himself, a living microcosm, a museum, reflecting the variety of his career. And it became his retreat.

Man Ray and Juliet travelled abroad from time to time, often staying at Cadaqués on the Costa Brava, long-time haunt of the Spanish branch of the surrealists – Dalí had a house nearby. But they settled into a life lived mostly at home, where friends came to him, into the sanctuary of the studio. They smoked, drank, listened to jazz. He politely turned away the hordes of fans who tramped to his door. Roland and Lee were frequent visitors, especially in the years when Roland was working on his biography of Picasso and spending time in France to research it. And in turn he and Juliet were often guests at Farley Farm. Man Ray played chess with Duchamp when his old friend was in Paris; chess was their conversation, the way they communicated with one another. Duchamp and his wife had been with Man Ray and Juliet in the evening before he died, in 1968. Duchamp's death was such a blow to his unequivocally adoring friend that he could barely speak about it.

Life had a good, easy rhythm. Man Ray wandered to flea markets, always on the hunt for objects and their potentialities, to claim and make new. There were regular dinners at a restaurant in the Place Saint-Sulpice, drinks at a cafe in the same square. Sometimes they'd go slightly further afield for dinner at La Coupole, in his old stomping ground of Montparnasse. Waiters and guests knew them, greeted them, were warmingly deferential to the famous artist who, even in old age, radiated an electricity, a magnetism that drew people to him. He became partial to berets; there's a photograph of him walking beside the Seine with Juliet. He's wearing one, with spectacles, a dark outfit beneath a light trench coat, clutching a pipe – the honorary Frenchman. Though there's archival footage of him in old age talking in his studio about his work, and his accent is distinctively Brooklyn. He would always be an American and never wished to be anything different. As he aged, he began to look to his own artistic legacy. He continued to recreate, to reconsider and often to redesign earlier works, things that had been lost in the war. He made copies of works and limited-edition replicas of others. These things sold and kept them afloat, he was unfazed by this process of commodification, of reproduction and dilution. And he continued to explore new forms, to invent objects, all with his surreal, irreverent, lyrical eye.

Man Ray thought that the idea of progress in artistic terms was a fallacy, just as there could be no progress in the way people had sex. And yet he was a pioneer, an innovator, an iconoclast. Perhaps this wasn't progress but endless curiosity and a desire to make his mark, driven by a fierce determination. The vast amount and the great variety of his work are a testament to his unending quest to be a great artist. His hunger to create and to belong, to be acknowledged, was an extraordinary driving force. He absorbed influence as he went along. He was good at it. He wanted to master something, to improve on it and then to claim it as his own. But that artistic recognition he craved had eluded him his entire life. He wanted to be taken seriously as a painter like so many of his friends and contemporaries, but it is as a photographer, with his poetic eye, his technical innovations, that he is remembered and celebrated. He helped to revolutionize the medium. A medium he scorned.

By the 1960s he was beginning to receive the attention that he felt he deserved, and his work was being shown in exhibitions around the world. He had two major retrospectives, in Paris in 1972 and in New York in 1974. Man Ray refused to attend the latter, held at the New York Cultural Center, but Lee and Roland flew to America for the opening. The exhibition was called 'Man Ray, Inventor, Painter, Poet', which must have made him happy. It later toured to the ICA in London, which he did attend. It was one of the last exhibitions Roland organized before leaving the Institute. He'd been determined to do it, for the sake of their old friendship.

Reviews were still mixed, sometimes dismissive, especially concerning his paintings. He continued to refuse permission for his photographs to be sold or exhibited, any interest from researchers or journalists or art historians was stubbornly batted away. After his death this changed, as the full extent of his achievement – and especially his photography – could be displayed. His work now commands incredibly high prices.

In November 1976 Man Ray died in his studio with Juliet beside him and surrounded by the work of a lifetime. He was eighty-six. He'd had a lung infection and been ill for some time. In October, hearing that he was failing, Lee flew to Paris to sit beside him and they talked of the past. It was the last time they met. Juliet moved out of the studio and into a more conventionally comfortable apartment following his death. She struggled to maintain his legacy and eventually recruited her brother and some of Man Ray's closest friends and his niece to help her. She kept Man Ray's studio exactly as it had been, down to the cigarette butts that Duchamp had stubbed out in an ashtray on his last visit. She hoped that it might become a museum to Man Ray, but by 1983 the building was in such a state of disrepair that she decided to sell it. The Centre Pompidou acquired hundreds of pieces of his rudimentary furniture and the ephemera of his life for its collection.

In 1963 Man Ray had published his autobiography, *Self-Portrait*. It's picaresque, and consciously vague, ambiguous, loose in its details. As he had done for most of his life, this was about image control, as edited and manipulated as the portraits he had made with his camera. Reading it one senses his self-protective cynicism, an honesty when he feels like it, a pluckiness, a puckishness. And all the while the urgent paddling of swan's feet beneath the untroubled surface of the water. For some years Man Ray's grave was unadorned, with only a small wooden plaque on which his name was written. Later Juliet added a gravestone, and she was buried beside him when she died in 1991. The stone is inscribed with the words 'Unconcerned but not indifferent'. An insouciance, a nonchalance in death, as he had aspired to effect in life.

MAN RAY

Paris – its streets, the weight of history, of past lives, its promise, the locus of dreams, the destination.

The canvas is smaller than many of his paintings. It's a street – Paris – blue sky, a bright white cloud, pale cobblestones, creamy warm limestone walls, vertiginous houses, mansard roofs, light and shadows, the chiaroscuro of the city. We're at the street's widest point, looking down as it winds and narrows into nothingness. Running along it is a large high wall which dominates the canvas. It's bathed in sunlight, and blank, impenetrable, but for the interruption of a little black door. We're forced to look at the wall, and to wonder what it conceals. Two dark green trees appear like verdant hot air balloons rising up from behind it. Sloping along in the shadows, almost incidental, almost unseen, is a handcart, pulled by a man in a beret. He's bent double, his load – like a burden – is a mystery, wrapped in tarpaulin and bound with a rope. Man and cart and load all painted as one in shades of darkest brown and black.

Otherwise the street's empty, and timeless. It could be an Impressionist painting, but equally there's something of the urban uncanny in the street paintings of Paul Delvaux or René Magritte, Man Ray's surrealist comrades.

Timelessness, the passage of time, echoes, repetitions, ghosts, kindred spirits. In 2012 the Dutch artist Jan Willem Bruins was commissioned to hand-paint the text of Arthur Rimbaud's poem 'Le Bateau ivre' ('The Drunken Ship') as a mural on the same wall. All 300 square metres covered in words. Written in 1871 by the sixteen-year-old poet at his family home in northern France, it was debuted in Paris (to which he fled by train to escape his provincial life that same year). His audience was a group of avant-garde poets who called themselves the Vilains Bonshommes (the naughty lads) and the location was a cafe on the corner of Place Saint-Sulpice at the end of the street. It was a pivotal moment for the poet. He'd arrived.

The poem's about a perilous, tumultuous sea journey – a boat abandoned, adrift, telling its own tale of terror as it heaves and tips between swelling sea and stormy sky. It's a delirious, disorientating, dreamlike poem – all symbols and synaesthesia – about transgression, an allegory for the journey through life and the quest for identity, and freedom.

Rimbaud – dazzling Symbolist poet, vagabond, revolutionary, anti-bourgeois, erratic and precocious. He was violent and often hateful. He was strident and passionate and open in his homosexuality. And he was violent too in his rejection of poetic tradition. He felt dislocated, alienated from society. He believed he was a visionary, his purpose to act as conduit for a great spiritual unknown. In the service of this, with the help of drugs and alcohol, he was unlocking, disorientating his senses. He's the drunken boat going he doesn't know where. Unmoored.

It's not hard to see why the surrealists worshipped him, why they saw him as one of their vanguard. And in many ways there's an affinity with Man Ray – both roamers, recalcitrant rebels, champions of sexual and personal liberty (for good or ill). And both were escaping their origins, rewriting their lives and making things new, both men of contradictions – of rebellion and commerce. Rimbaud eventually renounced his poetry just as Man Ray dismissed his photography.

Man Ray's painting is also about a quest, and arrival. He's the man in the beret, the immigrant, the wanderer, the outsider, pulling his cart, his life, along the street (the wrapped tarpaulin a nod to one of his early Dada works). At the end of the wall, at the end of the poem that was later painted there (it's designed to read from right to left as if to echo the poem drifting from the cafe), there at the end of the wall tucked away unseen was Man Ray's studio. And so, though he's in the shadows in this strange street and outside this high, mysterious wall, he now belongs inside. He'd finally stopped travelling. This is his street, the date – 1952 – and his name painted on the wall as a signature, but also to claim it. His painting, his sanctuary, he belongs here. He's home.

RECLAMATION

We catch only glimpses of Ady after the war ended. 'DD', her friend in Paris, continued to write to Man Ray in LA with news of her. She had fallen ill and had to undergo several operations in 1946 leaving her with abdominal scarring that put an end to any hope of a modelling career. Later that year, her friend wrote to Man Ray that Ady was feeling more and more rejuvenated, though very tired, as she was working at a black club on the Champs-Élysées. In another, undated letter, her new lover André Art – with whom it appears she'd begun a relationship towards the end of the war – tells Man Ray that Ady laments that she has to work in a kitchen as a 'negress'.

Ady didn't learn until after the war that Man Ray had been in a relationship with Juliet Browner since very soon after his arrival in Los Angeles back in 1940. If she had hoped that they would reunite, as her letters imply, her hopes must have been dashed entirely at their reunion in 1947, when Man Ray returned to Paris to retrieve his belongings with his lovely new wife in tow. Undoubtedly, he was grateful to Ady for protecting his archive with such care over the war years, but it seems that this did not translate into a reciprocal gesture. There's perhaps a suggestion in André's letters to Man Ray that he expected some financial support for Ady. Wendy A. Grossman writes that Man Ray never honoured his debt to Ady for her care of his work during the war. Ady's great-nephew, Patrick Mamberta, in an unpublished interview in 2017 with Sala Elise Patterson, recalled his aunt's feeling of abandonment by her avant-garde friends and that she was reluctant to talk about that time in her life.

In *Une muse oubliée?* (*A Forgotten Muse?*), a Radio France programme about Ady broadcast in 2022, Mamberta suggests this reluctance was out of respect for André, and he believes that she asked Man Ray to be discreet about their life together. By then she was living a different sort of life. In the same programme, the novelist Gisèle Pineau adds that Ady's family, who remained in Guadeloupe, on hearing that Ady was dancing in clubs and posing naked, feared that she'd become a prostitute. There was a concerted effort on their part to silence her story. She was no longer mentioned.

If there was bitterness towards Man Ray on Ady's part, there is no sense of it in the occasional correspondence between the two couples that lasted until the early 1960s. In 1950 Man Ray wrote to Ady that he was thinking of moving back to Paris, and André wrote in reply that he and Juliet would be welcome to stay with them if they couldn't afford anywhere, that there was space in their dining room. He also told Man Ray that Ady was dancing again, that she might travel in Europe with her black troupe with whom she'd developed new dance routines inspired by Guadeloupian drum dances, reminding Man Ray that she loved to dance, as much as life. And there were later postcards – from holidays in Corfu and Montpellier, friendly, chatty, talking about the weather, wishing Man Ray and Juliet well, talking about how much Ady swims. She also took some small film roles; Art told Man Ray in 1950 that they were minor, but that it helped to keep them afloat. It is interesting that it was Art and not Ady who seems to have written these notes to Man Ray and Juliet, as if it was he and not she who was trying to keep alive the connection.

Ady and André Art married in the late 1950s. They struggled financially. Perhaps Ady asked Man Ray for help, perhaps she didn't. It seems she didn't receive any. They stayed in Paris for some years and later moved south, where they lived in social housing in Albi, in the Languedoc region. There's a photograph of an older Ady, her features a little heavier with age, taken by Patrick Mamberta towards the end of the 1970s – a very different Ady to the one we see in Man Ray's photographs. It's a close crop of her face in profile and the top of her hand clutching a cigarette, its ash yet to be flicked away. She's looking ahead, unsmiling, as if lost in thought, as if unaware of the photograph that's being taken. Ady died in a retirement home in Lagrave near Albi on 5 February 2004. She was eighty-eight years old. Her death went unreported in the press. It was assumed by the art world – even those who were aware of her significance in the story of Man Ray's life – that she was already dead.

Since then things have changed. Space is being made to explore alternative narratives of the past, and the stories of lives previously overlooked or misunderstood or wilfully swept into the margins of history, because of skin colour or gender or sexuality or seeming inconsequence. It is a process of revision, of re-evaluation and reparation. And Ady – neglected, rendered doubly insignificant by both her gender and her skin colour, and also perhaps her comparative youth at the time she was in a relationship with Man Ray – is gradually taking her rightful place in this new canon of cultural history. In 2019 she was included in an exhibition at the Musée d'Orsay, *Le modèle noir de Géricault à Matisse*, which looked at black figures in the visual arts, and specifically at the black model, their relationship with the artist who paints them, the photographer who takes their picture. There were, it became clear, many stories like Ady's. In 2007 she was the subject of an extensive profile by Sala Elise Patterson in the *New York Times*. Wendy A. Grossman has reattributed Picasso's portrait of her. She is the subject of a novel, *Ady, soleil noir*, by Gisèle Pineau. Through this work, Ady's ethnicity and her story are being returned to her. In April 2022, she appeared in the *New York Times* in a series of obituaries dedicated to forgotten figures. It was called 'Overlooked No More'.

MAN RAY, ADY, ANDRÉ AND JULIET

At their reunion in 1947, Man Ray took photographs. His new wife, his erstwhile lover, her new lover. These are the last photos we have of Ady by Man Ray, at least in the public sphere. There she is, in a checked sundress, sitting snugly beside her new lover. They're in front of a curtain, in the bottom left corner of the photograph's frame, as if in a giant photobooth. André's in a shirt and tie, he's saying something, his arm's about her waist. A proprietorial arm perhaps, an arm that might want to claim in spite or because of Ady's beaming face as she looks at the camera. Another photograph. André sits in between Ady and Juliet, all their hands intertwined in a rather awkward embrace. But then perhaps the moment was awkward. There's a feeling of deter-mined jollity. But who knows, perhaps the mood was as bright as the smiles. Juliet is grinning at the camera. André looks wryly amused. Of course we cannot know what Ady is thinking; we can only ever see her. Again, she's smiling, whatever that means.

HOME

'What do we do now . . .?' British *Vogue* asked its readers in its pre-emptive 'Victory' issue in June 1945, after VE Day. The war over, as far as Europe was concerned, there was now a trepidatious pause, the magazine acknowledged, as the servicewomen shed their uniforms for civvy clothes, and the women who'd struggled to keep their homes going, to keep the factories and businesses in production, searched for new purpose. Except for Lee's Dachau photograph and article, this issue was a celebration of the nation's women, honouring those who had toiled for the war effort. The photographs that Lee had taken over the years of women at war were republished in tribute, along with mention of Lee herself still entrenched in Eastern Europe, to document the aftermath.

What now? was a question that women (and men) across the

country, across much of the world, were asking themselves. And no doubt Lee, too, as she eventually returned to London in early 1946. The moment of victory – a brief, bright, pure lacuna, a temporary vacuum into which reality was rushing back to recomplicate, to recloud, to disillusion. Lives needed to be rebuilt, and relationships. Bodies and minds needed to heal.

In *Plenty*, a 1978 play and later a film by David Hare, Susan is a former SOE agent. We see her post-war, bored, enervated, solipsistic, her mental health slowly deteriorating. And we see her during the war, at work behind enemy lines, active, with purpose, entirely alive. It's a narrative that played out for both men and women after the war. But for men there was the promise of new challenges. For women, more often than not, there was the expectation of a return to domesticity.

The Lee who returned from the war had been permanently damaged by it, by what she had witnessed, by the anger she carried within her and undoubtedly by how the trauma of war must have entangled itself with her own childhood trauma. Physically exhausted from living on adrenaline and amphetamines and alcohol, she was unravelling. There was also the issue of what she was to do with her life. She had been driven onwards by the overwhelming commitment to her work, by her compulsion to bear witness and, no doubt, by the addictive intensity of wartime.

Lee was given a hero's welcome at *Vogue* and she was sent on a celebrity tour to America, where she was interviewed on CBS radio about her wartime experiences. Travelling with Roland, they reunited with old friends, Man Ray, the art dealer Julien Levy, Max Ernst. They took the train out to Poughkeepsie to visit her parents. Lee loved them but she realized the extent to which her father was obsessed with control. She felt stifled to be home, felt anxious, perhaps because she knew that everyone was whispering about how much she'd changed – that she'd gained weight, was losing her looks, was looking old and unhealthy. Perhaps, too, it didn't help that Roland was continuing the affair he'd promised to end if she returned. They travelled on to

Arizona to visit Max Ernst and his new wife Dorothea Tanning at the small, simple home they were building for themselves amongst mountains and canyons at Oak Creek Canyon near Sedona.

After a further trip, to Los Angeles, where they met up with Man Ray and his new wife Juliet, they returned to London. Lee went back to working for *Vogue*, shooting fashion and travel features and trying to re-establish a peacetime version of her career. It was when she was on assignment in Switzerland in 1947 that she discovered she was pregnant and wrote to Roland from St Moritz with the news that she would soon have to start knitting for a new arrival. She told him that she felt strange, in body and mind, but was generally excited about it, which surprised her. She had been convinced that she was unable to have children, no doubt because of her years of treatment for gonorrhoea, and her miscarriage. She had a difficult pregnancy, suffering from pneumonia and a strange, lingering virus, and as she would be forty when the baby was due she was considered at high risk. All this must have exacerbated her anxiety about childbirth, her anxiety in general. Antony was born by elective caesarean in September 1947.

The morning of the operation she wrote a note to Roland, fearing that she might die. She told him that if she could have lived her life again, she would be even freer than she'd been – ideologically, physically, romantically. The letter forced her to acknowledge that she struggled to vocalize her love for him, something she told him she regretted. She wrote emphatically about how much she did love him. And also that she had accepted his affair as an expression of her love.

In 1949, when Lee and Roland bought Farley Farm, Lee attempted to settle into a new life in the country. With domesticity came stasis; finally, she was forced to stop blazing her trail. She struggled, and would always struggle, with motherhood and began to slide into a deep decline, infinitely exacerbated by post-traumatic stress, post-natal depression and undoubtedly by the simple exhaustion that comes with being a mother to a small child. And as the nation collectively tucked away its trauma instead of trying to heal its wound, so Lee put away her wartime photographs in the attic, just as she must have tried to tuck away the memories into that dark place inside herself where older traumas lay. But she could never unknow, unsee. She never spoke of the war again. She attempted to get on with her new life.

Lee and Roland were together, but apart. Often she was lost in her thoughts. Roland painted her sitting at the dining table, himself beside her, his arm around her. But they're rigid, formal, cold. In place of her face Lee has a giant eye. She can't stop seeing what she has seen. She was trapped in her misery and Roland struggled, and would continue to struggle, to support her. Though they would always love each other, deeply, profoundly, their relationship never returned to how it had been before the war. She found Roland's continuing affairs trying, and his belief that love and sex were two very different things, his belief that he could maintain the division between the two. Lee had also always believed in sexual freedom, but their lives – her life in particular – were different now. They muddled along together.

Farley Farm was gradually renovated and decorated in beautiful, bright colours. Roland painted a mural on the fireplace in the dining room. They filled the house with their art collection and the weird and wonderful collection of objects they had acquired over the years. It was their collaboration, a *Gesamtkunstwerk* – a living work of art. And the emphasis was on living with the art and the collections, not as if in a temple or a museum. Together they made the farm a sanctuary. Lee became the bountiful hostess, growing vegetables in the garden, cooking elaborate meals and entertaining their many friends, including Picasso and Dora, separately of course. There's a lovely photograph of little Antony in dungarees perched on Picasso's knee; they're smiling at each other in mutual appreciation. Man Ray and Juliet were frequent guests. Despite the wound Lee had inflicted on Man Ray in leaving him all those years before, despite how he'd tried to dominate and control her then too, they'd remained the greatest friends. They adored each other. They understood each other absolutely – an old intimacy – and would often sit in companiable silence side by side. He gave her paintings designed to amuse her, to cheer her up.

At times Lee worked for clients and for *Vogue*. Her final contribution was in July 1953. 'Working Guests' was a playful story featuring photographs of their grand visitors at work on the farm, including Alfred J. Barr, director of the Museum of Modern Art, feeding pigs and Max Ernst planting petunias. Her friend Robert Capa invited her to join Magnum, the photography collective he had founded with Cartier-Bresson in 1947. She didn't accept the invitation, perhaps because she valued her creative freedom too much to join anything. And so she had always been. She was only ever a surrealist in the way she saw and engaged with the world.

Lee and Roland travelled widely. She helped Roland at the ICA and shot photographs for his biographies of Picasso and others. But eventually she stopped taking commissions and refused access to her old work. The shadow of depression lay heavily on her. She continued to drink, which made things worse. She was prone to mood swings and could be cruel, though she was never violent. Alcohol rendered her incapable of writing or photographing. This was compounded by the death of her parents, by Roland's affairs and even more so by the mid-1950s when it became obvious that his relationship with Diane Deriaz was more than a passing fancy. Antony Penrose describes his mother's depression as 'a slow progressive decline'. In an interview with Lee's biographer Carolyn Burke, her old ally at British *Vogue* Audrey Withers admitted that Roland discreetly asked her to stop commissioning Lee, and that she reluctantly agreed. Withers told Burke that she felt that the war had been Lee's finest hour, and that she had made a mistake marrying, having a child, moving to the countryside. Domesticity, she believed, had stoppered her creativity.

But somehow, slowly, Lee managed to re-enchant her life, to redeem it for herself. A final act. Lee had always enjoyed cooking. And in the alchemical way that food and feeding people can heal so it began to work its magic on her. Cooking, at least non-professionally, offers easy, ephemeral and creative pleasure. And it allows for simple delight, and for sensual reconnection with the body, as a physical act, and as nourishment for the self and for others. Perhaps it was also a distraction, an avoidance technique, socially, and for the things she kept within herself.

But as with everything in her life, Lee threw herself into it with gusto. Only this time it was to develop something within her, rather than in pursuit of some external thing. She redesigned her kitchen down to the tiniest detail and bought thousands of cookbooks for which she eventually built her own library. She developed an obsession with gadgets, the freezer her loyal friend and the blender a firm favourite.

Lee went to Paris to train in Cordon Bleu. She won prizes and tried and failed to become *Vogue*'s cookery writer, losing out to Elizabeth David. Cooking became a way of sharing time with her friends, for whom she threw surrealist dinner parties. She served dishes like 'Green Chicken', 'Sour Grapes', 'Tomato Soup Cake', 'Cauliflower Breasts' (which were pink, with cherry tomato nipples) and mushrooms called 'Penroses' cut in the shape of roses. She was still finding pleasure in subverting the familiar into the strange, the everyday into the marvellous, the witty, the theatrical. These meals she served on silver platters and monogrammed serving dishes that she had stolen from Hitler's homes. British *Vogue* published an article on Lee as cook and hostess, called 'A Second Fame: Good Food, Lee and Roland Penrose'. She also started to write a cookbook to inspire her fellow cooks with her gastronomic flights of fancy. Notes for the book were found years after her death; it was to be called 'The Entertaining Freezer'.

With perseverance Lee managed to drag herself out of her alcoholism and, perhaps if not to heal, then to learn to live with the trauma she carried within herself. In 1976 she was diagnosed with terminal pancreatic cancer at around the same time as Antony's wife Suzanna announced she was pregnant. When she became too ill to leave her bed, Carolyn Burke writes that Roland stayed by Lee's side continually. Suzanna brought the new baby granddaughter for frequent visits, which delighted Lee in spite of her claim to dislike young children. And it was also thanks to Suzanna, according to Antony, that he and his mother were eventually reconciled. Lee died in Roland's arms on 21 July 1977.

As a suitably strange footnote to Lee's life, in 2009 declassified intelligence reports in the National Archives revealed that Lee (and Roland) had been spied on for most of the 1940s and 50s, for suspected communist sympathies. It was her relationship with Roland, who was perceived to have communist friendships, that put her under suspicion. Officers intercepted their post and observed their friendships. A Special Branch report, written in 1941, said she was an intellectual communist and passionately anti-Nazi, adding that she she was inclined to eccentricity and that her taste in clothes and food was 'queer'. It advised careful observation of the subject. Eventually the surveillance ended, an officer concluding that Lee's communism was more of a perspective on life than anything actively anarchic. While it is strange that someone who was not interested in politics in a formal sense, but rather the defence of personal freedoms, should have been considered an agent of a totalitarian state, the episode is a testament to the fevered paranoia of a country at war.

Only after Lee's death did her son Antony begin to understand her. She had always kept her secrets. He had known her as an incapable alcoholic and a mother whose love was not easily expressed. He recalls no instance of her telling him that she loved him. He had learned to avoid her, and her moods, and so Lee had remained an enigma. His nanny, Patsy Murray, had been his constant, his source of maternal love. But then he discovered Lee's papers and the sixty thousand or so negatives and prints in the attic of the family house. And he learned from Lee's brother of her childhood ordeal, something she had never even told Roland. Slowly Antony began to discover Lee, to make sense of his mother, her meteoric life, its pleasures and its deep pains, her extraordinary way of seeing the world. And not just her way of seeing, but also her great commitment to sharing what she had seen.

ROLAND AND LEE

1946. Lee's standing, framed in the doorway of the house Max Ernst and Dorothea Tanning are building in Arizona. She's wearing slacks rolled up to the knees, and sandals. She's naked to the waist. Her body faces the camera, her head's turned in profile. One arm is raised, a hand leaning against the door frame, the other arm is lower, its hand pressing forward against the flyscreen that fills the open doorway. Roland's outside with his camera, looking in at her, for her. Like a reversal of her *Portrait of Space* in Egypt. This time we're looking back at Lee through the gauze and not out, towards the promise of space, as she had done then. Perhaps this was the point. Perhaps this staging of herself allowed an appraisal of the state of things – of her self, her body. The body that her family was gossiping about, the body that had always been looked at, and judged. She's not looking glamorous. She probably didn't care to. She looks strong, even if she didn't feel it – a bare-breasted warrior, her hair swept back from her face and her arms aloft as if she's about to do something heroic. Outside the house there are planks of wood leaning against the wall either side of the door. There's a provisional feeling, of things under construction. Of lives, relationships, being rebuilt, and held together by bare arms.

ROLAND AND LEE (AND ANTONY)

Lee, as in many of Roland's previous paintings, as an elemental goddess, here a female Atlas, carrying the world not on her shoulders but in her belly. She stands against a yellow background, her legs encased in white fabric, perhaps a nightdress, and above this she is naked, her body rendered in bright pastel colours. One swollen breast is pale blue, the other is dark blue. Her face looks down – features foreshortened, expression ambiguous, half in blue shade – to the gibbous belly she cradles in her arms, forced to surrender to the blue and opaque unknown swirling within herself and the little skeletal, amphibian form with large eyes and the suggestion of a tail glowing at its centre. He called the painting *First View*.

LEE

'Gold Chicken'
Serves 6

1.8kg / 4lb whole roasting chicken
2 boneless and skinless chicken breasts
2 tablespoons cognac
salt and pepper to taste
edible gold leaf

STUFFING
340g / ¾lb lamb mince
4 tablespoons pine nuts or slivered almonds
2 tablespoons pistachios, peeled, scalded and coarsely chopped
8 tablespoons flat-leaf parsley, chopped
1½ tablespoons fresh tarragon, chopped
1½ tablespoons onion, grated
4 medium eggs
1 lemon, finely grated peel only
garlic to taste

Bone chicken by cutting it up the back and stripping the flesh from the bones.

Remove bones from thighs and most of the bone from the drum sticks.

Cut the bone off the poultry using shears inside the leg-skin just inside the joint. This bit of bone will act as a plug for the stuffing later. Do the same for the end of the wing part nearest the body. Sew up any holes accidentally made in the skin. Spread out the boneless chicken, skin side down on a board. Sprinkle with cognac, salt and pepper.

In a large bowl mix together the stuffing. Push some of the stuffing into each empty chicken leg and thigh skin, in such a way that legs can be folded back into their proper position. Push some into the wing hollow and spread most of rest on the open skin. The stuffing swells, the chicken skin shrinks, so don't fill it too full.

Observe where the white meat of the chicken lies naturally and distribute tender fillets of the supplementary chicken breast so that each portion, when cut later, will have some white meat. Be careful to keep the proportions of the thickish breast tapering to the rear.

Cover over the chicken fillets with more stuffing, draw up the back skin and sew it together. Re-form the legs into position, truss with string, rub with olive oil and roast in a 179C / 350F oven for 2 hours.

For some strange reason, this limp ragged looking beast resurrects itself into a lovely youthful shape again. While hot, apply pure gold leaf to the entire breast and other visible surfaces. Carve across. Good cold too.

Acknowledgements

Many thanks to the Lee Miller Archives for permission to reproduce Lee Miller's and Roland Penrose's photographs and for their help with my research. Thank you too, to Olivia Fraser for her generous permission to quote Eileen Agar's postcard. I am very grateful to the staff of all the archives I consulted, especially to the RAF Museum, the Getty Research Institute and the Tate Archive. Particular thanks go to the helpful and patient staff at the Scottish National Gallery of Modern Art and at the Musée d'art et d'histoire Paul Éluard.

A lot of people have helped me along the way. Thank you to Ian Massey, to Conor Mullan and to Robin Muir for the wonderful quote. Thank you also to Carol Redfern for her brilliant translation skills and for her help and patience. I am deeply indebted to Pierre Coquelet, to Wendy Grossman and to Sala Elise Patterson for all their help with Ady Fidelin. And thank you also to Mimi Beaumont, Peter Patrick and Marl'ene Edwin for their help with Creole pronunciation. Many thanks to Ludivine Broch for her help and insights into life during the Occupation, particularly for people of colour. Thank you to the Amar Gallery for revealing Dora Maar works I'd never seen before. Thank you to Kaye Donachie for her beautiful, inspiring paintings and for her inspiring and sensitive ideas about Nusch Éluard.

Many thanks to Antony Penrose for reading my manuscript with such care and for his insightful comments, clarifications and corrections. I would also like to acknowledge the work of the Lee Miller Archive in preserving and promoting the work and legacies of Lee Miller and Roland Penrose. I am especially grateful to David Boyd Haycock for reading my manuscript, for his diligence and the generosity of his comments. His help has been invaluable. Particular thanks to Andrew Lambirth for all his help and knowledge, for his ongoing support of my work, and especially for lending me precious items from his Eileen Agar archive.

Thank you to Karen and Richard McMinn, Jeremy McMinn, Sherman McMinn, Emma Powell and Roxanne Rogers. And long overdue thanks to my wonderfully inspiring teacher at MGC, Evelyn Thomas. Special thanks to my friend and fellow author Martin Williams, whose championing of my work means more than he knows.

At Picador, thank you to Elle Gibbons, Siobhan Slattery and Mia Lioni. Thank you to my proofreader Matthew Robertson and to Moesha Parirenyatwa for designing the wonderful book jacket. I am very thankful to Nicholas Blake for all his hard work. Many thanks to Stephanie Racine for reading the audiobook with such sensitivity, and to Perrin Sledge for taking such care in its production.

Huge thanks to my two editors. To the brilliant Georgina Morley, who commissioned this book many moons ago. She waited patiently and supportively as I sidelined the project in order to deal with other things in my life. I want to thank her profoundly for allowing me that time. It has been a pleasure to work with her. And to the wonderful Andrea Henry, who heroically took up the baton when Georgina retired. Thank you to her for all her hard work, enthusiasm and care, and for replying to my many emails and for understanding what I was trying to achieve with this book. I am so grateful for my lovely, wise, patient agent, Ed Wilson.

My aunt Julia Thomasson died in 2023. She was so supportive and enthusiastic about my work. We spent happy hours in search of Eileen Agar and Paul Nash in Dorset and whittling Agar-inspired sculptures at Lulworth Cove. I wish that I could thank her, and I miss her very much. Thank you to my wonderful friend Anne Marsham, I'm so lucky to have her in my life. Thank you to my dad, Peter Thomasson, for his support and encyclopaedic knowledge of the Second World War. And to my brother, Edward Thomasson, for his intelligence, sensitivity and love. Thank you to my wonderful mum, Annette Thomasson, for all her help. For being an enthusiastic travel companion, research assistant, reader, babysitter, and all the other countless things.

Thank you to my beloved husband Trent McMinn. I could not have written this without you. And thank you to our two lovely boys. This is for the three of you – who inspire me every day – with all my love.

Picture Acknowledgements

p. 1 Picnic, Île Sainte-Marguerite, Cannes, France 1937 by Lee Miller (P0146), © Lee Miller Archives, England 2025. All rights reserved. leemiller.co.uk

p. 17 Man Ray, Eileen Agar and Lee Miller, Côte d'Azur, France 1937 by Roland Penrose (P0202), Roland Penrose © Lee Miller Archives, England 2025. All rights reserved. leemiller.co.uk

p. 123 Picasso, Nusch and Paul Éluard, Elsa Triolet, Lee Miller, Roland Penrose and Louis Aragon, Picasso's Studio, Paris, France 1944 by Lee Miller (5981-16R), © Lee Miller Archives, England 2025. All rights reserved. leemiller.co.uk

p. 191 Lee Miller in her Kitchen, Farley Farm, Muddles Green, England c.1955 by Roland Penrose (FF0971), Roland Penrose © Lee Miller Archives, England 2025. All rights reserved. leemiller.co.uk

Bibliography

Archives consulted

Archive Collection, Royal Air Force Museum, London
Fonds Man Ray, Bibliothèque Kandinsky, Centre Pompidou, Paris
Fonds Paul Éluard, Musée d'art et d'histoire Paul Éluard, Saint-
　Denis
Man Ray Archives, Getty Research Institute, Los Angeles
Musée d'art classique de Mougins, Mougins
National Archive, Reuben Library, British Film Institute, London
Redfern Gallery, London
Roland Penrose Archive and Surrealism Archive, Gabrielle Keiller
　Collection, Scottish National Gallery of Modern Art, Edinburgh
Tate Archive, Tate Britain, London

Select Bibliography

Agar, Eileen, and Lambirth, Andrew, *A Look at My Life* (London:
　Methuen, 1988)
Alexandrian, Sarane, *Surrealist Art* (London: Thames and Hudson,
　1995)
Allmer, Patricia, ed., *Angels of Anarchy: Women Artists and Surrealism*
　(London: Prestel, 2009)
— , *Lee Miller: Photography, Surrealism and Beyond* (Manchester:
　Manchester University Press, 2016)
Annick, Lionel-Marie, *Paul Eluard et ses amis peintres* (Paris: Centre
　Georges Pompidou, 1982)

Anon., 'The Bushongo of Africa sends his hats to Paris', *Harper's Bazaar*, September 1937

Archer-Straw, Petrine, *Negrophilia: Avant-Garde Paris and Black Culture in the 1920s* (London: Thames & Hudson, 2000)

Atack, Margaret, *Literature and the French Resistance: Cultural Politics and Narrative Forms, 1940–50* (Manchester: Manchester University Press, 1989)

Attlee, James, *Guernica: Painting the End of the World* (London: Head of Zeus, 2017)

Auden, W. H., *Another Time* (London: Faber & Faber, [1940] 2019)

Baker, Josephine and Bouillon, Jo, *Josephine*, trans. Mariana Fitzpatrick (New York: Harper & Row, 1977)

Baker, Josephine, Sauvage, Marcel, *Les Mémoires de Joséphine Baker* (Paris: Éditions Dilecta, [1927] 2006)

Baldassari, Anne, *Picasso: Life with Dora Maar: Love and War 1935 to 1945*, trans. Unity Woodman (Paris: Flammarion, 2006)

Baldwin, Neil, *Man Ray* (London: Hamish Hamilton, 1989)

Baring, Louise, *Dora Maar: Paris in the Time of Man Ray, Jean Cocteau, and Picasso* (New York and London: Rizzoli, 2017)

Benkemoun, Brigitte, *Finding Dora Maar: An Artist, An Address Book, A Life*, trans. Jody Gladding (Los Angeles: Getty Publications, 2020)

Berger, John, *Hold Everything Dear: Dispatches on Survival and Resistance* (London: Verso, 2007)

— , *The Success and Failure of Picasso* (New York: Pantheon Books, 1956)

Bernard, Christine, et al., 'Adrienne Fidelin: Une femme dans la lumière', Radio France, Episode 1, 5 February 2022 <https://www.radiofrance.fr/franceculture/podcasts/une-his-toire-particuliere-un-recit-documentaire-en-deux-parties/une-femme-dans-la-lumiere-1752392>

— , 'Adrienne Fidelin: Une muse oubliée?', Radio France, Episode 2, 6 February 2022 <https://www.radiofrance.fr/franceculture/podcasts/une-histoire-particuliere-un-recit-docu-mentaire-en-deux-parties/une-muse-oubliee-7419586>

Bertrand Dorléac, Laurence, trans. Jane Marie Todd, *Art of the Defeat: France 1940–1944* (Los Angeles: Getty Publications, 2008)

Bohm-Duchen, Monica, *Art and the Second World War* (Farnham: Lund Humphries, 2013)

Bouhassane, Ami, *Lee Miller, A Life with Food, Friends and Recipes* (Chiddingly: Lee Miller Archives Publishing, 2022)

Brandon, Ruth, *Surreal Lives: The Surrealists 1917–1945* (New York: Grove Press, 1999)

Brassaï, *Conversations with Picasso*, trans. Jane Marie Todd (Chicago: University of Chicago Press, 1999)

— , *Picasso & Co.* (London: Thames & Hudson, 1967)

Brecht, Bertolt, *Svendborger Gedichte* (Frankfurt: Surhkamp, [1939] 1973)

Breton, André, *La Révolution surréaliste*, no. 1, 15 December 1924

— , 'Second Manifeste du Surréalisme', *La Révolution surréaliste*, no. 12, 15 December 1929

Broch, Ludivine, 'Colonial Subjects and Citizens in the French Internal Resistance, 1940-1944', *French Politics, Culture & Society*, Berghahn Books, vol. 37, no. 1 (Spring 2019)

— , 'History and Images', *World on Fire*, PBS, <https://www.pbs.org/wgbh/masterpiece/specialfeatures/world-on-fire-season-2-episode-3-history-images/>

Brooks, Tim, *British Propaganda to France, 1940–1944: Machinery, Method and Message* (Edinburgh: Edinburgh University Press, 2007)

Burke, Carolyn, *Lee Miller* (London: Bloomsbury, 2005)

Byatt, A. S., *Eileen Agar: 'An Imaginative Playfulness'* (London: Redfern Gallery, 2004)

Calvocoressi, Richard, *Lee Miller: Portraits from a Life* (London: Thames & Hudson, 2002)

Caws, Mary Ann, *Dora Maar: With and Without Picasso: A Biography* (London: Thames & Hudson, 2000)

— , ed. and trans., *Surrealist Love Poems* (London: Tate Publishing, 2001)

Caws, Mary Ann, Kuenzli, Rudolf E., and Raaberg, Gwen, eds., *Surrealism and Women* (Cambridge, MA: MIT Press, 1991)

Chadwick, Whitney, *The Militant Muse: Love, War and the Women of Surrealism* (London: Thames & Hudson, 2017)

— , *Women, Art and Society*, 5th edn. (London: Thames & Hudson, 2012)

— , *Women Artists and the Surrealist Movement* (London: Thames & Hudson, 1985)

Chadwick, Whitney, and de Courtivron, Isabelle, eds, *Significant Others* (London: Thames & Hudson, [1993] 2018)

Conley, Katharine, *Automatic Woman: The Representation of Woman in Surrealism* (Lincoln, NB: University of Nebraska Press, 1996)

Cosslett, Rhiannon Lucy, '"Picasso nearly fell over backwards when he saw her" – Lee Miller's son on their intense relationship', *The Guardian*, 5 September 2022

Cowling, Elizabeth, *Visiting Picasso: The Notebooks and Letters of Roland Penrose* (London: Thames & Hudson, 2006)

Desroches, Didier (Paul Éluard), *Le Temps déborde* (Paris: Cahiers d'Art, 1947)

Duras, Marguerite, trans. Barbara Bray, *The War: A Memoir* (New York: Pantheon Books, 1986)

Éluard, Paul, *À Pablo Picasso* (London: Secker & Warburg, 1947)

— , ed. Clive Scott, *Anthologie Éluard* (London: Methuen, [1968] 1983)

— , *Derniers Poèmes d'amour* (Paris: Seghers, [1962] 1973)

— , trans. Jesse Browner, ed. Pierre Dreyfus, *Letters to Gala* (New York: Paragon House, 1989)

— , 'Manifestation Philosophies', *La Révolution surréaliste*, no. 4, July 1925, p. 32

— , *Oeuvres complètes*, vol. 1 (Paris: Gallimard, 1968)

— , trans. Gilbert Bowen, *Selected Poems* (London: John Calder, [1987] 1998)

— , *Selected Writings* (London: Routledge and Kegan Paul, 1952)

— , *Souvenirs de la maison des fous* (Paris: Vrille, 1946)

— , trans. Gilbert Bowen, *Unbroken Poetry II* (Newcastle upon Tyne: Bloodaxe Books, 1996)

Éluard, Paul, Man Ray, *Facile* (Paris: Éditions G. L. M., 1935)

— , *Les Mains libres* (Paris: Gallimard, [1937] 2009)

Feigel, Lara, *The Bitter Taste of Victory: In the Ruins of the Reich* (London: Bloomsbury, 2016)

Felder, Rachel, 'Overlooked No More: Ady Fidelin, Black Model "Hidden in Plain Sight"', *The New York Times*, 29 April 2022

Fouchet, Max-Pol, *Un Jour, je m'en souviens . . . mémoire parlée* (Paris: Mercure de France, 1968)

Gateau, Jean-Charles, *Paul Éluard, ou, Le frère voyant* (Paris: Robert Laffont, 1988)

Gavin, Francesca, 'The Ephemeral Beauty of Kaye Donachie', *Beauty Papers*, issue 3, 2017

Gell, Alfred, *Art and Agency: An Anthropological Theory* (Oxford: Oxford University Press, 1998)

Gersh-Nesic, Beth, 'Art Historian Wendy A. Grossman on Man Ray's Muse Adrienne Fidelin', *Bonjour Paris*, 2020 < https://bonjourparis. com/history/the-first-black-model-in-a-major-american-fashion-magazine-was-french/>

Gildea, Robert, *Marianne in Chains: Daily Life in the Heart of France During the German Occupation* (New York: Henry Holt, 2003)

Gilot, Françoise, and Lake, Carlton, *Life with Picasso* (London: Virago, [1964] 1990)

Glissant, Édouard, trans. Betsy Wing, *Poetics of Relation* (Ann Arbor, MA: The University of Michigan Press, 1997)

Grossman, Wendy A., 'Les beaux jours avec Ady sur la Côte d'Azur, 1937', *Man Ray: Le Beau Temps*, 2023 <https://www. academia.edu/105424047/Les_beaux_jours_avec_Ady_sur_ la_C%C3%B4te_dAzur_1937>

— , ed., *Man Ray, African Art, and the Modernist Lens* (Minneapolis, MN: University of Minnesota Press, 2009)

— , 'Unmasking Adrienne Fidelin: Picasso, Man Ray and the (In)

Visibility of Racial Difference', *Modernism/modernity*, Vol. 5, Cycle 1, 2020 <https://doi.org/10.26597/mod.0142>

— , and Patterson, Sala E., 'Fidelin, Adrienne "Ady"', *Dictionary of Caribbean and Afro-Latin American Biography*, eds. Franklin W. Knight and Henry Louis Gates, Jr. (Oxford: Oxford University Press, 2016)

Hartman, Saidiya, *Wayward Lives, Beautiful Experiments: Intimate Histories of Riotous Black Girls, Troublesome Women and Queer Radicals* (London: Serpent's Tail, 2019)

Hester, Diarmuid, *Nothing Ever Just Disappears: Seven Hidden Histories* (London: Allen Lane, 2024)

Higgins, Charlotte, 'Picasso nearly risked his reputation for Franco exhibition', *The Guardian*, 28 May 2010

Holman, Valerie, *Air-Borne Culture: Propaganda Leaflets over Occupied France in the Second World War* (London: Routledge, 2000)

hooks, bell, *Black Looks: Race and Representation* (London: South End Press, 1989)

Hopkins, David, *Dada and Surrealism: A Very Short Introduction* (Oxford: Oxford University Press, 2004)

Hustvedt, Siri, *A Woman Looking at Men Looking at Women: Essays on Art, Sex, and the Mind* (London: Sceptre, 2017)

Kedward, H. R., *Occupied France: Collaboration and Resistance 1940–1944* (Oxford: Blackwell, [1985] 1993)

King, James, *Roland Penrose: The Life of a Surrealist* (Edinburgh, Edinburgh University Press, 2018)

Laing, Olivia, 'Separating art from life always needs the most delicate touch', *The Observer*, 18 October 2015

Lambirth, Andrew, *Eileen Agar: A Retrospective* (London: Birch & Conran, 1987)

— , *Eileen Agar: An Eye for Collage* (Chichester: Pallant House, 2009)

Lanzmann, Claude, trans. Frank Wynne, *The Patagonian Hare* (London: Atlantic Books, 2012)

Lawrence, D. H., *Assorted Articles* (London: Secker, 1930)

Leiris, Michel, 'Faire-part', *Cahiers d'Art* 12, nos 4–5, 1937

Lionel, Richard, *L'art et la guerre: Les artistes confrontés à la Seconde guerre Mondiale* (Paris: Flammarion, 1995)

Lord, James, *Picasso and Dora: A Memoir* (London: Phoenix, 1993)

Mabin, Dominique, Mabin, Renée, 'Art, folie et surréalisme à l'hôpital psychiatrique de Saint-Alban-sur-Limagnole pendant la guerre de 1939–1945', *Mélusine*, 17 October 2017 <https://www.melusine-surrealisme.fr/wp/art-folie-et-surrealisme-a-lhopital-psychiatrique>

Malraux, André, trans. June Guicharnaud with Jacques Guicharnaud, *Picasso's Mask* (New York: Holt, Rinehart and Winston, 1976)

Man Ray, *Self-Portrait* (London: Penguin, [1963] 2012)

— , *This Quarter*, vol. V, no. 1, September 1932

Martin, Russell, *Picasso's War* (London: Simon & Schuster, 2004)

Masó, Joana, 'Women of the Collective: Care and politics around Saint-Alban Psychiatric Hospital: 1930–1960', *Parapraxis* <https://www.parapraxismagazine.com/articles/women-of-the-collective>

Morris, Desmond, *The Lives of the Surrealists* (London: Thames & Hudson, 2021)

Mundy, Jennifer, ed., *Man Ray: Writings on Art* (London: Tate Publishing, 2016)

Nash, Steven, A., ed., *Picasso and the War Years* (London: Thames & Hudson, 1998)

Némirovsky, Irène, trans. Sandra Smith, *Suite Française* (London: Vintage, 2007)

Nowinski, Ira, 'Man Ray', *Gagosian Quarterly*, Spring 2017 <https://gagosian.com/quarterly/2017/02/23/man-ray/>

Nugent, Robert, *Paul Éluard* (Waterville, ME: Thorndike Press, 1975)

O'Brian, Patrick, *Pablo Ruiz Picasso: A Biography* (New York: W. W. Norton, 1994)

Parker, Rozsika, Pollock, Griselda, *Old Mistresses: Women, Art and Ideology* (London: Pandora, 1987)

Penrose, Antony, *Lee Miller: Summer of 1937* (Chiddingly: Lee Miller Archives Publishing, 2025)

— , ed., *Lee Miller's War* (London, Thames & Hudson, 2014)

— , *The Lives of Lee Miller* (London: Thames & Hudson, 1985)

Penrose, Roland, *Man Ray* (London: Thames & Hudson, 1989)

— , *Picasso: His Life and Work*, 3rd edn. (London: HarperCollins, 1981)

— , *Scrap Book* (New York: Rizzoli, 1981)

Patterson, Sala E., 'Yo, Adrienne', *T Style Magazine, The New York Times*, 26 February 2007

Patterson, Sydney-Paige, 'Sexualized Resistance: Black Women's Agency through the Erotic and Dance', April 2015 <https://www.academia.edu/11804500/Sexualized_Resistance_Black_Womens_Agency_through_the_Erotic_and_Dance>

Pepper, Terence, and Warner, Marina, *Man Ray: Portraits* (New York and London: Yale University Press and National Portrait Gallery, 2013)

Picasso, Pablo, *Desire Caught by the Tail* (New York: The Philosophical Library, 1948)

Pierre, José, ed., and Imrie, Malcolm, trans., *Investigating Sex: Surrealist Discussions 1928–1932* (London: Verso, 1992)

Poirier, Agnès, *Left Bank* (London: Bloomsbury, 2018)

— , 'Watching boxing with Picasso and a ménage-à-trois at home: my life with the surrealist elite', *The Observer*, 13 April 2014

Prose, Francine, *The Lives of the Muses: Nine Women & the Artists They Inspired* (London: HarperCollins, 2002)

Rave, Paul Ortwin, *Kunstdiktatur im Dritten Reich* (Berlin: Argon Verlag, 1987)

Read, Herbert, *Surrealism* (London: Faber & Faber, 1936)

Rémy, Michel, *Eileen Agar: Dreaming Oneself Awake* (London: Reaktion, 2017)

Richard, Lionel, *L'art et la guerre: Les artistes confrontés à la Seconde guerre Mondiale* (Paris: Flammarion, 1995)

Richardson, John, *A Life of Picasso, Vol. IV: The Minotaur Years* (London: Vintage, 2022)

Riding, Alan, *And the Show Went On: Cultural Life in Nazi-occupied Paris* (London: Duckworth Overlook, 2012)

Rose, Jacqueline, *Women in Dark Times* (London: Bloomsbury, 2015)

Rose, Phyllis, *Jazz Cleopatra: Josephine Baker in her Time* (New York: Doubleday, 1989)

Roth, Philip, *Shop Talk: A Writer and His Colleagues and Their Work* (Boston and New York: Houghton Mifflin, 2001)

Sartre, Jean-Paul, 'The Republic of Silence', *The Atlantic Monthly*, Vol. 174, no. 6, December 1944

Sayer, Derek, *Prague, Capital of the Twentieth Century: A Surrealist History* (Princeton, NJ: Princeton University Press, 2013)

Schwarz, Arturo, *Man Ray. Il rigore dell'immaginazione* (Milan: Feltrinelli, 1977)

Ségalat, Roger-Jean, *Album Éluard* (Paris: Gallimard, 1968)

Seghers, Pierre, *La Résistance et ses poètes*, 2nd edn. (Paris: Seghers, 1974)

Sheean, Vincent, *Dorothy and Red* (London: Heinemann, 1964)

Simpson, Ann, *Eileen Agar 1899–1991* (Edinburgh: Scottish National Gallery of Modern Art, 1999)

Sliwinski, Sharon, *Dreaming in Dark Times: Six Exercises in Political Thought* (Minneapolis, MN: University of Minnesota Press, 2017)

Slusher, Katherine, *Lee Miller and Roland Penrose: The Green Memories of Desire* (London: Prestel, 2007)

Smith, Laura, *Eileen Agar* (Bath: Eiderdown Press, 2021)

— , ed., *Eileen Agar: Angel of Anarchy* (London: Whitechapel Gallery, 2021)

Solnit, Rebecca, *Hope in the Dark: Untold Histories, Wild Possibilities*, 3rd edn. (London: Canongate, 2016)

Sontag, Susan, *Literature is Freedom: The Friedenspreis Speech* (New York: Winterhouse Editions, 2003)

Spender, Stephen, *World Within World* (London: Readers Union, 1953)

Stein, Gertrude, *Paris, France: Personal Recollections* (London: Peter Owen, 1971)

Tancons, Claire, 'Women in the Whirlwind: Withholding Guadeloupe's Archipelagic History', *Small Axe*, vol. 16, no. 3, November 2012 (No. 39)

Utley, Gertje R., *Picasso: The Communist Years* (London: Yale University Press, 2000)

Vieuille, Chantal, *Nusch: Portrait d'une muse du Surréalisme* (Paris: Artelittera, 2010)

Walden, Lauren, 'Cosmopolitan Surrealism: an investigation into photographic circulation and the intercultural relations of an avant-garde movement', Coventry University, September 2018 < https://core.ac.uk/download/pdf/519709315.pdf>

Warner, Marina, *Forms of Enchantment: Writing on Art and Artists* (London: Thames & Hudson, 2018)

Withers, Audrey, *Lifespan* (London: Peter Owen, 1994)

Zeavin, Hannah, 'We Took Care of the Network', *The New York Review*, 17 August 2024 < https://www.nybooks.com/online/2024/08/17/taking-care-of-the-network/>

Notes

Preface: Picnic, 1937

p.2   'There is certainly another world: Paul Éluard, *Oeuvres complètes*, Vol. 1 (Paris: Gallimard, 1968), p. 986, lines trans. Anna Thomasson.

p.3   The empty plates: Lee Miller, *Picnic (Nusch Éluard, Paul Éluard, Roland Penrose, Man Ray, Ady Fidelin)*, Île Sainte-Marguerite, Cannes, France, 1937.

p.7   'It is impossible,' writes Glissant: Édouard Glissant, *Poetics of Relation*, trans. Betsy Wing (Ann Arbor, MA: The University of Michigan Press, 1997), p. 194.

p.9   'Paris was where the twentieth century was: Gertrude Stein, *Paris, France: Personal Recollections* (London: Peter Owen, 1971), p. 11.

p.12   'In the context of Nazi Germany: Jacqueline Rose, *Women in Dark Times* (London: Bloomsbury, 2015), p. 74.

p.12   'From now on,' he ranted: Paul Ortwin Rave, *Kunstdiktatur im Dritten Reich* (Berlin: Argon Verlag, 1987), p. 101.

p.15   'hounded by external events': Stephen Spender, *World Within World* (London: Readers Union, 1953), p. 117.

I: A Dance of Freedom

p.18   They all owed each other a tender nudity: Paul Éluard, Man Ray, *Les Mains libres* (Paris: Gallimard, [1937] 2009), p. 101, lines trans. Anna Thomasson.

p.19   Eileen Agar is dancing: Joseph Bard, *Eileen Agar dancing on a roof outside Mougins*, 1937.

p.19   'after a bat-infested night: Eileen Agar, Andrew Lambirth, *A Look at My Life* (London: Methuen, 1988), illustration caption.

p.23   'seized with a diabolical playfulness': Roland Penrose, *Picasso: His Life and Work* (London: HarperCollins, 1981), p. 311.

p.23   'a happy family': Man Ray, *Self-Portrait* (London: Penguin, [1963] 2012), p. 227.

p.24   He told her that he would never return to Spain: *A Look at My Life*, p.140.

p.24   And somehow he absorbed the energy: Charlotte Higgins, 'Picasso nearly risked his reputation for Franco exhibition', *The Guardian*, 28 May 2010.

p.25   There are six portraits in all: Pablo Picasso, *Arlésienne* series, 1937.

p.27   Lee's son Antony believes they did: Antony Penrose, as told to the author.

p.27   As if it was merely an organic aspect: Rhiannon Lucy Cosslett, ' "Picasso nearly fell over backwards when he saw her" – Lee Miller's son on their intense relationship', *The Guardian*, 5 September 2022.

p.27   this was one of the first of many photographs: Lee Miller, *Picasso*, Hôtel Vaste Horizon, Mougins, France, 1937.

p.27   Roland is crouching on the tiled floor: Lee Miller, *Roland Penrose making a postcard collage*, Hôtel Vaste Horizon, Mougins, France, 1937.

p.28   And then one work becomes two: Man Ray, *Drawing by Pablo Picasso on the sand in Mougins*, 1937.

p.28   A few sketched lines in pencil: Pablo Picasso, *Nusch Éluard*, 1937.

p.30   MILLE BOMBES INCENDAIRES: *L'Humanité*, 27 April 1937.

p.31   'No, painting is not done to decorate apartments: *Les Lettres françaises* (Pablo Picasso interview with Simone Téry), 24 March 1945.

p.32   'Where is the protest then?': John Berger, *The Success and Failure of Picasso* (New York: Pantheon Books, 1956), p. 169.

p.32   'for artists as for every person: Louis Aragon, *La Commune*, 1936, in Richard Lionel, *L'art et la guerre: Les artistes confrontés à la Seconde guerre Mondiale* (Paris: Flammarion, 1995), p. 85, lines trans. Anna Thomasson.

p.33   'Picasso sends us our letter of doom: Michel Leiris, 'Faire-part', *Cahiers d'Art* 12, nos 4–5, 1937, pp. 152–3.

p.34   'Éluard always has an air of availability: Paul Éluard, *Selected Writings* (London: Routledge and Kegan Paul, 1952), p. x.

p.38   'La femme est l'être qui projette la plus grande ombre: André Breton, *La Révolution surréaliste*, no. 1, 15 December 1924, p. 18.

p.39   'The problem of woman': André Breton, 'Second Manifeste du Surréalisme', *La Révolution surréaliste*, no. 12, 15 December 1929.

p.39   'There is no total revolution: Paul Éluard, 'Manifestation Philosophies', *La Révolution surréaliste*, no 4, July 1925, p. 32.

p.41   He told her that one night: *A Look at My Life*, p. 141.

p.41   Breton called him '*le partouzard*': Brigitte Benkemoun, *Finding Dora Maar: An Artist, An Address Book, A Life* (Los Angeles: Getty Publications, 2020), p. 60.

p.42   'You hold the flame between your fingers: Paul Éluard, *À Pablo Picasso* (London: Secker & Warburg, 1947), p. 67.

p.47   'I heard moans: Claude Lanzmann, trans. Frank Wynne, *The Patagonian Hare* (London: Atlantic Books, 2012), p. 227.

p.49   Lee, who, while in a relationship: *A Look at My Life*, p. 121.

p.50   she wrote to Picasso, trying to justify her outbursts: John Richardson, *A Life of Picasso, Vol. IV: The Minotaur Years* (London: Vintage, 2022), p. 156.

p.50   She's sitting on a bright red van Gogh-like chair: Pablo Picasso, *Portrait of Paul Éluard*, 1937.

p.51   Nusch is wearing a swimsuit and a sarong: Lee Miller, *Nusch Éluard by the side of a car*, Golfe-Juan, France, 1937.

p.52   'Headless. And also footless: Mary Ann Caws, 'Seeing the Surrealist Woman: We Are a Problem', in *Surrealism and Women*, eds. Mary Ann Caws, Rudolf E. Kuenzli and Gwen Raaberg (Cambridge, MA: MIT Press, 1991), p. 11.

p.53   An early self-portrait: Dora Maar, *Self-portrait with fan*, early 1930s.

p.53   'Some lives', writes Olivia Laing: Olivia Laing, 'Separating art from life always needs the most delicate touch', *The Observer*, 18 October 2015.

p.58   A man in a suit is walking along a pavement: Dora Maar, *Man looking inside a sidewalk inspection door*, London, c. 1935.

p.58   They're at the picnic table on the Île Sainte-Marguerite: Man Ray, *Lee Miller, Adrienne Fidelin / Lee Miller, Adrienne Fidelin, Paul Éluard / Group in the Rocks*, 1937.

p.59   'he wrote the most passionate defence: Arturo Schwarz, *Man Ray. Il rigore dell'immaginazione* (Milan: Feltrinelli, 1977), p. 75.

p.63   'No one knows any longer: Sarane Alexandrian, *Surrealist Art* (London: Thames and Hudson, 1995), pp. 44–5.

p.65   'Cut out the eye from a photograph: Man Ray, in *This Quarter*, Vol. V, no. 1, ed. Edward W. Titus (Paris: September, 1932).

p.65   'Keep going to the limit of endurance: ibid.

p.65   Man Ray described these fifty or so drawings: Neil Baldwin, *Man Ray* (London: Hamish Hamilton, 1989), p. 209.

p.67   They all owed each other a tender nudity: *Les Mains libres*, p. 101, lines trans. Anna Thomasson.

p.67   Man Ray spotted a traditional flat-iron: Man Ray, *Cadeau (The Gift)*, 1921.

p.68   He's lying in bed, appearing to be asleep: Man Ray, *Man Ray (Asleep)*, 1930.

p.69   'the delightful girl from Guadeloupe: Roland Penrose, *Man Ray* (London: Thames & Hudson, 1989), p. 128.

p.69   'a self-effacing young woman: Baldwin, *Man Ray*, p. 213.

p.69   at lunch one day at the Vaste Horizon: *A Look at My Life*, p. 136.

p.70   'Ady is in fine shape: Man Ray, letter to Roland Penrose, 19 May 1940, in *Man Ray, Writings on Art*, ed. Jennifer Mundy (London: Tate, 2016), p. 73.

p.70   'hidden in plain sight': Wendy A. Grossman, 'Unmasking Adrienne Fidelin: Picasso, Man Ray and the (In)Visibility of Racial Difference', *Modernism/modernity*, Vol. 5, Cycle 1, https://doi.org/10.26597/mod.0142.

p.71 'What was the good of having the statue: Josephine Baker and Jo Bouillon, *Josephine*, trans. Mariana Fitzpatrick (New York: Harper & Row, 1977), p. 42.

p.72 'Paris is a dance: Josephine Baker and Marcel Sauvage, *Les Mémoires de Joséphine Baker* (Paris: Éditions Dilecta, 2006), p. 63, lines trans. Anna Thomasson.

p.72 'the white imagination sure is something: Phyllis Rose, *Jazz Cleopatra: Josephine Baker in her Time* (New York: Doubleday, 1989), p. 81.

p.72 'a silenced body': bell hooks, 'Selling Hot Pussy', in *Black Looks: Race and Representation* (London: South End Press, 1989), p. 63.

p.75 Ady is standing in front of a window: Man Ray, *Ady with a Bust of Man Ray*, 1937.

p.76 a party, a tableau: Man Ray, *Nusch and Adrienne Fidelin in Martiniquan costume, with Man Ray, Paul Éluard, and an unidentified man*, c. 1937.

p.77 Her face and body look like the inner workings: Pablo Picasso, *Seated Woman on a Yellow and Pink Background II (Portrait of a Woman)*, 1937.

p.78 Looking at the painting: Antony Penrose, as told to the author.

p.78 Picasso requested another print of the washboard: 'Unmasking Adrienne Fidelin'.

p.79 Ady and Man Ray are sitting back-to-back: Lee Miller, *Man Ray and Ady Fidelin*, Mougins, France, 1937.

p.80 'It isn't that she hasn't got a mind: D. H. Lawrence, *Assorted Articles* (London: Secker, 1930).

p.81 'an escape-hatch': *A Look at My Life*, p. 52.

p.82 'People were very shocked to hear: Susanna White, dir., *The Colour of Dreams*, 1989.

p.87 Joseph is sitting in a cane chair: Eileen Agar, *Photographs of Joseph Bard nude on the balcony and on a bed at the Hôtel Vaste Horizon*, Mougins, France, 1937.

p.88   A section of moulded Coade stone column: Lee Miller, *Eileen Agar*, Brighton, 1937.

p.89   DEAROLANDLEE: Eileen Agar, *Postcard to Lee Miller and Roland Penrose from the Hôtel Vaste Horizon*, September 1937.

p.90   Picasso is sitting on a rock: Dora Maar, *Picasso with an Ox's Skull*, 1937.

p.90   'female figments': Siri Hustvedt, *A Woman Looking at Men Looking at Women: Essays on Art, Sex, and the Mind* (London: Sceptre, 2017), p. 6.

p.92   Eileen discusses Picasso in her memoirs: *A Look at My Life*, p. 138.

p.92   Apparently, he then sauntered off: *A Life of Picasso*, Vol. IV, p. 70.

p.94   Picasso's old friend: *Picasso & Co.*, p. 43.

p.95   Dora had always been a weeping woman: Françoise Gilot and Carlton Lake, *Life with Picasso* (Melbourne: Thomas Nelson, 1965), p. 122.

p.95   'Women are suffering machines: André Malraux, *Picasso's Mask*, trans. June Guicharnaud with Jacques Guicharnaud (New York: Holt, Rinehart and Winston, 1976), p. 138.

p.95   'All his portraits of me are lies: James Lord, *Picasso and Dora: A Memoir* (London: Phoenix, 1993), p. 123.

p.96   as evidence of Dora's strength: *Dora Maar*, p. 120.

p.96   This is not weeping: Pablo Picasso, *Weeping Woman*, 1937.

p.96   His face – in her hands, on her canvas: Dora Maar, *Portrait of Pablo Picasso*, 1938.

p.97   Two women dressed in shades of grey: Dora Maar, *The Conversation*, 1937.

p.97   There's a frame: Lee Miller, *Portrait of Space*, 1937.

p.99   'There is certainly another world: Paul Éluard, *Oeuvres complètes*, Vol. 1 (Paris: Gallimard, 1968), p. 986, lines trans. Anna Thomasson.

p.100   'There are acts of cruelty towards women: *Women in Dark Times*, p. 19.

p.100 Her brother remembered her screams: *Lee Miller*, p. 18.

p.104 'rather take a picture: *Lee Miller*, p. 128.

p.105 In 1938 Lee wrote a letter to Aziz: *Lee Miller*, epigraph.

p.106 A triptych, a sequence: Man Ray, *Lee Miller (Triptych)*, 1930.

p.106 After witnessing a radical mastectomy: Lee Miller, *Untitled (Severed breast from radical surgery in a place setting 1)*, Paris, France, c. 1929.

p.106 the surgeon, Dr Dax: Antony Penrose, as told to the author.

p.108 Their life is like art: Francesca Gavin, 'The Ephemeral Beauty of Kaye Donachie', in *Beauty Papers*, Issue 3, 2017, pp. 84–9.

p.109 At Mougins Picasso inscribed an ink portrait: Patrick O'Brian, *Pablo Ruiz Picasso: A Biography* (New York: W. W. Norton, 1994), p. 332.

p.109 Picasso was moved: *Life with Picasso*, p. 131.

p.111 Silvery images of her naked serpentine body: Man Ray and Paul Éluard, *Facile* (Paris: Éditions G. L. M.) 1935.

p.112 The painting is unmistakeably Nusch: Pablo Picasso, *Portrait of Nusch Éluard*, 1937.

p.118 'Picasso widow': Elizabeth Cowling, *Visiting Picasso: The Notebooks and Letters of Roland Penrose* (London: Thames & Hudson, 2006), p. 12.

p.121 Boisgeloup, Picasso's château in Normandy: Dora Maar, *Roland Penrose, Paulo Picasso, Pablo Picasso, Paul Éluard, Cécile Éluard and Nusch Éluard, Boisgeloup*, March 1937.

p.122 In reality she'd been wearing: Roland Penrose, *Night and Day*, 1937.

p.122 *Night Fishing at Antibes*: Pablo Picasso, *Night Fishing at Antibes*, 1939.

II: Occupations

p.124 In the dark times: Bertolt Brecht, *Svendborger Gedichte* (Frankfurt: Surhkamp, 1973), p. 35, lines trans. Anna Thomasson.

p.129 He'd recently had a dream: Man Ray, *Le Beau Temps* (*Fair Weather*), 1939.

p.137 A cosy image: David E. Scherman, *David E. Scherman, Lee Miller and Roland Penrose, Downshire Hill, Hampstead, London, England*, 1943.

p.137 It could be a Catholic relic: Eileen Agar, *Angel of Anarchy*, 1936–40.

p.140 'There is one artist I know: *The Daily Sketch*, London, undated.

p.140 At the centre of the collage: Eileen Agar, *Erotic Landscape*, 1942.

p.144 '[At Le Catalan] on some days: Alan Riding, *And the Show Went On: Cultural Life in Nazi-occupied Paris* (London: Duckworth Overlook, 2012), p. 106.

p.145 there was a young theatre teacher: *And the Show Went On*, p. 184.

p.145 'It says nothing of human destiny: Pablo Picasso, *Desire Caught by the Tail* (New York: The Philosophical Library, 1948), p. 2.

p.146 'Never were we freer: Jean-Paul Sartre, 'The Republic of Silence', in *The Atlantic Monthly*, Vol. 174, no. 6, December 1944.

p.146 It was one of the paintings he kept all his life: Pablo Picasso, *Café at Royan*, Royan, 15 August 1940.

p.147 Man Ray tells Ady he's arrived in New York: Letters between Man Ray and Ady Fidelin, Getty Research Institute, Man Ray letters and album (930027).

p.148 And Strauss adds that: Sala E. Patterson, 'Yo, Adrienne', *T Style Magazine, The New York Times*, 26 February 2007.

p.148 People of colour were 'to ride in the last carriage: Ludivine Broch, 'History and Images', *World on Fire*, PBS. https://www.pbs.org/wgbh/masterpiece/specialfeatures/world-on-fire-season-2-episode-3-history-images/.

p.149 'little black sun': Adrienne Fidelin, letter to Man Ray, 17 April 1945, in Fonds Man Ray, Box 3, Bibliothèque Kandinsky, Centre Pompidou, Paris.

p.152 'I saw him grow pale: Paul Éluard, *Selected Writings* (London: Routledge & Kegan Paul, 1952), p. vii.

p.152 'The time has come for poets to proclaim: Paul Éluard,

'L'Évidence poetique', trans. George Reavey, in Herbert Read, *Surrealism* (London: Faber & Faber, 1936), p. 171.

p.155 Cicero Dias: Antony Penrose, as told to the author.

p.155 In the early 1980s: Antony Penrose, as told to the author.

p.156 'dark night of total German occupation': Archive Collection, Royal Air Force Museum, London.

p.156 the literary arm of the Resistance had triumphed: Valerie Holman, *Air-Borne Culture: Propaganda Leaflets over Occupied France in the Second World War* (London: Routledge, 2000), p. 225.

p.156 'Poetry makes nothing happen: W. H. Auden, 'In Memory of W.B. Yeats', in *Another Time* (London: Faber & Faber, 2019), p. 75.

p.157 'it survives / A way of happening, a mouth': ibid.

p.158 Love and freedom: Paul Éluard, 'Liberté (or Liberty?)', 1941.

p.158 Dora cut the paper in half: Dora Maar, *Self-Portrait Cut in Two by a Razor, c. 1943*.

p.159 In Royan in 1940 Dora had written to Picasso: *Life with Picasso*, p. 77.

p.160 when she was in a relationship with Picasso: *Picasso and Dora*, p. 115.

p.164 'Well, now I had everything again: *Self-Portrait*, p. 335.

p.167 'a profoundly conservative country: Susan Sontag, *Literature is Freedom: The Friedenspreis Speech* (New York: Winterhouse Editions, 2003), p. 7.

p.167 'a beautiful prison': *Man Ray*, p. 240.

p.167 He glowers out of the frame: Man Ray, *Self-Portrait with Half Beard*, 1943.

p.171 'now I owned a private war: *Lee Miller*, p. 225.

p.173 A fleeting calm in Saint-Malo: Lee Miller, *Lee Miller, Reflection in Mirror*, Saint-Malo, France 1944.

p.173 Fellow photographers Robert Doisneau: Lee Miller, *Woman Accused of Collaborating with the Germans*, Rennes, France 1944.

p.174 Two photographs. In the first, Paul is sprawling on the ground:

Jacques Matarasso, *Paul Éluard at the Saint-Alban Asylum, Winter 1943/1944* and *Nusch and Paul Éluard at the Saint-Alban Asylum, Winter 1943/1944*.

p.177 Paul's poem about the cemetery: Paul Éluard, 'Le Cimetière des fous' from *Souvenirs de la maison des fous* (Paris: Vrille, 1946).

p.178 The horizontals and verticals: Pablo Picasso, *Tomato Plant*, 1944.

p.180 He told an American journalist: Peter D. Whitney, 'Picasso is safe', *San Francisco Chronicle*, September 1944 in Monica Bohm-Duchen, *Art and the Second World War* (Farnham: Lund Humphries, 2013), p. 112.

p.183 'Why should we hide the emotion: Charles de Gaulle, 'Paris Liberated' speech, 25 August 1944, lines trans. Anna Thomasson.

p.183 'the first dame photographer': *Lee Miller*, p. 228.

p.189 only a few days earlier: Derek Sayer, *Prague, Capital of the Twentieth Century: A Surrealist History* (Princeton, NJ: Princeton University Press, 2013), p. 393.

p.189 'like God or the Devil': *Picasso*, p. 347.

p.190 His father Roland told him: Antony Penrose, as told to the author.

p.190 'They were all in tremendously high spirits: Roland Penrose, *Scrap Book* (New York: Rizzoli, 1981), p. 104.

p.190 Another gathering with Lee, Nusch and Paul: Henri Cartier-Bresson, *Lee Miller, Paul and Nusch Éluard, 1944*.

III: Time Overflows

p.192 'Nothing is simple or singular': Paul Éluard, 'Death, Love, Life', from *Derniers Poèmes d'amour* (Paris: Seghers, [1962] 1973), p. 7, lines trans. Anna Thomasson.

p.194 the magazine's 'greatest publishing excitement: Audrey Withers, *Lifespan* (London: Peter Owen, 1994), pp. 52–3.

p.198 Roland sent her a long letter: Katherine Slusher, *Lee Miller* and *Roland Penrose: The Green Memories of Desire* (London: Prestel, 2007), p. 69.

p.198 It was the dust of Dachau: Lee Miller with David E. Scherman, *Lee Miller in Hitler's bathtub, Hitler's apartment*, 1945.

p.199 'tell it slant': Emily Dickinson, from 'Tell All the Truth but Tell It Slant', c. 1872.

p.200 helping Paul to sell signed copies: Claude Lanzmann, *The Patagonian Hare*, p. 227.

p.200 Three days after writing to Gala: *Prague*, pp. 397–8.

p.201 they gave him the will to live: ibid., p. 398.

p.201 Nusch's death had caused Paul to lose faith: Brassaï, *Conversations with Picasso* (Chicago: University of Chicago Press, 1999), p. 376.

p.201 'Orpheus had lost his Eurydice': Jean-Charles Gateau, *Paul Éluard, ou, Le frère voyant* (Paris: Robert Laffont, 1988), p. 309.

p.201 'Je dors dans un lit: Antony Penrose, as told to the author.

p.202 'who did everything to dispel the night: Didier Desroches (Paul Éluard), *Le Temps déborde* (Paris: Cahiers d'Art, 1947), lines trans. Anna Thomasson.

p.202 Twenty-eighth of November: *Le Temps déborde*, lines trans. Anna Thomasson.

p.203 'Poor Paul, I thought: *Self-Portrait*, pp. 289–90.

p.204 Paul, he says in an interview: Philip Roth, 'Conversations in London and Connecticut with Milan Kundera', in *Shop Talk: A Writer and His Colleagues and Their Work* (Boston and New York: Houghton Mifflin, 2001), p. 96.

p.205 she revealed in an interview: Agnès Poirier, 'Watching boxing with Picasso and a ménage-à-trois at home: my life with the surrealist elite', *The Observer*, 13 April 2014.

p.205 'Nothing is simple or singular': *Derniers Poèmes d'amour*, p. 7, lines trans. Anna Thomasson.

p.206 June 1951. Saint-Tropez: Lee Miller, *Françoise Gilot, Paul Éluard, Dominique (Odette Lemort) and Picasso at the wedding of Paul and Dominique, Saint-Tropez, 1951.*

p.207 They and many of his friends: Henri Cartier-Bresson, *Funeral of Paul Éluard*, Père Lachaise Cemetery, Paris, 1952.

p.207 Valentine Penrose attended: Antony Penrose, as told to the author.

p.207 A naked woman dances: Pablo Picasso, *La Joie de Vivre*, 1946.

p.210 he had joined a family: Charlotte Higgins, 'Picasso nearly risked his reputation for Franco exhibition', *The Guardian*, 28 May 2010.

p.214 Finally he began to look at himself: Pablo Picasso, *Self-portrait*, 30 June 1972.

p.216 *'un surrealiste dans l'amitié'*: Scrap Book, p. 60.

p.216 'full moon augmented by solar Lee: Paul Éluard, *Selected Writings* (London: Routledge & Kegan Paul, 1952), inscribed copy from Paul Éluard to Roland Penrose, Keiller Library, Edinburgh.

p.218 When a French friend asked: James King, *Roland Penrose: The Life of a Surrealist* (Edinburgh: Edinburgh University Press, 2018), p. 259.

p.219 When Lee died: *Lee Miller and Roland Penrose*, p. 89.

p.219 La Californie, Picasso's house in Cannes: Lee Miller, *Roland Penrose and Picasso with an edition of 'Portrait of Picasso'*, La Californie, Cannes, France, 1957.

p.220 'What is surrealism today: David Hopkins, *Dada and Surrealism: A Very Short Introduction* (Oxford: Oxford University Press, 2004), p. 143.

p.222 'like a transparent skirt': *Colour of Dreams*, dir. Susanna White, 1989.

p.223 'in a sparkling moment': *A Look at My Life*, p. 235.

p.223 Joseph is drawn in warm sunlit shades of yellow: Eileen Agar, *Man Reclining (drawing of Joseph Bard)*, 1986.

p.224 Two profiles of one head: Eileen Agar, *The Horned Woman*, 1978.

p.225 Dora wrote an untitled poem: *Dora Maar*, p. 177.

p.229 'Do you think I care?: *Picasso and Dora: A Memoir*, p. 123.

p.229 A series of four tiny prints: Unknown photographer, *Dora Maar*, undated.

p.229 A negative from 1935: Dora Maar, *Woman with Hands in Hair*, 1935/1980.

p.235 The canvas is smaller: Man Ray, *La rue Férou*, 1952 / Jan Willem Bruins, *Le Bateau ivre d'Arthur Rimbaud*, 2012.

p.238 his aunt's feeling of abandonment: 'Unmasking Adrienne Fidelin'.

p.238 she was no longer mentioned: Adrienne Fidelin, Episode 2/2: Une muse oubliée: https://www.radiofrance.fr/franceculture/podcasts/une-histoire-particuliere-un-recit-documentaire-en-deux-parties/une-muse-oubliee-7419586.

p.240 There she is, in a checked sundress: Man Ray, *Juliet Man Ray, André Art, Adrienne Fidelin* and *André Art and Adrienne Fidelin*, 1947.

p.240 'What do we do now . . .?': British *Vogue*, June 1945, p. 5.

p.242 she wrote a note to Roland: *Roland Penrose*, p. 179.

p.244 'a slow progressive decline': Antony Penrose, as told to the author.

p.245 British *Vogue* published an article: 'A Second Fame: Good Food, Lee and Roland Penrose', British *Vogue*, 15 April 1965.

p.246 thanks to Suzanna: Antony Penrose, as told to the author.

p.246 of her telling him: Antony Penrose, as told to the author.

p.247 Lee's standing, framed in the doorway: Roland Penrose, *Lee Miller*, Sedona, Arizona, 1946.

p.247 Lee, as in many of Roland's previous paintings: Roland Penrose, *First View*, 1947.

p.248 'Gold Chicken': Ami Bouhassane, *Lee Miller, A Life with Food, Friends and Recipes* (Chiddingly: Lee Miller Archives Publishing, 2022), p. 297.

Index

References in *italics* indicate photographs.